JUN 1 5 1996

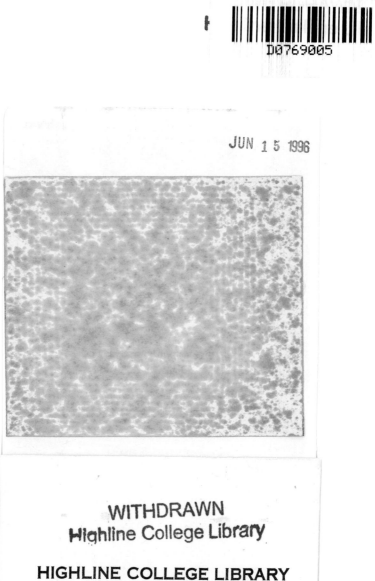

Children of the Enemy

Children of the Enemy

Oral Histories of Vietnamese Amerasians and Their Mothers

by

STEVEN DEBONIS

McFarland & Company, Inc., Publishers
Jefferson, North Carolina, and London

Frontispiece: The author between two of his Vietnamese and Amerasian students in the Philippine Refugee Processing Center.

British Library Cataloguing-in-Publication data are available

Library of Congress Cataloguing-in-Publication Data

DeBonis, Steven, 1949–
    Children of the enemy : oral histories of Vietnamese Amerasians
and their mothers / by Steven DeBonis.
      p. cm.
    Includes bibliographical references and index.
    ISBN 0-89950-975-4 (lib. bdg. : 50# alk. paper) ∞
    1. Amerasians—Vietnam—Social conditions. 2. Children of
military personnel—Vietnam. 3. Abandoned children—Vietnam.
I. Title.
DS556.45.A43 1995
959.7'00413—dc20   94-28735
                                                               CIP

McFarland & Company, Inc., Publishers
  Box 611, Jefferson, North Carolina 28640

In memory of my grandfather, Irving May,
and for my grandmother, Sonia May,
and their great-grandson,
Noah David DeBonis

ACKNOWLEDGMENTS

My deepest appreciation goes to the Amerasians and their mothers, who despite the stress of refugee camp life, the sorrow of leaving friends and family behind in Vietnam, and the uncertainties of their futures in the United States, were kind enough to share their stories with me.

Mr. Khuyen D. Pham spent hours reviewing the narratives, explaining the arcane, ferreting out the implausible, and correcting my spelling of Vietnamese words. Our long discussions provided me historical and cultural perspectives on the the personal accounts that appear in this book. Mr. Khuyen is an interpreter par excellence and assisted me in that capacity as well. He also contributed "Changes in Province and City Names in Vietnam after 1975," which appears in the Appendix.

Tuan Anh Pham and Michelle Noullet patiently responded to my many letters and faxes, answering questions and providing information essential to the completion of this book.

A number of people acted as interpreters and cultural informants. Several of them have also contributed their own narratives to this text. Most were at the time refugees themselves, subject to the same demanding refugee camp schedule as the interviewees for whom they translated. In days filled with English study, mandatory community work, and waiting in line for scant rations of water, they graciously found time to work with me, often for hours at a stretch. They are Nguyen Thi Thanh Xuan, Nguyen Trong Chinh, Ngo Nhu Trang Lieu Thi Duong, Chanh Thi Mai, Le Thi Thu, Phan Vinh Phuc, Chau Van Ri Raymond, Lam Thi Cam Thu Lien, Minh Chau Thi Tran, Mr. Thanh, and Nguyen Kim Long, whom I also thank for his superb saxophone playing.

Captain Dung Q. Nguyen of the United States Air Force, based in Misawa, Japan, reviewed much of my work, making comments and checking the spelling of Vietnamese words.

Anita Menghetti of the Lutheran Immigration and Resettlement Services, Washington, D.C., Julie Macdonald of Lutheran Immigration and Resettlement Services, New York, Michael Kocher of InterAction,

Washington, D.C., Don Ranard of the Center for Applied Linguistics in Washington, D.C., and David Deas all shared with me their insights into Amerasian resettlement in the United States.

David Derthick and Gerry Collins offered their comments and assistance.

The staff of the Overstreet Memorial Library at Misawa Air Force Base in Misawa, Japan, was extremely helpful in accommodating my many requests for help in locating research materials.

My wife, Laurie Kuntz, supported this project in every way. Her ideas, suggestions, and influence are mirrored in the text. In addition, she conducted the interview that led to the oral history of Lan.

Steven DeBonis
Misawa, Japan
September 1994

CONTENTS

The guard says, "Raymond, what's the song you singing?" I say, "I'm singing my father's song." He says, "Well, you know that if you singin' that song, that mean you are the enemy."

Raymond, an Amerasian, describing an incident in a Vietnamese reeducation camp

She came out of that trance so common to us all and whispered in my ear: "Can you describe this?" And I said: "Yes, I can."

Anna Akhmatova, *Requiem*

INTRODUCTION

August on the Bataan peninsula is the heaviest month of the monsoon. This is not a rainy season of fair days punctuated by intermittent storms, but one of weeks of drenching rain and terminal humidity. Clouds blow in from off the South China Sea and bump up against the southwestern fringe of the Zambales mountains, where they sit, like overladen ships caught on shoals, loosing their cargo on the land below. The peninsula, brown and thirsty from the remorseless sun of the Philippine summer, turns billiard-table green. Any place mold spores can grab hold and multiply, they do. Leather belts, the suede trim of track shoes, the cloth spines of hardcover books, all mildew to the color of a rice paddy.

Manivong has his most important belonging tucked safely inside his shirt against the August deluge. He carried it this way when he arrived in the Philippine Refugee Processing Center (PRPC) in Bataan a month ago. From layers of plastic and paper he fishes it out, a five-by-seven photo of a blonde, crew cut American military man wearing a pair of horn-rimmed glasses. "Father," he exclaims proudly, pushing the photo across the table to me.

Superimposed over what would be the heart of his dad is a tiny likeness of Manivong's Vietnamese-Khmer mother. On back of the photo is printed a Milwaukee address and inscribed in an almost childlike scrawl:

> To Sapim, you are the number one girl of my life. I love you and want you so much.
>
> > Love always,
> > Lt. Ballman (Batman)

I look at the photo and back at Manivong. The likeness is unmistakable. Lt. Ballman was about the same age when the photo was taken as his twenty-year-old son is today.

I have seen scores of such photos in the PRPC, carried by Vietnamese Amerasians fortunate enough to own even that tiny scrap of their past. Many have had the impression that once they get to the United States,

1

waving these snapshots will almost magically cause their fathers to appear. The reality, unfortunately, has been quite different.

"Before I came here, I wrote my father sixteen letters from Vietnam," Manivong says. "I think someone received them because they were not sent back, but I never got a reply."

In a country where postage for a single overseas letter can eat up an average day's wages, sixteen letters represent a substantial investment. Manivong, however, is far from discouraged. He is now using the Red Cross tracing services to try and track down his dad and will continue when he gets to the United States. His chances are not good; only a tiny percentage of the Vietnamese Amerasians who have left Vietnam for America have been successful in finding their fathers.

AMERICAN RESPONSE TO AMERASIANS

The battle of Dienbienphu in 1954 marked the end of the French Colonial Era in Southeast Asia. That same year the French brought 25,000 Franco-Asian children to France and guaranteed them citizenship. The response of the United States to the thousands of half–American children left in Vietnam after its ill-fated venture there has been considerably less immediate.

In 1982, ten years after the majority of U.S. military withdrawal from Vietnam, seven years after the fall of Saigon, Congress passed the Amerasian Immigration Act. Designed to expedite the immigration of half–American children from a host of Asian countries, it did not affect Amerasians in Vietnam, as the United States and Vietnam had no relations. Amerasians, however, often with their immediate relatives, did begin leaving Vietnam for the states in September of that year under the auspices of the Orderly Departure Program (ODP).

In light of the horrific plight of the Vietnamese boat people, ODP was "created in 1979 to provide a safe, legal alternative to dangerous flight by boat or overland from Vietnam."[1] United States ODP officers from Bangkok travel to Ho Chi Minh City to interview applicants for resettlement in the United States. These applicants have already successfully negotiated the intricate maze of Vietnamese bureaucracy in order to obtain the prerequisite exit permit, often leaving a trail of well-greased palms in their wake.

In 1984, Secretary of State George Shultz, under the prodding of American voluntary agencies, announced the creation of a specific Amerasian subprogram within the Orderly Departure Program. Still, the rate of Amerasian departures remained slow. In 1986, claiming that the United States had let a backlog of 25,000 applicants build up, Vietnam halted the processing of new Amerasian cases. Amerasian departures from Vietnam dropped from 1,498 in 1985 to 578 in 1986 and to 213 in 1987.[2]

In September of 1987, the United States and Vietnam signed an agreement to expedite Amerasian emigration from Vietnam. In December of that year, Congress passed the Amerasian Homecoming Act, also known as the Mrazek Act after its sponsor, U.S. Representative Robert Mrazek. This act, which went into effect on March 21, 1988, allows for Vietnamese Amerasians and specified members of their families to enter the United States as immigrants, while at the same time granting them refugee benefits such as preentry English-as-a-Second-Language training in the Philippine Refugee Processing Center and resettlement assistance in the United States. The cumulative effect of these two events in accelerating Amerasian departures from Vietnam can be seen in the numbers: from 1982 to 1988, ODP brought approximately 11,500 Vietnamese Amerasian children and accompanying relatives out of Vietnam. Extend the period out to December of 1991 and the number jumps to 67,028.[3] Also factored into this increase is the effect of a 1990 amendment to the Homecoming Act which allows both the spouses and mothers (or primary caregivers, including bona fide stepfathers) of Amerasians the right to immigrate with them to the United States. Previously Amerasians had to choose one to the exclusion of the other, a wrenching decision that often tore families apart.

AMERASIANS IN THE PHILIPPINE REFUGEE PROCESSING CENTER

My own interest lies not in numbers of departures and cases processed, but in the stories behind them. From 1982 to 1992, I worked in the Philippine Refugee Processing Center in Bataan as a supervisor in a State Department–funded educational program. This program was mandated to prepare U.S.-bound refugees for life in America. Three hundred and seventeen thousand Khmer, Lao, Hmong, Vietnamese and Amerasians passed through the center from its inception in 1980 to December of 1991, to take five-month courses in English-as-a-Second-Language (ESL), Cultural Orientation, and Work Orientation, prior to their resettlement in the United States. Amerasians and accompanying family members began trickling into the PRPC in 1985.

In most of these Amerasians, the genes of their fathers predominated; there was little of Vietnam in their looks. Freckle-faced girls, lanky young black men, blondes, red heads—one expected to hear Brooklyn rasps or southern drawls, but though many identified strongly with the American half of their parentage, they were indeed Vietnamese in language, culture, habits, in all ways but appearance. By 1988, uncorked by the Homecoming

Act, this trickle had become a torrent, overwhelming many of the services set up to meet the needs of earlier populations.

Teachers in the various educational programs of the PRPC, accustomed to the deference of earlier waves of Lao, Khmer, and Vietnamese refugees, were unprepared for the young Amerasian adults now flooding their classes. By 1988, the Amerasians were no longer children. Many were already in their late teens and early twenties or beyond, and quite a few had children of their own. A significant number had been street kids or children from dysfunctional families and were arriving in the refugee camp without any accompanying relatives. Many had had little, if any, education in Vietnam, having lacked the necessary documents for admission to school, the money for tuition, or the willingness to endure the taunting that Amerasians are often subjected to from their classmates. These were the disenfranchised, shunned by their countrymen for their American blood. They lacked the support of strong family ties, and had often been forced into marginalized lives in the underbelly of Vietnamese society. For these adolescents and young adults, many accustomed to the freedom of the street, the transition to five hours a day, six days a week of school, plus two hours daily of unpaid community service, was not without its difficulties.

Disruptions and fights, once relatively rare in PRPC classrooms, now became commonplace. Drunkenness and brawling in the refugee quarters also increased substantially. Those Amerasians involved in disruptive behavior were a definite minority, generally from the more disadvantaged segments of the population, but they were highly visible. Not surprisingly, those who were unaccompanied by relatives or who had grown up on the street with little or no family supervision experienced the most problems in adapting to the structured environment of the refugee camp. Those who made the transition smoothly often expressed dismay at the behavior of the others, worrying that in the PRPC, as in Vietnam, Amerasians as a group would suffer negative stereotyping for the actions of the minority.

Counseling and recreation services were created to meet the needs of these new arrivals. Subsequent waves of Amerasians arriving at the PRPC proved a bit more restrained. Service providers were less besieged, classes ran more smoothly, and though Amerasians as a group remained problematic, the turmoil caused by the early Amerasian arrivals subsided somewhat.

AMERASIANS IN VIETNAM

Why had they opted out of the land of their mothers, the country of their birth and upbringing, for passage to the unknown land of their anonymous fathers? Most wished simply to escape discrimination and poverty.

In relatively homogeneous Vietnam, foreign blood carries a strong stigma. Outsiders in the land of their birth, fatherless children in a culture where identity flows from the father, Amerasians were generally relegated to the fringe of society. These offspring of Americans were considered fair game for abuse. The taunts *My lai* and *con lai,* suffered by almost all Amerasians, and *My den* by those of black descent, carry stronger negative connotations then their approximate English equivalents: "Amerasian," "half-breed," and "black American." Abuse often went beyond the verbal. Joe Nguyen, an Amerasian now serving in the U.S. Air Force in Japan, reports:

> I remember one time, going to a movie and walking home by myself at night. I was probably thirteen at that time. There was a whole bunch of kids hidden out in the bushes, and they just ran out on the street, beat me up, and took off. . . . That's their game, going around, finding us, teasing us, and beating up on us, and the parents don't do anything about it. That's how they treat us.

Black Amerasians generally feel that they have suffered greater abuse than whites. Vietnamese negative attitudes towards blacks may have been initially shaped by their experience with the "black French," the North African troops of France's colonial army. Generically referred to as *Ma roc,* these troops acquired a terrible reputation for pillage, cruelty, and especially rape. Whatever the reason, the brunt borne by those fathered by blacks seems to have been heavier. Hoa, mother to both a black Amerasian girl and a white Amerasian boy, puts it this way:

> Vietnamese say, "You go back to America, you dirty American, go back to America. You lose the war already, go back." They say like that many times to my daughter, 'cause she is black. My son is white, not so many problems.

Huong, a black Amerasian woman of twenty-four, concurs:

> All my life people had been mean to me there *[in Vietnam]* because of my color. My skin is black, and my hair is curly, not like the Vietnamese, and they didn't like that.

School was generally torment for mixed blood children. Many quit early, unable to stand the taunts of their classmates, and sometimes, even the classmate's parents. Mai Linh, a young black Amerasian woman, explains:

> So I go back to school, and a man and woman over there, they slap me. They say, "You black, you can't sit down with my children." . . . So I tear up that paper *[school registration]*, and I never go to school no more.

Lessons emphasizing the "American imperialists" could be equally devastating. History classes decrying America's role in the destruction of Vietnam were intensely embarrassing for the Amerasians because they emphasized their status as children of the enemy, often turning their classmates against them.

Amerasians coped with the prejudice directed against them in different ways. Phuc is one whose features allowed him to pass for Vietnamese:

> Sometimes I would go somewhere, and in a social situation people might whisper to me, discreetly, "Are you French Vietnamese, or are you Amerasian?" I would say, "No I'm pure Vietnamese, it's just the way I look," and they would say, "Oh, sorry, forget about that, no problem." I was shy about being Amerasian, and that was one way I could avoid the problem.

Huynh, a black Amerasian girl, was also able to sidestep the onus of being pegged as the daughter of an American:

> Nobody made trouble for me, because they think I'm Indian. I knew I was Amerasian, but I didn't say anything. It's easier to be Indian than American.

Some whose features didn't allow for the option of concealing their racial identities sometimes avoided confrontation by simply keeping to themselves, staying at home. Others fought back physically against their tormentors, sometimes spiraling into lives of violence, alcohol abuse, crime, and incarceration. Mr. Loi recounts his Amerasian stepson Dung's reaction to the taunts of the Vietnamese:

> They teased him with the My lai rhyme. *[A nonsense rhyme used all over Vietnam to taunt Amerasians. It says that the Amerasians have twelve assholes, and if you plug one, gas and shit come out the others.]* He would fight every time. He always had problems with the police, he fought with them.

Abandoned and orphaned children and those raised by abusive or unloving stepparents were, not surprisingly, among those who most easily fell in with the underseam of Vietnamese life, the so-called *bui doi*, the "dust of life," joining gangs, engaging in street crimes, getting busted, and doing time. This segment has found it most difficult to adapt to life in the Philippine Refugee Processing Center and in the United States as well. A substantial number have mutilated themselves grotesquely. Cigarette burns and razor slashes on the arms, legs, and occasionally the torso are common among both males and females. Also not unusual among men is the lopping off of a part of a digit, generally the pinky, occasionally the index finger.

Two young men, who told me their stories over a period of several months, began the telling with a full complement of ten fingers each, but finished with nine and a half. During the months in which we spoke, one lopped off the upper joint of his little finger, the other took off half his index finger with a bolo, a Filipino machete. Another, Charlie, whose oral history appears in this book, slashed at his own hand in a drunken rage, but managed only to pare off the very tip of his pinky.

On a blistering afternoon in the PRPC, I was present when My, a nineteen-year-old white Amerasian with a history of disruptive behavior in his English-as-a-Second-Language class, was told that he would be recycled. This entailed delaying his graduation date from class and, subsequently, his date of departure from the Philippines for the United States. Moments later My had disappeared. We found him shortly, squatting in a drainage ditch on the side of the road, his left forearm dripping with blood, a razor blade nestled between the thumb and forefinger of his right hand.

I have heard a number of explanations of these self-destructive behaviors. One American counsellor/social worker who was raised in Vietnam and now works extensively with Amerasians calls them "the externalization of inner pain." Several of my interpreters mentioned that those Amerasians who scarify and tattoo themselves are emulating the behavior of the Vietnamese underclass with which they associate. Raymond, a black Amerasian, interprets the behavior this way:

> This is very common in Vietnam, among the Amerasians and the Vietnamese. They prove that they are tough, they aren't scared of anything. If it's a girl, then that means she's a wild girl, maybe a drug user or a prostitute. And sometimes if you don't see many of scars, just one, or one cigarette burn, they might *[do it]* to prove their love to someone, or *[their pain]* over a misunderstanding.

The Amerasians themselves, when asked why they have mutilated themselves, invariably answer, "depression." This depression is sometimes suicidal, as Hung, a black Amerasian whose torso is horrifically scarred, explains:

> All my life people despised me, they called me a "bastard," a "nigger." I didn't care about myself, I wanted to die. So I took a razor and slashed myself all over. People see my scars and they think, "Oh, he's a tough guy, he's a trouble maker." They judge me. But it's not like that, I just wanted to die.

Despite widespread prejudice against them in general, a number report normal lives, not being targeted for discrimination as a result of their American connections. Den, a twenty-one-year-old black Amerasian from Phan Rang province:

My grandparents advised me to go to America so I could help my relatives, but now I feel very sad. I miss my village, everyone there knew me and loved me. I feel I am Vietnamese, not American, and I wish I could go back.

MOTHERS OF AMERASIANS IN VIETNAM

During the war, the American bases in Vietnam were magnets for young women from the villages, who migrated to find jobs either inside the bases themselves or in the thriving economies outside the base perimeters that were fueled by the influx of American goods and dollars. Inside the bases, these women found employment as maids, laundresses, waitresses in the base clubs, and, for those with more schooling, secretaries and clerks in the offices and hospitals. Outside the base they worked in restaurants, markets, and shops. Some had food stalls or wagons where they sold fruit or drinks. And, of course, a number found employment as bar girls in the watering holes that sprung up wherever there was an American presence.

American civilians were in Vietnam as well, in various support roles for the military, as embassy staff, and in any of the numerous international companies doing business in Vietnam. Vietnamese women also found employment in these sectors of the economy, often as clerical staff for American businesses. Whatever their work, the jobs of these Vietnamese women put them into contact with Americans who, in many cases, eventually fathered their children.

Although a stereotype persists of Amerasians being conceived through casual encounters of American military men with Vietnamese bar girls, this was the case for only a small number of the women I spoke too. Most of the mothers of Amerasians report living with the fathers of their Amerasian children, sometimes for periods of several years. Eighty-one percent of mothers of Amerasians responding to a 1992 survey claimed to have lived with the American father of their children.[4] These relationships are generally viewed in a positive light. Seventy-eight percent of the women surveyed "had positive regard for their American husband."[5]

For the vast majority, the end of the husband's tour or stay in Vietnam meant the end of the relationship. Men often implored their Vietnamese sweethearts to accompany them back to the United States, but many demurred, bound by family ties and obligations. Van, married to an air force officer, was one who put off leaving Vietnam until it was too late:

We stay together until he goes to the U.S. in '72. He wanted me to come with him, but I cannot go. I cannot leave my mother. . . . Before "Charlie" *[the Viet Cong]* came, my husband writes me, he tells me that the VC are coming . . . but I don't think so, I think never the VC come. He tells me, sure. He says, "Please honey, take my baby, come to America. Charlie will come kill you." I don't believe him but in 1975 Charlie comes. My husband cannot write me anymore, and I feel very stupid. I feel crazy that I didn't listen to him.

For many others, however, husbands and lovers slipped silently out of their lives. Hanh, who had five Amerasian children with two men, talks of her second American boyfriend:

When he goes back to America, he don't even tell me nothing. His friends say, "Oh, Gleason, he went back already."

In April of 1975, as the Communists marched southward, women with American ties frantically disposed of evidence that might link them to the United States. Photos, documents, U.S. military base ID's, all went into bonfires. A minority severed their most tangible connection to the enemy, abandoning their own Amerasian children. Many children report having been left with baby-sitters and simply never picked up. The market also seems to have been a common venue for discarding infants, as My, a white Amerasian male from Da Nang, relates:

I was abandoned at the Da Nang market when I was a newborn and picked up there by a lady who had a stall selling fabric. She says that I was about three days old when she found me.

Rumors flew of the terrible vengeance to be exacted against Amerasians and their mothers by the new government. Many mothers hid their kids. Others cut off or dyed their children's hair and rubbed them with dirt to darken white skin in an attempt to disguise their parentage. There was, however, no bloodbath, nor any national policy of violence against Amerasians and their families. Institutionalized discrimination certainly did exist, but appears to have been more of a local matter, varying from place to place. Some mothers claim that it was worse in the urban areas, others say that rural Amerasians and their families suffered more. Policies affecting them seem to have been largely dependent upon the attitudes of the local officials.

The new government enacted a policy of clearing the cities of their excess population and using those evicted as laborers to develop uninhabited, undeveloped tracts of land, the so-called "New Economic Zones." By revoking their household registrations, the documents that entitle Viet-

namese to live, work, and study in a specific area, the government was able
to force many families to relocate to these New Economic Zones. Families
with Amerasians were often among those targeted. Some families hid;
others flatly refused to go and sometimes got away with it. Many, however,
were forced to comply. For city dwellers, unaccustomed to rural life, the
spartan conditions and heavy labor of the New Economic Zones often
proved unbearable.

Chau, mother of an Amerasian son and stepmother to two other
Amerasians, was forced out of Ho Chi Minh City to one of the New
Economic Zones:

> They sent me and my kids to Tay Ninh. I stayed there two years and
> worked as a farmer. There was no school, no hospital, nothing. I go to
> work, and the kids just stay in the house all day. One day I think my kids
> will die, because they tell everybody to go to work, but they don't give us
> no rice, no nothing.

Like many, Chau eventually returned to the city, living on the pe-
riphery of society without the indispensable household registration.

> Our children don't have food. My kids are all laying down, sick, hardly
> moving. I realize then that if I stay there we die, so I have to get out of
> that place. . . . So we left Tay Ninh. I walked, me and many people . . .
> from seven at night to four in the morning we walked. We had no ride,
> no bus. We walked for two days. We walked to Saigon, all the way.

Confiscation of their property by the Communist government is mentioned bitterly by a number of mothers of Amerasians, some of whom, like
Nam, wound up on the street when her house was seized:

> In 1975, the VC took my house, took everything. I had nothing. My
> children and I had no house for eight years. We slept in cars, anywhere.

Many mothers report being harassed by local officials sometimes they
dragged out of bed in the middle of the night and interrogated; sometimes
imprisoned for varying lengths of time, and in extreme cases, sent to prison
camps. Hoa, mother of a black Amerasian daughter and a white Amerasian
son, is one of these:

> They [the police] talk about Ho Chi Minh. They say he is so good because
> he work very hard and he don't need no money, he only want to help peo-
> ple. But I say, "I'm not sure," I never saw him, so how can I say anything
> about him? So VC get very angry at me, and one night, at about two

o'clock, when I was sleeping, he *[the police]* come to my house and take me to the monkey house. He don't even tell me where they take me, and my family, they don't know where I go. . . .

The VC tell us that we would only go to school for ten days and then go back home. . . . Yeah, ten days, that's what they say, but they take me go for more than two years.

A number of Amerasians and their mothers report having suffered no special persecution at the hands of the government, but fewer were spared social opprobrium. Mothers of Amerasians were lumped together in the national eye as whores, and their children as bastards. The ostracization of Amerasians and their mothers intensified after the war, when, along with being the wives and offspring of foreigners, they were the children and mistresses of the enemy. Hanh describes the situation in her home province of Kien Giang:

Before 1975, nobody talk nothin' to me . . . just behind my back, so I can't hear. They don't talk loud, but I know that they say that I have a GI boyfriend. Nineteen seventy-five, I go back there, and some people look me the same as a dog.

GOLD CASES

If after 1975, many Amerasians were consigned to the "dust of life," with the passage of the Amerasian Homecoming Act in 1988, that dust turned to gold. Ironically, those who had reviled the Amerasians for their American blood were now eager to exploit them as tickets out of impoverished Vietnam to the United States. In socialist Vietnam, a market in Amerasians developed, with people at many levels of society profiting, though least of all, in general, Amerasians and their bona fide families.

Obtaining a Vietnamese exit permit from the Vietnamese Ministry of the Interior is a prerequisite for the interview with the American Orderly Departure Program and eventual acceptance by the United States. The procedure has several steps. First, the applicant's name must be on a valid household register. Then completed Orderly Departure Forms must be submitted to the local neighborhood leader, who is entrusted with forwarding them up the chain to national authorities, where they eventually reach the Ministry of the Interior. The Ministry of the Interior has the responsibility of interviewing the applicants and, if all is in order, issuing the coveted exit permit. Sharks often hide in the shoals of Vietnamese bureaucracy, and gold is their preferred sustenance. If they are not amply fed, an applicant's case can founder for years.

Many Amerasians and their legitimate families lack the resources to make the necessary payoffs and must turn to outside sources or face hideous delays. There is no shortage of Vietnamese willing to pay the requisite bribes in exchange for passage out of Vietnam to America. They approach the Amerasian directly or through one of the many brokers that for a fee find Amerasians for prospective "family members." The Amerasian then claims these newfound "relations" as legitimate family. Bribes are paid, documents forged, and the Amerasian and his or her bogus family are on their way to the ODP interview, and if lucky, eventually to America. In this way, thousands of Vietnamese who would not otherwise have been eligible, have entered the United States in the years since the passage of the Amerasian Homecoming Act.

All too often in this scheme, the Amerasian's real family must be left behind, and many Amerasians hope to sponsor their bona fide relations once they reach the United States.

These "gold cases" rarely end happily for the Amerasian. Once in the Philippine Refugee Processing Center, relations between the Amerasians and their families of convenience generally deteriorate rapidly. Families that were warm and caring in Vietnam when their own interests were at stake often turn hostile and abusive now that the Amerasians have successfully served their purposes. The Amerasians, who have often left their real families behind, once again find themselves ostracized. Phuong, a twenty-four-year-old Amerasian woman, says this about her "family":

> When we were in Vietnam, being interviewed, they were very nice to me, sure. But now that we are here, they don't need me anymore. They treat me like dirt. They even tell me, "We're on our way to America already, we don't need you anymore." They insult me, berate me, the daughters even have attacked me. They loved the Amerasian when they needed to leave Vietnam, but now they despise me.

In other cases, bogus families have remained cordial, even warm, through their stay in the PRPC, often out of fear that discovery of the details of their fake relationship with the Amerasian might affect their resettlement. Once they are resettled in America, however, any such restraint vanishes. Loc, a twenty-three year old who had grown close to his family of convenience in the PRPC, wrote his friend the details of his resettlement:

> As soon as we got to California, they turned on me and threw me out. I feel like I am in hell.

Although the high incidence of fraud in the Amerasian program has been common knowledge for years, little was done about it. Once a family reached the PRPC, the policy was, in most cases, to push them through to the United States, regardless of the genuineness of their relationship to the

Amerasian. Over the past year however, this policy has changed radically. The Joint Voluntary Agency, the agency responsible for facilitating resettlement from the PRPC, has begun to move against fraudulent families, putting many on hold, delaying or terminating their resettlement in America. What will eventually happen to them is still unclear, as at the moment, Vietnam seems disinclined to take them back.

It must be pointed out that Vietnamese resorting to fraud to get out of Vietnam are not necessarily base or evil. Living in a country with a repressive political system and one of the lowest per capita incomes in the world, many are desperate to leave at any cost, as witnessed by the mass exodus of boat people in the face of well-publicized risks. Many Amerasians and their families have, not surprisingly, used the market that has grown up around them to their own advantage. Some have received payment in gold for taking bogus relations to the United States. Truong, a black Amerasian in his early twenties, has a picture of his family sitting in front of a newly built cement house. He explains how his impoverished family was able to afford it:

> A man from Saigon came to see me and said he had a family that wanted to go to America with me. He said they would give my family some gold. So I said okay, and they gave my family enough to build this new house.

Recently, a new scam has surfaced. Amerasians and their families go through the application process, and once they are approved and ready to go, noneligible Vietnamese take their place at the airport. In this way, an Amerasian, changing his name and using easily obtainable falsified documents, can sell himself many times and realize a tidy profit. A number of these stand-ins have been caught recently at Tan Son Nhut airport in Ho Chi Minh City, and in the PRPC.

RESETTLEMENT IN THE UNITED STATES

More than 70,000 Amerasians and family members have left Vietnam and resettled in America; about 21,000 are themselves Amerasians, the rest are accompanying relatives.[6] It is estimated that only a few thousand bona fide Amerasians remain in Vietnam.

A 1989 study indicates that Amerasians with limited schooling, those arriving in the United States without their mothers or accompanying family members, and those fathered by African-Americans are especially at risk for problems in adaptation.[7] Indeed, for many Amerasians, particularly those who fall into these categories, resettlement has not been easy. Most

Amerasians come as "free cases," having no relatives to welcome them in the United States. These free cases are resettled in "cluster sites," selected cities that have social service providers experienced in dealing with Amerasians and that can potentially provide adequate support. With strained budgets and increasing caseloads, this is not always the reality.

The majority of the new arrivals, like most refugees and immigrants, wind up where apartments are available and rent is cheapest, in run-down inner-city neighborhoods. Unlike most other refugee groups, Amerasians rarely have strong family or community support to rely on. Most of the Amerasians I spoke with in the PRPC were quite adamant in their avowal not to live with Vietnamese in the United States. Once here, however, their options are limited by language, finances, and a lack of familiarity with American culture. Many find themselves in the ironic predicament of having left Vietnam to escape life on the fringe of Vietnamese society, only to find themselves in the same situation in one of the various little Saigons around the United States.

Amerasians who have developed unrealistically optimistic expectations about their futures in America are often disappointed. Those who grew up in Vietnam reviled as Americans and as a result identified themselves with the United States find out quickly that culturally, linguistically, in all ways but appearance, they are Vietnamese. For those who banked on easy acceptance and integration into American society, this can be a shattering realization, confusing already fragile identities.

Given general backgrounds of limited education, poverty, parental loss, and discrimination, the hurdles these Amerasians face are formidable. Not surprisingly, in the United States, as in the Philippine Refugee Processing Center, many find it difficult to deal with the structured environment of school, as well as the intricacies of the English language. Few U.S. high schools are set up to deal with non–English-speaking students who lack even minimal academic backgrounds. Dropout rates are high. A large number of the Amerasians coming over now are too old for the public school system, but are eligible for adult English-as-a-Second-Language Programs. A case worker formerly working in Virginia reports difficulty in motivating her Amerasian clients to attend. "Many worked in Chinese restaurants owned by Vietnamese," she says, "and had only Vietnamese-speaking friends. They never had to learn English." She also lists low self-esteem and fear of failure as deterrents.

Blacks, who often bore the heaviest load of discrimination in Vietnam, can face special adjustment difficulties. Having grown up with their race the object of scorn, many have internalized negative racial stereotypes about people of color. This has sometimes made attempts at matching black Amerasians with black American sponsors or black Big Brothers/Big Sisters problematic.

Mothers of Amerasians face their own set of problems. Many are unmarried and must meet the challenges of single motherhood in an unfamiliar land at the same time they make the difficult transition to American life. A large number have limited education and few marketable job skills. Some find themselves isolated in the Vietnamese community in America, as they were in Vietnam, by virtue of having had Amerasian children. Support groups for these women have formed in several cities, venues where they can find empathy and assistance.

The search for long-gone fathers and husbands, often described by the Amerasians and their mothers in the Philippine Refugee Processing Center as a priority, is usually put on hold while they adjust to American life, look for jobs, and settle in. Many come with far too little information on which to base a search. For others, fear of rejection probably plays a role in their reticence. A significant number, however, do pursue the father search, generally through the American Red Cross. If the father is located, he is apprised of the situation, and the decision to contact the Amerasian or to supply his address or phone number is left up to him. The men who lived and fathered children with Vietnamese women during the war have gone on with their lives, often remarrying and raising families. The appearance of a child and spouse from twenty years past is not always welcome. Only about 2 percent of the father searches end positively.

Anita Menghetti, a consultant for Amerasian resettlement with the Lutheran Immigration and Refugee Services in Washington, D.C., describes disenfranchisement in Vietnam as the root of the Amerasians' difficulties. "They were denied legitimacy as Vietnamese persons," Menghetti states. "Hope has been bludgeoned out of them. *[Bringing the Amerasians to America is]* just like taking any group of disenfranchised people from the United States and plopping them in a foreign culture and asking them to adapt."

At the same time, Menghetti stresses that too much publicity has been given to the problems Amerasians have encountered and very little has been written about the numerous success stories. Many Amerasians have gone to Job Corps or skills training programs and are successfully holding down steady jobs. A number have graduated from high school, some with honors, and have gone on to college. One black Amerasian, despite only five years of schooling in Vietnam, graduated in the top ten of her high school class, no mean feat. Joe Nguyen, whose narrative appears in this book, received hardly any education in Vietnam, but in America he graduated from high school, went through a year of college, and eventually joined the U.S. Air Force. Joe came to America at fifteen with his mother and had the good fortune of being befriended by a concerned American who patiently acted as his mentor. In general, those Amerasians who, like Joe, come to America with the person who was their primary caregiver in

Vietnam, find the transition easier. Those who hook up with American mentors often thrive. These mentors may be found through Big Brother/Big Sister type programs, through churches or schools, or through foster families in the case of Amerasians under eighteen.

Dr. Julie Macdonald, program director of Children's Services at the Lutheran Immigration and Refugee Service in New York City, succinctly summarizes the Amerasian plight. "Amerasians have had a rougher time *[than most Vietnamese]*, lacking family acceptance, and community acceptance. When they come here, they find that their fantasies that they are American are untrue. They have a lot to get over. We do a disservice to refugees if we believe that all we have to do is to get them into the country, and that no other help is needed."

Amerasians and their mothers have walked a long road to get to this country. They are survivors and will persevere here as they did in Vietnam. The spirit of the "Homecoming Act," by its very name, is one of providing comfort and nurture. With adequate support from resettlement agencies, from community groups, from concerned individuals, Vietnamese Amerasians can adapt and prosper. Without it, for those lacking in education and family support, survival may be all that the country of their fathers can offer.

MAKING *CHILDREN OF THE ENEMY*

The idea for *Children of the Enemy* grew out of a project in the Philippine Refugee Processing Center aimed at providing English reading material for mothers of Amerasians. I interviewed fourteen women, and the resultant oral histories were transcribed for use in their classrooms. Although the literacy project was completed in a few months, my own interest was piqued, and I continued the interviews, expanding them to include the Amerasians themselves. Between January of 1991 and August of 1992, I conducted over a hundred such taped interviews in the refugee center. In May of 1993, I interviewed Tung Joe Nguyen and his wife Julie Nguyen, a Vietnamese Amerasian couple living outside the gate of Misawa airbase in Japan, where Joe was serving in the U.S. Air Force. They were the only interviews I conducted outside the refugee camp, and Joe and Julie were the only interviewees who had already been through resettlement in America.

The Philippine Refugee Processing Center is divided into ten neighborhoods, each containing refugee quarters, rudimentary classrooms, and a tiny clinic. It was in the refugee housing, referred to as billets, that the majority of the interviews took place. These narrow two-story asbestos and wood units, laid out in rows of ten, house up to twelve refugees in less space than a American might devote to storing his automobile. Ads and articles from old American and Filipino magazines are taped to the bare asbestos walls; *Time* magazine accounts of Iran-Contra, Playtex bra advertisements, cutouts of Arnold Schwarzenegger, Fidelity mutual fund advertisements. None of these are intelligible to the Vietnamese-speaking occupants; their function is decorative, to provide a shot of color in the drab surroundings.

Another venue for interviews was the PRPC jail, generally called the "Monkey House," a generic term used by the refugees to refer to any type of detention facility. Refugees who run afoul of the often capricious PRPC regulations do time here, as do those arrested for criminal offenses. In the PRPC, arrest equals conviction; there is no judicial process. Several of the Amerasians whose oral histories appear here were interviewed, at least in part, while they were detainees at the PRPC jail.

Despite the immense heat, the hectic daily schedules of five hours study and two hours of mandatory "volunteer" work, and the June 15, 1991, eruption of nearby Mt. Pinatubo, which blanketed the refugee camp in six inches of sand and ash, turning lush tropical land into instant moonscape, people were generally eager to tell their stories. Twice, however, after agreeing to be interviewed, mothers of Amerasians declined once I arrived at their billets. Despite my assurances of complete anonymity, they feared that the repercussions of what they might say would endanger their relatives still in Vietnam. They were not alone in their fears; a number of interviewees voiced this concern, even as they agreed to speak. One who assented to tell her story but later backed out explained, "Even if you change my name, the VC will know, they know everything." I was to hear similar statements many times, eerie testimonials to the government of Vietnam's success in controlling the lives of its citizens.

The decision of whether or not to use real names in the oral histories was left up to the interviewee. A number indicated that they preferred not to be referred to by name, or simply to be called by their given names, which in Vietnam, are generally the last. There were those who asked to be referred to by specific pseudonyms or nicknames. Some former bar girls had aliases for work, some Amerasians had changed their names when they were "bought" by Vietnamese who claimed them as kin to get out of Vietnam, some mothers of Amerasians had pet names which their American husbands called them. There were those too who requested that their real names appear, sometimes in the hope that a long-gone husband or father might read their narratives and recognize them. Even when permission to use a real name was given, if potentially embarrassing or sensitive disclosures had been made, I changed the name. An oral history headed by a single name indicates either that the narrator's name has been changed or that only the given name is being used. The use of pseudonyms or nicknames is mentioned in the introduction of the oral histories in which they appear.

The names of the American boyfriends and husbands, the fathers of the Amerasians, have been changed in the interests of privacy. Three exceptions are those of Henry Higgins and Terry Reynolds, who are deceased, and Lloyd Grow, whose name appears with his permission.

I note in the individual introduction to each oral history whether the narrator spoke to me in English or in Vietnamese through an interpreter. The interpreters usually were other refugees with good English skills, often those who worked as volunteer translators with one of the agencies in the PRPC. When a narrator did speak in English, I generally edited the resultant narrative as little as was practical in order to retain the color of the account. Therefore, somewhat ironically, the oral histories of those who spoke in English often contain grammatical irregularities and nonstandard usages, while those done through an interpreter have been edited into standard English.

Saigon is now called Ho Chi Minh City, and a number of provinces and towns have also been renamed since 1975. Old habits die hard, and many still use the former names. In the oral histories, I let the preference of the narrator stand. The Appendix lists the major changes in Vietnamese geographical place names that have occurred since 1975.

Almost all mothers of Amerasians refer to the American fathers of their children as their husbands, regardless of whether or not they were formally married. This usage is retained in the oral histories.

The oral histories in this book are divided into three sections. In the first section, the narrators are Amerasians. In the second, they are Amerasians and their mothers. In the third section, the narrators are mothers of Amerasians. The children of the women in this section were not interviewed.

Some who tell their stories here delivered brief sketches of their lives into my tiny recorder. Others spoke at length, sometimes meeting with me over a period of months. Many became my friends, my frequent companions, and I found myself drawn into the torrent of emotions that the tellings released. Their accounts deal with loss of husbands, of parents, of family, of freedom, of country. Feelings that lie beneath the surface were often dredged up; voices quivered, tears flowed, but the telling went on. Their stories are far from over.

NOTES

1. *The United States Orderly Departure Program.* American Embassy, 1/92.

2. *Home to America, If Not to Daddy, The Economist* 19 May 1990: 40.

3. *The United States Orderly Departure Program Statistical Summary.* December 1991.

4. *Vietnamese Amerasian Mothers: Psychological Distress and High-Risk Factors.* (Washington, D.C.: Office of Refugee Resettlement, 1992) 23.

5. Leong and Johnson 20.

6. *Amerasian Resettlement. Arlington, Va., June 25–27, 1992.* Washington, D.C.: InterAction Amerasian Resettlement Program under agreement with the Office of Refugee Resettlement, 1992. Unpaginated.

7. Donald A. Ranard, rev. of *Vietnamese Amerasians: Practical Implications of Current Research,* by Kirk Felsman, Mark C. Johnson, Frederick T.L. Leong, and Irene C.Felsman, *In America* October 1990: 9.

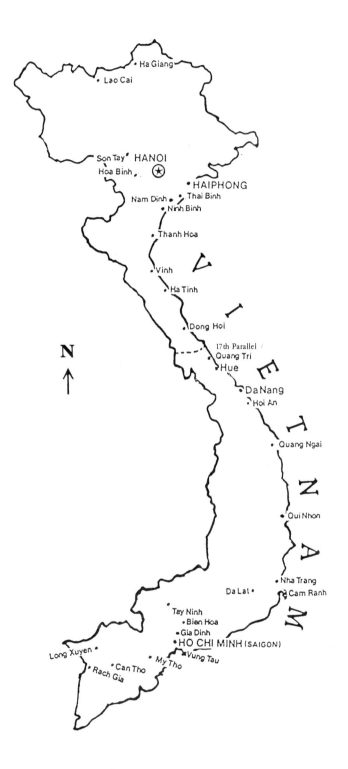

- Ha Giang
- Lao Cai

Son Tay
HANOI
Hoa Binh
⊛
HAIPHONG
Nam Dinh • Thai Binh
Ninh Binh
Thanh Hoa
Vinh
Ha Tinh
Dong Hoi
17th Parallel
Quang Tri
Hue
Da Nang
Hoi An
Quang Ngai
Qui Nhon
Nha Trang
Da Lat
Cam Ranh
Tay Ninh
Bien Hoa
Gia Dinh
HO CHI MINH (SAIGON)
Long Xuyen
Vung Tau
Can Tho
My Tho
Rach Gia

VIETNAM

N
↑

AMERASIANS

Difficult times, some of my brothers
gone east, some west; wars
have left fields and gardens desolate;
families have scattered and refugees
wander like ghosts or fall like autumn leaves...

Bai Juyi, "Thinking of My Brothers
and Sister," *Two Hundred Selected Poems*

I will leave my homeland
as I have lived in it, with nothing,
but a ticket to my father's land.

Laurie Kuntz, *Nguyen Van Phuong*
Imagines: Speaking to my American Father

I consider Vietnamese as my family, as my people
too, but they don't think of me the same way. They
always think of me as a stranger, uneducated, with
an uneducated mother.

Airman E-4 Tung Joe Nguyen, Amerasian

Raymond

"Singing my father's song."

"When the prisoners are working, most of them like for me to sing American songs. When I get caught, the guard says, 'Raymond, what's the song you singin'?' I say, 'I'm singing my father's song.' He says, 'Well, you know that if you singin' that song, that mean you are the enemy'." Raymond and I are sitting in an empty conference room in the PRPC. The monsoon rain is pounding against the windows; small rivulets of water form beneath them as Raymond describes life in a Vietnamese reeducation camp. Certainly, singing his father's song was not done without cost in postwar Vietnam.

We first met in the billet of one of my Amerasian students. He greeted me with a perfectly fluent, "Hi, how ya doin'?" From his appearance, accent, and gestures, I took him to be a black American, possibly a Vietnam veteran who'd come to the refugee camp to search for a lost son or daughter. Continuing in fluid English, he mentioned that he had recently arrived at the PRPC and was living in neighborhood one. Only then did I realize that I was speaking not to an American, but to an Amerasian refugee.

Raymond's speech, gestures, and body language are acquired from the black GI's who cared for him as he grew up on and around the bases near the coastal town of Vung Tau. His experiences "Americanized" him, and for twelve years after the fall of Saigon, the Vietnamese government tried in a series of labor camps to purge him of his Western influence. Raymond, however, would not be changed. "This is my way," he explains, "I cannot forget it."

For the Amerasian, language is power, and few, if any, have the command of English that Raymond displays. When journalists came to Vietnam to research the Amerasian situation, it was often Raymond they spoke to or who translated for them. When Vietnam vet John R. returned to Vietnam to set up an English program for Amerasians, Raymond was his contact. For many Vietnamese refugees, especially Amerasians, it was Raymond they sought out in "Amerasian Park," located near the Ministry of Foreign Affairs, to fill out their applications for the Orderly Departure Program. In the PRPC, he has worked as an inter-

preter for numerous people, including myself. His skills at translating are excellent.

Raymond's makeshift scrapbook is stacked with his clippings from a number of American papers, and his name appears in several books about Vietnam. He is well known, and those that do know him tend to form strong opinions about him, whether positive or negative. He is seen by some as a samaritan, utilizing his skills to teach and aid other Amerasians. Raymond certainly sees himself in this light. Others view him as a con-man who exploits his language abilities for his own ends at the expense of others, making sure his side of the story is always heard. In reality, there is probably something of both aspects in Raymond.

Controversy seems to follow Raymond. Shortly after our first meeting, he was arrested and sent to a Filipino prison in Balanga, the provincial capital of Bataan, for his alleged part in the stabbing of another refugee, a small-time tough named Duc. Three other Amerasians were charged in the attack and incarcerated together with Raymond. The oral histories of two, Tuan Den and Charlie, also appear in this book.

After several months of detention, the charges of "Frustrated Murder," the Philippine equivalent of attempted homicide, were dropped, and the four were sent back to the PRPC. Although no longer suspects under Filipino law, they were put on hold by JVA, the organization responsible for expediting refugee departures to the United States from the PRPC. Raymond and the others found themselves in a bureaucratic limbo, their scheduled departures for the States postponed indefinitely.

In our early conversations, Raymond denied any involvement in the stabbing, ostensibly to protect himself. Months later, when the issue was already moot, he was to admit to me a role less benign.

Raymond appears considerably older than his documented age of twenty-six and readily admits that, as an orphan, he knows neither his true age nor his paternity. Some believe him to be the son of an African soldier from the French colonial forces, rather than an Amerasian. Because of his fluency in English, he has even been suspected of being an American GI who remained in Vietnam after the war and is trying to reenter the United States through the Amerasian program to escape detection and possible prosecution. The former, Raymond admits, is a possibility, the latter he characterizes as "absurd."

As Raymond's speech is fluent and colloquial, I have retained many of the nonstandard pronunciations and tense changes in order to preserve the original flavor of the narrative.

MY EARLIEST MEMORY is of an orphanage, a Catholic orphanage in Vung Tau. I just cut out of there, you know. I left with a bunch of kids, Amerasian, Korean, Filipino, all mixed race kids. I was seven or eight, out on the street, shinin' shoes day by day. I was hangin' around this black bar, shinin' shoes there, when I met one black American soldier, his name is

Robert Handler *[not a real name]*. He adopted me and took me to live with him inside the base. I learned English from him and his friends. They were all black, and most of the time I was just hangin' around with all these GI's, and I'd be listenin' to them talk. I was young; they didn't want to let me go off the base because they be afraid that the VC might give me a box of cookies, and it might have a bomb inside. But most of the time I just sneaked out. I just wanted to stay outside in town and run around with my friends, playin', swimmin', sometimes stayin' at the beach all day.

I can't remember exactly how long Robert Handler stayed in Vietnam, but I tell you, I think it was a long time because I can remember him more than the others who took care of me after he went back to the States. *[After Robert Handler]* there was a teacher, a black American, he taught for what they call the American-Vietnamese Association. He was in the army. He took care of me for . . . I don't know how long, but many times I ran away from home. That guy, he's so strict you know, he wanted to put me in school. That time I could speak English already, and I thought I was good, too good to be put in school. I liked to be out runnin' more. When Robert was in Vietnam, he put me in school, and I stayed only two days. I spoke English, you know, more outstanding than the other students, so I just was . . . self confident, that's it. . . . I didn't have to learn more, I liked to play more than study.

In '72, when all the troops were gettin' out, I met this lady, she says she's my mother, you know. I was an orphan, I didn't know who my mother was. Then this lady comes, says she's my mother, and takes me with her. I thought, "Hey, I got a mother," and I'm just so happy, I didn't think about who she was. I was in heaven. Later, some people told me that she was not my real mother, but I don't know. . .

She took me up to Saigon, but after about a month, a month and a half, I was bored, so I just sneaked out of there. You know, I liked to live on the street. I was just runnin' around, and I was tryin' to look for Americans. I met this marine, he was guarding the U.S Embassy. His name was Albert McClean *[not a real name]*. He's young, about twenty or so, a black guy. You know the guards, they don't live inside the U.S. Embassy. They live in the billet, and I was staying there with him. He's takin' care of me, and he also was tryin' to put me in the school, but I said no.

Then in '75 Saigon fell, and I was runnin' away from the place where I lived with the marine guard. The VC, they started comin' in. I was worried, so I went back to my mom, and she took me out to the countryside. She thought it would be safe there, but once we get there the VC is comin' in there too. She gets real scared, and after four or five days she brought me back to Saigon. She burned all the pictures, all the photos that I have, that I took in the base. She destroyed them all. Even the letters that Robert Handler wrote to me she burned, she burned everything.

Raymond, spring 1992

She was afraid, and so was I. When I lived inside the base, I looked at the movies for instruction for soldiers on duty. They always say, "VC, they hate Americans." I feel that I'm an American also, and I think, "They gonna get me too." I'm afraid, and I cannot deal with it myself. I must depend on my mother, and at that time I be afraid to separate from her.

She brought me back to Saigon, but she got sick and could not take care of me. I had to go around to neighbors, friends, and I ate there. I went out to the center of Saigon. The VC are comin' in with their tanks. They're celebrating, kinda proud. People are robbing, looting, breakin' into houses, carrying all the property out.

I go over to the U.S. Embassy and just walk inside. All the cars are torn up, the doors are broken in. I just go in and look at all the rooms, and I think, "Everything is gone, and I'm still here." I heard people say the helicopter picked everybody up here, and I think, "If my mom didn't take me to the countryside, maybe I would have got away already." I think about that, and I suffer.

You know, the marine who was my friend, he told me before, he tell me like this, he say, "Raymond, I'm worryin' about you, because I think the VC are gonna come in, in maybe one more month." And I think he's trying to frighten me, you know, scare me. He always was jokin' with me, you know. And he say, "You know, Raymond, I'm tryin' to take you back to America, but it's too short to make the papers."

I just walked around in the street, and I met this old man who was a cigarette vendor. He was sitting there eating, and I was kinda hungry, you know, so I was just standing there, watching him eat. He asked me, "Where your home, where your parents?" And I say, "I have no parents." So he ask me, "You want something to eat?" I say, "Yeah," and he buy me a piece of bread. And he tell me, "Okay, you just sell this cigarette, this candy, and I will give you some food." And I did. I was selling and selling.

Around June of 1975, they had a campaign about peace and order. After Saigon fell, people was breakin' into houses and takin' everything. So the police arrested vendors, beggars, criminals, anybody. That's when they pulled me in and sent me to the reeducation camp. They say it's reeducation, but it's a prison, hard labor, working.

First, they bring us all together in the city prison, Chi Hoa. I stayed there about four months. Then they transferred me out to labor camp. They sent me to Nong Giao, they call it Nong Giao base. It used to be for basic training for the South V.N. army, but now they use that for the detainees. I was still young then. I didn't have to work too hard, I just did all these cleaning things. I didn't have to go out and work on the farm like the adults.

They transferred me to many different locations. I been to about six places, including the central highlands, in the twelve years they kept me locked up in those camps.

The guards, they treat the South Vietnamese who had relations with the Americans especially bad. They always tell them, "You are the enemy." So I was treated worse, 'cause at that time I didn't speak Vietnamese fluently. I spoke more English, you know, street English. I sang only American songs, like "My Girl," and "Since I Lost My Baby," songs by the Temptations. I don't know how to sing Vietnamese songs, and most of the stories I know about are the American stories.

Now, I am fluent in Vietnamese, but about writin' and readin', I can't do them well, 'cause I never been to elementary school, I was taught by a Vietnamese prisoner. I can read and write English, but not too well.

There were many rules in the labor camps—don't speak any language except Vietnamese, and don't practice any religion or create any group for praying or anything like that. Don't fight, don't talk about the politics. Three people cannot group together talking, they think you may be trying to escape.

When the prisoners are working, most of them like for me to sing American songs. When I get caught, the guard says, "Raymond, what's the song you singing?" I say, "I'm singing my father's song." He says, "Well, you know that if you singin' that song, that mean you are the enemy," and he start givin' me the instructions about Communism. They not allow you to sing a blues song in camp, you always sing red songs—fight, fight, fight, fight the Americans, fight the French, how we won the war, all that stuff. I can't stand that music.

So, afterward they make a statement. They say that I was breakin' the rules of the camp, speakin' a different language. They don't beat me, because I'm too young to beat. They put me in the cell, and they chain my leg. Every day they give me a meal, but only half, because they say, "You don't work, you just layin' there in the cell so you don't need to eat much."

I never knew when I would get out of prison camp. When I was in jail in Saigon, I asked them how long they gonna keep me there, and they said about three months. That was the penalty for street vendors. But then three months passed, and I didn't get out, and they transfer me to the reeducation camp. When I get there, someone says to me, "The Communists, they have no limit on the sentence. They say that if you good, your brain has been "washed," you a good worker, then they let you free." I wanted to try to escape, but at that time I was very young. The adults don't let the young follow them, so they don't let us know when they escape. But I saw them, and when they escape, if they got caught, the VC shoot them. Sometimes you don't try to escape, sometimes you just crawl out of the camp, trying to steal some manioc and some potatoes, 'cause everyone is hungry, they don't feed you enough. They know, they know that the prisoner is not trying to escape, that they just trying to get something to eat, but they shoot them anyway.

We have to get up at five-thirty in the morning, and by six we're already out on the farm working. We don't get no food before we work. There are teams, about fifty workers on a team, one team leader, a vice–team leader, a secretary. Every day we get a work assignment. The guards say, "Okay, if you finish this as early as you can, you can go home and rest. But if you just keep trying to delay, you stay there until you finish." We work outside the camp perimeter, big jobs, cuttin' and diggin' deep to build canals. There is no water in the prison camp, you have to go out to the stream to get water. Most of the time that's where the prisoners escape, so they wanted to build a canal to bring the water inside the camp.

At lunch they give you a bowl of rice and some vegetable soup with fish sauce, no meat. You only can have meat when they have a celebration, a holiday, a Communist holiday. Then you can have a piece of thin, thin meat. They make people hungry, but you have to work hard. Many people violate their rules, because you cannot be good if you hungry. You steal;

if you get depressed, angry, you might turn wild, kill somebody. This happened a lot inside the camp.

We work every day, no holiday. They say we have one day off, Sunday, but Sunday you don't work outside the camp, you work inside the camp. They say that's for doin' your own things, your clothes, but you work hard. When you work outside the camp, maybe you can go and find some wild fruit. You can maybe rest a little bit, but inside, aw . . . it was terrible inside the camp. No trees and all this hot sun, and you cannot go inside the hut where we sleep. If you go inside the hut, they just beat you up and they give you a punishment. So we have to work all day in the sun . . . aw, it's awful.

You get teaching at seven in the evening, until nine-thirty when you go to bed. They give you your instructions for tomorrow, and they give you feedback for that day, what you have done, what is your mistake. The first instruction is that you have to finish the assignment that is given to you. They don't care how hard it is. If you don't, you have to receive the punishment. The punishment depends on how bad your work is. If you really lazy, or you be late they give you long punishment.

They give you Communist training, especially for minors, like me at that time. We minors not working too hard, but they training us hard. They point to the American, and they always say, "That's the enemy. They are the reason that our country became poor and suffers." When I'm in class, I don't really listen to them. I'm always playin' and not payin' attention, so when they ask me the question, I cannot answer. For the punishment, I have to go to the cell. They say that I . . . what do you call this word . . . oppose them. But I don't actively oppose them. Some people oppose by acting, but me, I'm too young to act. I can't do nothing, they gonna beat me to death if I act. So I just don't answer, I don't talk, I don't sing their songs. They say raise your hand and say, "America is damned." I don't do that. So they say I'm hard-headed, and they put me in the cell.

The prisoners are all in miserable circumstances, all the same, just thinking "I want to be full." So the Communists they use you. . . . They pick one prisoner out, they give him a lot of food, and they send him back to give reports, you know, to give them information every day. So some prisoners start doin' like that, informing, and many time I get caught by one of them. It's nighttime, the cell is locked, you cannot go outside, we're supposed to be sleepin'. I be layin' in bed or in a group talkin' about a story and a man turns me in. The next morning the team leader announces, "Raymond, after you come back, go see a counselor, and I say "Aw, I got trouble," but I can't even imagine what I did. I didn't fight, I didn't steal, so what's the problem? All the trouble is that I told about American stories and sang American songs and they lock me in the cell again. If the other prisoners find an informer, they kill him. They might stab him, throw some boiling water on some part on his body or even his head as a warning.

If people get sick, they got a clinic, with this one kind of medicine. If you got fever, if you got a cold, if you got a headache, they give you the same medicine. Many people got sick, especially with malaria. I never got malaria, you know why? I always follow this one old guy, he's an ARVN officer, a colonel. He been in training in America, and he speaks English fluently, so he always speaks English with me, and he taught me to read and write some Vietnamese too. He's a preacher also, He comfort me and he give me patience, you know, to believe in God. Sometimes I think of everything back when I was livin' in the base. I lost everything, and now I'm in hell. Then I want to kill myself, I just think about dying. But he tell me, "If you die, you have to die for something. If you die, you have to hurt them. Kill one or two of them, and then you can die. Don't kill yourself, you got to be tough enough to survive." That colonel, they never let him go, he was still there when I was released.

He and his friend, they have a secret group, you know, they have meetings in camp. They loved me because I always oppose the VC. The other children they don't, they just follow, but I always say, "I grow up with Americans, I didn't grow up on Vietnamese food." The other Amerasians, they did not grow up on the base, so they cannot realize, you know, how it is. They don't know if it's true or not, what the VC say. So, they be in the middle, but me, I know.

One time I ask the VC, "Why you say, you know, that I am the sign of the enemy that was bombin' this country, that was rippin' this country off?" I was standin' in front of the whole camp, with two more black Amerasians and one white Amerasian. They all been violating the rules, fighting. But for me, it was my spirit, so they make an example of me. This VC was giving instructions and gettin' kinda angry. He say, "You hard-headed, but we have punishment for hard-headed people." So what do they do? They squeeze you, they make you hungry, and you will be weak, then you will obey. They don't beat me up. They just put me in a cell, and I don't have to work. But I don't have much to eat or drink either. It's hot in there, and the mosquitoes and bed bugs... Oh jeez, many people die in that cell. They put me there four times. And then I was thinkin' about escapin'. I was thinkin', "Aw, when I'm gonna be released, when they gonna free me?"

They always say, "Oh, Raymond, he's a contrary person," always. That's how come many Amerasians who know me there respect me, because I'm tough, but not tough by fighting or troublemaking. I'm tough because I don't listen to the VC politics. I just say it's not true. My adopted father used to train me a lot about the slaves in the States, about the white and black people, and I got all that in my mind when I was young. Most time when I hang around with GI's they say about me, "This is a smart guy." Sometimes I write in English, "Peace," "Make love not war," "Black power," You know, I learned it before with the American GI's when I was young. When they was doin' somethin', I just look at them, and I act like them. A group of guys be by the stereo, sittin' there talkin', I be sittin' there listenin', and I go home and act just like them. It's always like that. So when I get to the prison camp, I still act just like that. Just like now. I'm not walkin' slow just like Vietnamese walkin', I'm walkin' fast. When I'm talkin', I'm just like an American black, talkin', movin' a lot. This is my way, I cannot forget it; but in Vietnam it kind of shocked them. I shocked many Vietnamese children, you know, when I was talkin' to them, touchin' them. If it's a girl, in Vietnam you don't touch them, but when I talk, tryin' to analyze or explain something, I move my hands a lot. They say if you talk, don't point your finger like that. They don't like that. But I always have a problem, because I cannot talk like this [Raymond hugs his arms to his sides].

In the prison camp, if you die, you die. They don't even report to your parents. Until around '86 or '87, you couldn't even have any visitors. At that time it became a little easier. Before then, you could not even write a letter. I could not contact my mother.

Every morning before you go to work you have to line up in the big square. They call your number, and you go out to get your head count. One morning I think, "Why we go out late today? Maybe something happened, maybe somebody be released." But to myself, I say, "No, Raymond, it's not you." I lost my hope to be released, but not to survive. I always think, "I will go out somehow, but not in the legal way. They never gonna let me out after twelve years, yeah, twelve years." But that one day, June 20, 1987, I'm just sittin' there, and I'm the one that they call first. I don't even hear it, because I don't listen. When they call my name, I just . . . I was not ready to hear that. After they call my name twice, people in the front line, they just look at me and they say, "Raymond, your name." I think they was jok- ing, but I hear many guys saying, "Raymond, it's you, they gonna let you out." And I stand up, and they say, "Don't you want to go out?" And I just sit down quietly, and I hear them calling another name, and another. I was having a deep breath, and thinking, "I survived, oh, I survived."

I got back to Saigon seven o'clock in the evening. I was lookin', I was walkin' around. I went back to my neighborhood, my locale, and they tell me, "Your mama, she's dead," and I suffer. I say, "Oh, now I live on the street again." And then the neighbors, they give me clothes, they give me food, and they say, "If you were out here you be in America already, because now they have the policy to let the Amerasian out. You come late, you know." I had heard about that in the prison camp, about the "Homecoming Act," but I just didn't believe it. "America has no relations with Vietnam," I think, "How they gonna let all the Amerasians go to America?" But it was true. I say, "If I knew that, I would have escaped [from prison camp] already."

I went out to the central city, Nguyen Hue, the main road. I was lookin' for Americans. I was thinkin', "How can I get in touch with Robert Handler, with anybody I knew so that they can help me to get out?" And then I saw this one guy with a mustache, he looked Spanish, and a girl with blonde hair. I looked at the way they dressed, and I think, "They're not Russian, I can tell. They don't look French, they must be American." So I walked over and talked to them. They had a tape recorder, and they recorded everything I said. I was talking about how difficult the life is for the Amerasian, and I say, "If you are a journalist, I will give you a letter, so you can talk to the people in America and try to help Amerasians, get us all out. We cannot stay here with the Communist regime. We don't have any education, and we are not able to work anywhere. The employer won't hire us." So I gave him the letter, and he promised that he would give it to the government, talk about my story.

Then I met one nice Vietnamese prisoner friend who was released before I was, after maybe seven years in the camp. He had a motorcycle repair shop. He say, "Raymond, what you doin'?" And I say, "I have no job, my mother's dead, I'm homeless." He says, "I know you don't know how to repair motors, but I can teach you." So I come stay with him for about two months, and I get paid maybe two hundred piasters for a day.

I smoke, that costs money. I like to drink milk, but it's expensive to drink milk in Vietnam. Tea, ice, and coffee are cheap, but milk is expensive. But I don't like coffee, I can't drink tea. I just like milk, 'cause I used to drink it when I was on the base. But I can't afford it. Two hundred piasters is not enough for a day, I have no breakfast. So I think, "I'm workin' and still the money's not enough," and I look for another job down at the market. I find a job as a porter, but I'm too weak. I been twelve years in the prison camp, and I been locked up. My legs are weak. To be a porter you got to be strong, like a farmer. But I'm not a farmer. I never worked that hard, even in the camp. I cannot carry that stuff, about sixty or eighty kilos of onions.

So I started sellin', standin' and sellin', it's okay for me. But then I get sick, 'cause when you work in the onion stockroom, that smell is so powerful, many people are allergic. So I cough a lot, and I think, "How much do I make a month . . . if I get sick and I got to pay for a doctor, for medicine? Don't even talk about a doctor, just for medicine, it's not enough. How can I work for this little bit of money just to get some lung disease?" So I had to stop workin'.

I started hanging around behind the Catholic church, they call it "Amerasian Park." You can make your application there, to apply for America, if you want to leave Vietnam. I can write, I got a good handwriting, so I became an application writer. I write for the Vietnamese who have Amerasian children and are trying to get to America.

Many don't have the money to make the document, so I'm the one helpin' them. I do it for free, or they offer me fifty or a hundred piasters. If they go to someone else, sometimes it costs them five thousand, but for me, no price, I don't demand nothin'. So the people come and crowd around me, and when they go back to their town, and they see the local Amerasian who is jobless, they tell him, "You should go out and see Raymond, tell Raymond to make the application for you." So they came from all over. From the country, from the province, and in Saigon. They come behind the Catholic church, lookin' for Raymond. They come to me, and they say, "Are you Raymond?" I say, " Yeah." They say, "I have no mother, I have no father, I want to leave this country, can you help me?" I say, "yeah," and I write everything down for them on the application.

I met a lot of Amerasians who been robbin' at the market, stealin', pickpocketing. If they get caught, they get beat up. I think, "Hey, if they were in my shoes, if they been twelve years in prison camp, they wouldn't be doin' this. It's no fun in there, because I'm an Amerasian, I been there, and I know." But they say, "I have no job. Nobody will hire me, so how can I survive?"

I was tryin' to think about how to get them together and have them sleep in one place. Because I see a lot of beggars sleepin' on the side of the street. Many of them are hooked on drugs, droppin' pills and things like that. You see a lot of Amerasians, they got scars on their arms. They do drugs, and then they cut themselves up. They learn this from the Vietnamese. They want to prove they tough, not scared of anything. Girls do it too. They might be prostitutes, or a drug user, or just a wild girl.

But, I also saw many Amerasians who are street vendors, sellin' postcards, makin' a livin' that way. Some are doin' bicycle repair on the sidewalk, drivin' pedicabs, sellin' bread, and I'm thinkin' about why the other Amerasians don't do like these. I met this one black Amerasian, and I say, "Why don't you go out and repair bicycles, something like that?" And he say, "Nah, I don't like to do that, because people always pay me low wages and treat me bad. They use me like a slave."

The Amerasians feel upset about this. They don't want to work for the Vietnamese. These people don't call you by name. They call you *con lai*— that mean mixed blood, Amerasian. That sounds bad, it hurts an Amerasian, and they don't want to work. So they group up with some Vietnamese street kids, who already been in jail many times, you know, and they get hooked into that group. Soon they will be doin' the bad things.

I gathered a small group of these Amerasian children, and we sleep in the park. One night the police came by. They say, "Hey, where's your home? Go home." I say, "We have no home, sir." "Well," they say, "Just go somewhere else. You know, this is a public place, in front of the administration office. You cannot sleep here, it makes it look bad." I say,

"Well, we want to sleep here to let people know that we need help." Many American people were around there also. Orderly Departure Program people, they worked right by there.

I was trying to think of how to support this group. If you want to avoid crime, you have to support them, you have to feed them. So I just walk around town, just looking for Americans and askin' them to help. I met John R., who is a Vietnam veteran. He left his Amerasian daughter behind, and he came back and found her. He brought her back to Hawaii, where he lives. He is married to a Vietnamese woman, and he speaks Vietnamese fluently.

I tell him we need help, and I brought him to the park where we sleepin'. He says, "Okay, I'm goin' back to America in three days, but I will come back, and I will help." We asked him for money to buy some rice, and he gave us some, but at that time it's not enough.

Meanwhile, more and more Amerasians are coming to the park. I begin teaching them English. You know the Vietnamese are kind of nosy. They see somethin' strange, they just come and look. So they come and crowd around, and then a police car comes. The police say, "Raymond, we want you to come down to the police station." And I went down there, and crowds of Amerasians follow me, and they wait for me there in front of the police station. And the investigator, he tells me, "Don't gather up these Amerasians again, if you do, we put you back in the prison." And I'm scared. I already been in twelve years, and they gonna put me back again.

So I went back out and I told the Amerasians, "Okay, you sleep here. Don't go nowhere tonight, you stay here in the area. Stay together. I'm not gonna sleep here with you, but I'm gonna be watchin' out for you." And I go sleep in a small alley near the park.

At this time the Amerasians were all living in the park without any shelter. I would feed them with money I made from writing applications. Sometimes the people whose applications I made have Amerasian children themselves, and they feel pity for the street children, so they donate some rice or a cooking pot. So the Amerasians are happy because they are together. Before, they don't look friendly at each other. Even if I am Amerasian, when I meet another Amerasian I kinda feel ashamed, a stranger, because we grow up in the Vietnamese community. So, I always put in their mind, "He's your brother, she's your sister. We should love each other, help each other." Some of these Amerasians they are tough guys, they be in gangs. They listen to the Vietnamese and beat up the other Amerasians.

So the police, they arrest me again, for grouping the Amerasians. They don't charge me with anything, they just say that I'm a troublemaker. And so, just a few months after I get released from twelve years of reeducation camp, they sentence me to twenty-four months in a labor training camp for youth. It's not supposed to be a jail. It's a place where they send people who

don't want to work, people who drink too much, people like that, for training. It's on a small island, where they have some salt fields to produce salt.
Water all around you, very difficult to escape. You have to swim good to
escape.

I arrived there, and I saw Tuan Den, this black Amerasian. He is here
in the PRPC now. Anyway, he was a detainee, but he been there in that
labor camp so long that they had made him like a guard, except he didn't
have a rifle, he only had a stick. He's like one of those Amerasians I told
you about, that listen to the Vietnamese and beat up other Amerasians. He
was always around, with that stick in his hand, like he was God, or something. I look at him, it's my first day there, and I say to myself, "This is absurd. I want to know how is this different from the place I been for twelve
years, because it was hell there, and if this is another place like that, I'm
gonna escape even if they kill me." He look at me also, and I know why.
He wants to know whether I'm tough or not. If I'm a tough guy, he's the
one who will face me. That's what they use him for.

My first night there, they make like a long bed. Everybody sleep in a
line. One student, they call them students, he's movin' in his sleep. He's
knocking into another guy, 'cause there is no room, and the other guy gets
angry and starts hittin' and cursing him. Tuan Den, he's the guard, he's the
team leader. He comes in and he got a long whip, not a leather whip. It's
steel, like a bicycle chain, and he whips that guy so bad. I stand up and I
look at Tuan Den, and I say, "In jail, it's the Communists treat us like that.
But this is not a jail, not prison. It's a training center. Why you treat the
people like this?"

I stand up. At that time it's curfew, you cannot even nod your head
up, but I stand up. He look at me, I look at him, and he walks out.

The next morning, they say we have to get dressed and line up for the
toilet. I tell them, "I don't line up because I'm not a criminal." So I feel
very, very angry, and I say no, and I just walk out.

They try to put you at their mercy. I'm a newcomer, and usually as a
newcomer you cannot be in a private place by yourself. After you there one
or two months, they trust you. But your first few months, they always follow
you. You always must be with your team. If you in a line, and one person
violates [a rule], the whole team will pay with punishment. They be runnin'
in a circle at noontime, and no one can eat, all day like that. So I tell them,
"I'm not involved with the team, if I'm in trouble, it's me. If the team
violates, that's the team. If I do wrong, punish me. I don't want to get involved with any people around here."

Most of the Amerasians I met there were treated real bad. They make
them work like a slave, carry water for them to take a bath, cook, wash their
clothes, sometimes even massage them at night.

There are girls out there too, Vietnamese girls, Amerasian girls, picked

Tuan Den in front of his billet

up for prostitution. One time at noontime, one girl dropped a block. She's hungry and tired, she been working since six or eight in the morning. So they give her a punishment, she has to kneel down and look at the sun. But I don't like that kind of thing, and I say, "Hey," to the girl that runs the team, and she says, "You talkin' to the team leader." I say " Hey, you hear me?" And she says, "It's none of your business. You ain't been workin' all this morning, why you interrupt my business?" I say, "I just want to ask you if you're a human. If you a human, you don't treat people like that. If you get out of your uniform and you go down and do the same work, you will drop that block too."

That woman is the nurse, and she is so corrupt. Sometimes you get sick. You got a headache, or you got a stomachache, and you need an excuse slip for the day, you want to be absent. She will not allow you. You got to give her some food, some gift, or she won't sign your paper. It's unfair. She thinks nobody knows what she's doin', but I observe, I find it out, what they have done in this place. All the employees abusing drugs, they all shootin', all drinkin' alcohol. That nurse was working there ten years, and she has so many enemies that she can't go back on the outside. She has to stay there to be safe. They say the camp is for training young people, but it's a punishment camp. It doesn't help anybody.

I refused to follow their rules. I refused to work. I say, "I am not a prisoner. This is a training center, not a prison, but this is not training, it's forced labor." So they just let me be. They cannot do nothin' to me cause I don't talk nasty words. If you talk nasty words, they beat you. If you think you're tough, they beat you. That's why I don't use that kind of behavior. It's here in my heart.

Before they release me, I talk to that black Amerasian, the one with the stick. I ask him, "Why you be in here?" and he start talkin', "I been stealin', robbin', like that. I got no job, and they put me in here." And I ask, "What your mother and father say?" And he says, "I have no mother or father." And I say, "Okay, I been hearin' about you a lot. A lot of people been tryin' to escape and you caught them and beat them up. You work for the Vietnamese, but they don't treat you like Vietnamese. They make you hurt people. They don't give you no rights. I ask him, "Do they pay you any salary here?" He says, "No." I say to him, "They just usin' you here. Those people you caught when they tryin' to escape. If they see you when you get back to society, what's gonna happen to you? They're going to want to kill you. I tell you what, your country is not here. Why don't you get out of here and try and go to America?" And you know, he did. He is here in the PRPC now, and he got here before I did.

When they release me, I went back to Saigon. The local police station gave me a warning to stay out of the Amerasian Park. They tell me, "Don't ever hang out there any more, if you want to leave the country. If you don't listen to us, you gonna have big trouble. You will go in [prison] for a long time." Then I ask, "Okay, what do I need to apply to leave the country?" So they told me you got to have your birth certificate and your household register. But I don't even have a birth certificate, because I come from the orphanage I only have my release document from reeducation camp. They tell me to go back to my local [neighborhood] and look for the old people that's been residing there long enough to know my background, who can give information about me.

So I do that, and I go through all this paperwork, applyin' to leave Vietnam to go to America. They accept my documents, but they always put my paperwork on hold. They don't process it, because it looks like they don't like me at all. They know about me, that I'm the leader of the Amerasians at the park, that I been twelve years in the reeducation camp. They know that I speak English fluently, and they suspect that I am an American spy.

That's the way Vietnamese Communists are. When they don't like you, but they cannot put you in jail, they put your paper on hold. See, when they put your paper on hold, you might be depressed, you become bored. You might go the wrong way, commit a crime. Then they can arrest you easier. That's the way the Communists do it.

So I went to the Tan Son Nhut airport. At that time there was an ODP interview group who was working there, doing the interviews with Amerasians. I went there tryin' to talk with someone, but the policeman won't let me in. So I'm just hanging out until lunch time, and I see this one very tall black American walking out. I approach him, and I say, "Sir, I need your help." So he says, "Write it down and give it to me." I wrote a letter, and the next day I went back, but when that man walked out, his hands were so full of files that he cannot even get my envelope, so I just put it in his pocket. He went down to his van and took a picture of me, and he went back to Bangkok the next day. About three weeks later I received a letter from the Bangkok office of the ODP program. They gave me an ID number, that means they opened my file. So I'm thinkin' everything is goin' to be fine, I don't have to register in Vietnam anymore. Then, I met this white American, they call him Bill, but his name is William Flamby. He's got a Vietnamese wife, and he speaks fluent Vietnamese. I ask him, "What do I need to follow up, to get out of the country?" He say, "I think you should register again, because your old records, they [the Vietnamese authorities] might tear them up." So I went back and I made another application, and while I'm waiting I still try to help the other Amerasians.

We set up tents in Amerasian Park because the rainy season is coming. Everything is legal. The police say we can stay there now. But they tell me that I'm responsible for all these Amerasians, and if anything happens, they are going to get me.

During that time, Mr. John R., he comes back again, and I was talkin' to him about rentin' an apartment so we can move off the street. The tents were no good for the rainy season. The wind was blowin' so hard we were all gettin' wet inside. So we decided to rent two apartments, we call them half-way houses, and I would run them. John R., he gave me the money, and he told me to take care of all that. But I just don't want him to think that I will use it for other things, so I tell him, "You go with me to rent the apartments."

So I take him to the landlord, and we talk to the landlord about the price. Then we count the money and pay the landlord. Everything is complete, and we get the receipt. And he tells me, "You know, Raymond, you can rent it all yourself. Why'd you bring me here? They charge more if they see there is an American here." I say, "I know that, but I want to make sure that you trust me. Because I know that someone might think that I use that money." Because it's big money he give me, about three million piasters *[three to five hundred dollars]*. So after that he gave me money for rice and some food, charcoal, everything, and he said, "Okay, Raymond, I will go back to America next month, but I will be back here every month to try to support you." So he went back to America tryin' to call up people to get donations.

I try to set up two English classes, one in the morning and one in the evening, but we can't find volunteer teachers. Everybody wants to get paid, and we don't have much money, so I wind up doing the teaching myself. At the same time I have to write up a list every day of who's staying at the apartments. The police, they want that because they be afraid that the Amerasians could cut out of that place and do the crime. It's very hard for me, I have so much to do. So I meet Tuan Den, the guy who was the Amerasian guard in the second camp, and he says he will help me to keep peace and order. That means he will give them instruction about following the rules of the apartment—everybody goin' to bed at nine o'clock, no noise. Don't fight inside the apartment, don't steal, no drink, no drugs. I'm afraid if there is a lot of noise, we may get kicked out.

Some of the Amerasians don't like those rules, they are too strict. So they just cut out and go back to the street again, even though it's rainy season. They want to drink, you know, do anything they want. This they cannot do. We can't mess up because it's very difficult for me to ask permission to rent the place.

Some of the Amerasians obey the rules, some not. But Tuan Den, he's not like me. He don't like to talk, he beats them up. When they drinking, they come back to the apartment and try to raise hell, make all this noise, and make trouble for the other guy, he just say, "Okay," and he uses the stick, whippin' them on the butt. I got to tell him, "Please don't do that, that's not the way. This isn't a prison, it's a halfway house. What are people gonna think about this place?"

Also, a lot of people come lookin' for me. They want to buy some Amerasian, you know what I mean. They pay an Amerasian to say that they are a son or a daughter, and then their family can go to America with that Amerasian. But I don't go tryin' to deal, I always refuse that.

After three months, John R. comes back, and the Vietnam administration wants to see him. So we go up there, and they say, "Okay, we have no relationship with America yet, so you only here like a tourist, you on vacation. If you want to run this organization, you got to have permission from the government. If not, we gonna close it down." And they tell John R. that they want him to give them all the money he collected for the Amerasians and that they will use it to help all orphans, Vietnamese and Amerasians. They want his money in their hand.

So John R. says, "Who is responsible for the Amerasian? You are. But you can't take care of them, because you say you poor. So why don't you take care of the Vietnamese children, and I take care of the Amerasians. This money is not enough for both."

They say, "No. Unfair, inhumane." So John R. says, "If you don't let me continue, I just go home." And they say, "Okay," and they stand up, and that's the end of the meeting. After that, they got this undercover agent always followin' John R. I don't know what kind of information that agent gave to the officials, but later, they call John R. back again. They say, "How do we know you not abusing these Amerasians. How do we know you not using the money for yourself?" So John R. say that he got all these documents. Everything is organized, everything is legal. But these Communists, they so dumb, they don't know what it's all about. They insist that he's a spy. They say, "You have to leave the country in twenty-four hours," and they fine him one hundred dollars for opening his organization illegally.

They take a picture of him, and about two days later, after he's gone, the newspaper comes out, and he's on the headline. "Don't listen to this black American. He's a veteran, a spy, he comes here trying to abuse the Amerasian, tryin' to fool the people, tryin' to get the money." They talk bad about John R. in the newspaper, but all he was trying to do was help Amerasians.

So they give the order, "Raymond, you should close down *[the apartments and the English program]* in two more days." Now, when John R. came, he gave all us number tags. They got little American flags outside. So the police tell me to get all the tags back, don't let the Amerasians wear them anymore, because it don't look good in Vietnam when you wear the American flag. So I have to get the tags back, and when I turn them in they say, "Some are missing." And I say, "Well, some Amerasians, I don't know where they went to." And they say, "What about yours?" I have one also, mine is number one, I was the first to get one. I just say, "I lost mine," but I still got it until now. I brought it with me, and I got it here.

I see now we have to be independent, because John R. cannot come back no more. So I try to do some business. I order some bread, and I give it to the Amerasians to sell so that we can make money for food. So they do that, and the first day they bring the money back, but second day, I am waitin' for them, they don't bring the money back. I see one of them on the street, I say, "How come you don't come back with the money? Your friends have no food." And he say, "Oh, somebody beat me up and took it." I know he's tellin' me a lie, he's so scared. I say, "Tell me the truth." He says, "Oh, yesterday I see a friend of mine and we have a party, and I drink away all the money." And I say, "Oh, how am I gonna pay the guy who gave me the bread?" But I don't let Tuan Den know. If he knows about that, he would beat that guy to death.

So we have no money for food, and we have no money for rent, and we have to move out of the apartments. But at that time, Dam Sen Transit Center for Amerasians is already built, and the Amerasians who already applied to go to America and are waiting to be called, they can stay there. They don't have to live on the street anymore.

The time I organized the two apartments, many Americans came and visit us. They wanted to see how we live in the house, you know, they donate a bit of money. I met two persons there, they from Boston, and they ask how I can speak English. So I talk about how I be growin' up on the base with Robert Handler, and they ask me if I know his address. I say, "My memory is that he's from Philadelphia, Pennsylvania," and she say, "Okay, let me write down his name. I try to locate him for you, the best I can." About a month and a half later I got a letter. When I received the letter, I saw in the corner of the envelope the name Robert Handler. I was so surprised. I was so happy, but I was kind of nervous, you know. It took me a while to cut open the envelope, and I started readin', and I was cryin'. Any journalist, any reporter I met, I was talkin' about Robert Handler, tryin' to find him. I never had any luck, but this time I got a letter from him. He asked me, "How tall is you now, how you been doin'?" He read an article that talked about me, and he said, "People talk about you, I'm proud of you." And I think, "I still got a father there, I be more lucky than any other Amerasian."

When I was making applications in Amerasian Park, many Vietnamese people approached me and said they had information about MIAs. They come behind me and just blow in my ear, "Raymond, I have some information about MIAs, but I am afraid to approach Americans, so can you help?" One time, I say, "What you got?" and they show me a little dogtag, you know, and a piece of bone. And I ask, "How do you know this is from American GI? They say, "Look at the dog tag, and we got a letter from him also." Then I give them to John R., and he went back to Hawaii and had it analyzed, and they say, "It's phoney, it's not real." So John say, "Stay away from that, it get you in trouble." I met one lady, she gave me a photo of a black American. She says he was an MIA, still alive, and that people still takin' care of him, near the central highlands. She says he lives deep inside the jungle. I really don't believe it. I look at the photo, I see he's kinda small. He doesn't look American. I say, "This could be an Amerasian, he doesn't look American." She says, "It's true, he's American." I say, "Can you bring me a picture, a new picture? Can you get me his handwriting, information about his parents in the States, his address?" She says, "Yeah." So she brings back to me another photo with his name, his family name, his parents, his address, his fingerprints. But I still don't believe it. I say, "I can do all of this also, I got a good handwriting in English. Can you take me there?" She says, "No, Raymond, we can't take you there, because if the people see you, they will move the guy inside more, and then we can't find him anymore." I say, "Okay, what can we do now to bring this guy out?" She say "The Montagnard people are keeping him. They live in the jungle. They don't want to go to the States. They just want to trade some gold." I still don't believe them. I think, "How can I know for sure that this is an American?" So I tell them, "One more thing I want you to do. You do this and I will inform the U.S. Embassy about your evidence. You tell this man to list down for me four kinds of soul food." The black American always knows about soul food. The Vietnamese, I don't care how good his English is, he cannot know about soul food. If he really is a black American, I know he knows about soul food. She says, "I'll try." I waited, but she never came back. So I still have that information with me, piece of paper, his handwriting, and a photo of him. I just keep it here.

When I left Vietnam and arrived here in the PRPC, Tuan Den, he's here already. He came in June, I came in July. The first day I am in camp I meet him, and he asks me to stay with him in neighborhood one. He says, "Raymond, we need you to stay by us to teach us more English." I say, "That's great." And I start to work as an interpreter in the Cultural Orientation program and also at the Youth Center. I request for an empty class at night, to teach English to some Amerasians who want to learn. I'm tryin' to help.

My other role in this camp is with the INC, the Inter-Neighborhood Council. I am on the Inter-Neighborhood patrol. They assign me that kind of work because they know most of the Amerasians here are troublemakers. They don't ever listen to the Vietnamese. They hate Vietnamese, so most INC members they cannot work with them. So they say, "Raymond, I know the Amerasians respect you, so can you help us to keep the peace and order?"

Now there was a guy, he was here before, he was a long-stayer here in camp. They call him Dung Dai Bang, that means like Dung "big boss." He was this big Vietnamese guy, and he was the head of the extortion/protection racket here in camp. He went to America already.

One time Tuan Den, he went to the gold seller in neighborhood five, and he took a gold chain. Now that chain cost eight hundred pesos, but he only pay two hundred. He tells the gold seller that he will give the rest later. Now the seller, he don't know Tuan Den, but he sees that Tuan Den's a big guy, and he's afraid to say anything. That seller is under Dung's protection, and he reports to Dung, and Dung goes lookin' for Tuan Den.

They meet at the coffee shop in neighborhood one, and Dung asks

Tuan Den, "How come you come in my brother's store and you bought the necklace and you don't pay the money?" Tuan Den asks, "It's your real brother?" and Dung say, "No, I protect him." So Tuan Den says, "It's not your real brother. If it's your real brother, I won't bother him. But he's only the guy that makes money for you, so don't bother me about it."

At that time, Duc, a Vietnamese troublemaker, he was in the monkey house. He spent almost five years in this camp, and he got rejected by America. He been in and out of jail, and his brother is in a Filipino jail for life, for rape. Duc hears that Tuan Den stood up to Dung Dai Bang, and Duc asks, "Who is this Tuan Den, who is this Raymond?" The other Amerasians say that Tuan Den, he's this tall black Amerasian tough guy. He runs all these Amerasian groups. Duc says, "I really want to face this guy, 'cause I'm the number one guy here, not the number two."

Minh, this Amerasian that we know, he was in jail with Duc. When he gets out, he comes to Tuan Den and he says "Duc, he threatened you and me, he says he will get our heads." We're sittin' in the billet drinkin', and I say, "Hey stop talking about that in here, while we're drinkin'. Take it easy, just wait and see." But Tuan Den, he doesn't like it. He always likes to make something happen.

About a month later, Minh comes to us and he says, "Hey, I heard Duc is released. He's having a party in neighborhood nine. I'm going to get him, because he threatened me." But Tuan Den says, "No. He threatened me also, so if you go get him, he'll think I'm a chicken, let me go get him."

So I say, "Hey, let's vote to see who will get him." So we vote, and Minh gets the mission to get Duc. So Minh, he prepares two small knives, and he bands them around his legs and he's gone. Me and Tuan Den, we sit at the billet. Tuan Den, he says, "Raymond, I think Duc is a tough guy, and Minh is only talk, he won't do nothing. Let me go down there." I say, "Hey, don't go by yourself, they may have a gang down there in neighborhood nine. Let me go with you. Wait, let me get a small knife so we can protect ourselves."

So I put a small knife in my pocket, I don't give it to Tuan Den 'cause I know he's a crazy guy. We jump on a tricycle and we get down there. We go around lookin' for the billet where they're partying. We ask the other Amerasians, "Where's Duc?" and they show us.

So me and Tuan Den, we come inside the billet while they drinkin' and playin' the guitar. When they see us, they all break out and run. Duc is the only one to still remain inside the billet. He jumped near the kitchen to get a knife. One big Amerasian grabbed Duc. I say to Tuan Den, "Here, take my knife," and I give him the small knife.

I talk to the guy who's holdin' Duc and say, "Turn him loose, let him go get a knife. Let him go." So the guy turned him loose, and Duc tried to get away, but Tuan Den, he just stabbed him.

When I saw that, I said, "Stop, you could kill him," and I grabbed the knife back. At that time Duc, he was beggin', "Tuan Den, I didn't say anything," like that, "forgive me, forgive me."

One guy in the back tried to jump inside with a guitar and beat Tuan Den on the head. I grabbed the guitar, and he ran away. I went back to Duc, I see he's still movin. I took the guitar, and I beat him. I don't mean beat his head, I just beat on him. When he was not even movin' anymore, we say, "Let's go," and we get out of there. Minh, and another Amerasian called Charlie, they come after that. Charlie brought a knife, but we say, "Hey, what you bringin' all that stuff here for? We're finished, we're through."

So when the security guards come to neighborhood nine, the witnesses say that Tuan Den and Raymond were there. So security comes to my billet and they say, "Raymond, the eyewitness say they saw you there." I say, "Yeah, I was there, because it's my patrol." Because my job is the Inter-Neighborhood Patrol. They say, "Someone says you stabbed him." I say, "No." They say, "Someone says you beat him with a guitar." I say, "No." I'm not stupid, to say that I did that. So Tuan Den says, "I stabbed him because he was tryin' to stab me. I'm not goin' wait for him to hurt me. He threatened me, so I gotta get him first." So, they bring Tuan Den to the monkey house.

I have a friend, he works here. He is a Vietnamese, but he is a Filipino citizen. He tells me, "Raymond, I heard security say they gonna get you." And I say, "Get me for what?" He tells me, "Because you involved, and they don't like you." You know, one time I complained to Mr. Deles, their boss, about how security mistreats the Amerasians, and he disciplined them. So security don't like me at all.

I read the statement Duc give after they brought him back from the hospital. It's very clear and accurate, but Duc didn't recognize me, didn't even identify me. He only identified Tuan Den as the one who stabbed him, but then security talked to him and gave him some reason to hook me into the case. Duc's companions, they don't like Charlie, they don't like me, they don't like Tuan Den. They gave statements, and the police came and arrested us all, even Charlie and Minh.

We spent five months in the Filipino prison in Balanga. Finally, I think my *[American]* friend who I work with, he convinced Duc to drop the charges, and they dismissed the case and let us out. But Tuan Den and I are still on hold. They not lettin' us go to the States yet. I heard someone say that policies on refugees going to America are a little stricter now because many of the refugees comin' through ODP committed crimes in the United States. The charge against me was frustrated murder *[attempted homicide]*, and even though it was dismissed, it affects, you know, my record. So all I can do is wait.

Tuan Den and Charlie

When I got back from Balanga, Mr. D. from JVA called me to his office and asked me if I ever heard anything about an MIA named Robinson T. Water, who applied to leave Vietnam as an Amerasian. I tell him that I never heard of that, but I gave him the photo and the piece of paper that the lady in Vietnam gave me, the photo of the black guy she said was being kept by the Montagnards.

So recently, Mr. J., from the U.S. Embassy, calls me to the office, and he asks me to sit down. He brings me the photo, and he asks me, "Raymond, can you recognize this person?" I say, "No sir, I cannot recognize the person, but I recognize the photo, because it is my photo. I gave it to Mr. D. before when he was working here with JVA. But this person, I have never seen him before in my life, I don't know who he is." Then Mr. J., he sort of looks at me, straight in my face, and he says, "Okay, you look over there," and I see that he is trying to compare the photo with me. He says,

Tuan Den, Charlie and Raymond

"How old are you?" I say, "My documents say I'm twenty-six, but I don't know exactly how old I am." He asks me many questions, and he tells me to write down everything about the woman who gave me the photo.

So my case worker, Marivic, she says, "Raymond, the people been talkin' about this thing. They think that you are the MIA." I say, "How could it be? I'm not an MIA." She say, "Yeah, but that's what people think." Of course I'm not an MIA. I learned English from living with black Americans on the base. I wish I was the MIA, then I could go to America.

I ask her, "When I'm gonna leave?" She says, "It's not sure if the United States will reject you or not. If they don't want you to go to America, what you gonna do?" I say, "My expectation is I want to get out of here and look for an opportunity to study, to help people. I can get my opportunity in America. If they reject me and send me back to Vietnam, no way. They should just kill me, that's the easier way."

The Vietnamese people have the prejudice that I am more American then Vietnamese. My custom, my culture, my accent is more American than Vietnamese, and they don't like me at all. You think I will agree to go back? No. I would rather drink some medicine so I can die easy. No future, if I be sent back there, no future.

Postscript: *Raymond left the PRPC for Hawaii in April 1992. His sponsor was John R., the American Vietnam veteran who had returned to Vietnam to set up the Amerasian programs.*

Nguyen Thi Hong Hanh

"I grew up without love."

Her ebony skin is from her American father, her high cheekbones and al-
mond eyes from her Vietnamese mother. Hanh is in the refugee camp with her
Vietnamese husband and their one-year-old daughter.
    We are speaking on a clear, hot February day outside the Buddhist temple.
Hanh speaks little English, and we converse through an interpreter.

I WAS BORN in Pleiku. I lived on
Nguyen Ky Hoc Street, in a cement
house, with my stepparents and their five
Vietnamese children. When I was four
years old, my mother left me. I have a picture of her, but I don't remember her. I
never knew where she went.

When my mother gave birth, she
hired a baby-sitter to take care of me. She
worked as a waitress at the American base
in Pleiku. When I was four, my father
returned to America, and my mother went
away. She just left me with the baby-sitter
and didn't come back, and that baby-sitter
became like my stepmother.

My mother didn't tell the baby-sitter
that she was leaving. She just abandoned
me there. The baby-sitter never told me
anything about my mother, but the neigh-

**Nguyen Thi Hong Hanh, in
the PRPC, February 1992**

bors said that my mother got remarried and lived in Kon Tum. I never saw
or heard from my mother again.

I never went to school in Vietnam, not even one day. I learned to read
Vietnamese from some friends, mostly other Amerasians. Vietnamese

46

didn't let me be friends with their children. Some people wouldn't even let me work for them. That's what my stepmother told me. Black Amerasians have a lot of problems.

My stepparents treated me badly. When I was about six years old, they sent me out to work to make money for them. I took any job, like maid or baby-sitter. My stepparents were teachers, but they never sent me to school or taught me at home. They just made me work. They didn't love me, I grew up without love.

Minh

"I rarely left the temple, so I know only
a little about the life outside its confines."

The Buddhist temple of neighborhood seven sits on a bluff overlooking a
tranquil valley framed by the slopes of the Zambales range. The river below, barely
a trickle in the dry season, brings life to acres of rice when swollen with monsoon
rain. Refugees wander into the temple grounds to worship, to admire the statue
of Quan Am, or merely to watch the river wind through the valley on its way
to the South China sea, five kilometers distant.

Minh listens attentively as my interpreter introduces us. He is a fine-boned
young man of twenty. His light skin and Western features mirror an unknown
American father; his pensive demeanor bespeaks the teachings of the Buddha.
Adopted by Buddhist nuns when still a toddler, Minh has lived in Buddhist
temples for twenty years. His hair is cropped close to the scalp, and he wears the
saffron robe and gray pants of a monk.

We sit with my interpreter on a concrete embankment outside the temple
wall, sharing a tiny patch of shade. Chanting wafts through an open window,
a feeble breeze teases wind chimes in a nearby tree, and the mid–February sun
blazes in premonition of the approaching hot season. As we speak, the sun shifts.
The spot of shadow we inhabit moves, and we follow it.

I WAS LEFT in an orphanage in Saigon, and so I know nothing of my
real mother. When I was still an infant, maybe two or three, I was adopted
by a Buddhist nun, and she took me to live in the Hue Lam temple at 130
Hong Vinh Street, in the 11th district of Ho Chi Minh City.

There were five Amerasian children adopted by the temple and
brought up there and probably about twenty-five Vietnamese children. I
rarely left the temple, so I know only a little about the life outside its confines, and I did not experience the many problems of the Amerasians who
lived outside of the temple.

Some of the orphans adopted by the temple went to school in the

Minh

temple. Others went outside, if they wished. I studied only inside the temple. There were many things I wanted to learn about Buddhism and I became a monk. The Buddhist monk follows several rules. The Buddha doesn't permit us to kill any animals. We cannot eat meat or fish, so I am a vegetarian. Monks can't steal, rob, or do bad things. We cannot have sex, tell a lie, drink alcohol. We are told not to be talkative, to boast, exaggerate, or use foul language, and to take advantage of no one. I believe the most important rules are "Don't kill any animal, and don't take advantage of anyone else." All monks and nuns must honor the teachings. I have grown up with these precepts, so it is not difficult for me.

Minh by the statue of Quan Am in the PRPC Buddhist temple

Before 1975 the Hue Lam temple was for nuns only. There were only four nuns in the temple, no monks, and these nuns brought in many orphans to care for. The nun who adopted me took care of myself and one other child. There were many orphans there, maybe thirty. Of these children, some went to America, some left the temple and were drafted by the government into the military, and about five remained in the temple to become monks or nuns. When I reached seventeen, the local authorities no longer allowed the adopted boys to remain in Hue Lam temple. They said that since the temple was for nuns, all males must leave. Of course the nuns did not want their adopted children to leave, but we had no choice. We were forced to move to another temple, and I went to Vang Duc temple in Tu Duc, on the outskirts of Ho Chi Minh City. The local authorities often make difficulties for the monks. They don't want them to continue their [religious] studies.

My life here in the PRPC is similar to Vietnam, I live in the temple. In Vietnam I studied, and here I study as well, but I'm studying English for the first time. The teacher teaches well, but I feel that I don't have ability in learning it. I never studied any English in Vietnam, and it is very difficult.

I have no sponsor in America. I don't know where I will go. I hope to improve my English there and to be a Buddhist monk, but I don't wish to wear the robe. I left Vietnam in order to know different things and go to different places. I want to be part of society. I don't want to hide in the temple. I would like to be active in the community. The robe is not important.

Tuan Den

"If I am attacked, I might not be able to be patient."

Although it is not his real name, everyone calls him Tuan Den, roughly translatable as "black and smart." Always well dressed and sporting a stud in his left ear, he is well known in the refugee camp by Vietnamese as well as Amerasians, and certainly by the camp security. His size, his imposing demeanor, and his reputation for toughness all contribute to his notoriety.

At five feet, ten inches, slender but strong, he towers above most of his countrymen. With his height, his black skin and curly hair, there is little in Tuan Den's appearance that suggests the country of his birth. (See photos pp. 35, 44 and 45.) As with so many Amerasians, it is the American side of his parentage that is most evident.

Shortly after arriving in the PRPC, Tuan Den spent five months in prison with three other Amerasians, charged with the stabbing of another refugee, a Vietnamese named Duc. The narratives of two of these Amerasians, Charlie and Raymond, also appear in this book. The details of the stabbing vary depending upon whose version you hear. Speaking through an interpreter, Tuan Den, though he is vague in his account, claims that he was simply defending himself from Duc's knife attack and is not sure how Duc received his injury. Duc recovered and eventually dropped the charges of "frustrated murder," the Filipino equivalent of attempted homicide. The Amerasians were then freed from prison.

Also in dispute is Tuan Den's account of his stay in Dang Thao camp in Vietnam, a facility for youth who run afoul of the Communist government's rules. Raymond, who was there at the same time, claims that Tuan Den, after being admitted as a prisoner, eventually became a much-feared guard. Tuan Den disputes this, claiming that he was just a common detainee.

The top two joints of Tuan Den's left pinky are missing. This is not uncommon in Amerasian males and seems to be done for various reasons, generally to show courage or sincerity. This is what Tuan Den says about it: "I had a girlfriend in 1989. She was treating me bad, and I was suffering, so I chopped off my finger." The implication is that he proved the depth of his love in this manner.

WHEN I WAS A CHILD, I did not live beside my mother. She was a bar girl, and when she went to work, she left me with a baby-sitter, an old, poor lady who made some money by watching people's kids. One day my mother just dropped me off there and never came back, so it was that old lady who raised me. She never told me much about my mother, only what I just told you.

I suffered a lot because I was Amerasian. People embarrassed me, discriminated against me. Other children called me *My lai* and *lai den* *[Amerasian and Black Amerasian]*. I had no chance to go to school because I had no birth certificate.

When I was a teenager, I went out to live on the street and to earn some money. I was part of a group of kids, shining shoes and sleeping on the street. When we went out to work, we would go our own ways, but when night came, we would come back and stay together in one place.

I was the only Amerasian in the group. The others didn't treat me as an equal, they stuck together. Sometimes when I came back, they would take my money, but there was nothing I could do because I was only one. If I separated from them, I could not work that area, where most of the business is. So I had no choice.

Eventually, I got into street crime. We cornered people at knifepoint, at night, in dark places. We'd tell them to give up their money. If they gave us the money, we'd let them go. If they resisted . . . *[Tuan Den makes a stabbing motion with his arm.]*

When we got the money, we had to give it to the gang leader, a Vietnamese about twenty years old. Even if I was the one who did the robbery, he would let me keep just a little of the money. I didn't like that, but there was nothing I could do. I didn't feel close to the people in the gang, but I needed them to survive. The life of crime didn't bother me. I just thought of it as business.

Even though I am big and black, I never really worried about being identified by our victims, but somebody made a complaint, and the police came and picked me up. They sent me to Dang Thao prison, a camp for youth offenders on an island near Saigon.

When they told me they were sending me there, I didn't know how bad it could be. It was terrible, the worst time of my life. We got up at six-thirty and worked till eleven-thirty. We'd get a little to eat and then go back to work until six, and go back to the barracks. We worked everyday, there were no holidays.

I had to do farm work, growing manioc, sweet potatoes, cutting grass. I was not familiar with the work, and when I made a mistake, they would scream at me, call me an animal, an American. I thought about escaping, until I saw what happened to people who tried to escape and were caught. They were beaten badly.

After three years, they released me, and I went back to Saigon. I got a job as a porter in a market, but after a month I left. I heard the people saying that the Amerasians could apply to leave the country, so I went out to the Amerasian Park and made the application to leave Vietnam and go to America.

I stayed in Amerasian Park, sleeping there and waiting for my name to be called. One day a woman came to me and showed me a picture. She said that the picture was of me as a baby and claimed she was my mother. I looked at the picture, but I was suspicious because she didn't raise me. She said that she had been looking for me a very long time. Now that she met me, she said she wanted me to come home and live with her, but I said, "You didn't take care of me when I was a child, so I don't want to go with you now." Many women come and try to tell Amerasians that they are their mothers, to try to go to America, so I was suspicious about that, but she never asked me to take her to United States, and she never told me why she had abandoned me.

She came and visited me often. The last time I saw her she asked me to say hello to her friend in PRPC, and she wished me luck. I still don't know if she was really my mother.

My happiest day in Vietnam was the day I got the ticket to leave, in June of 1990. I arrived in the PRPC on July 2, 1990. When I got here, I met many Amerasians who knew me in Vietnam. Most of the Amerasians here had been drinking and dropping pills, doing the bad things. I always advised them to stop. So, many people were saying that I am the Amerasian gang leader. That's the reason why Duc, who is a troublemaker and a long-stayer here, gave the word to threaten me.

I went to neighborhood nine to visit my girlfriend. Duc lives down there. He saw me and he attacked me with a knife. He was drunk, and I defended myself. I pushed him, and he got hurt. It took place so fast that I don't exactly know what happened [Duc was stabbed]. So they sent me to jail in Balanga for five months, and when Duc dropped his charges they sent me back here to the PRPC. I am still here on hold, my departure for America has been delayed.

When I went to Balanga, I thought about why I was here. And I thought that since I arrived in the PRPC, the security had a bad impression of me, because I'm with the Amerasian group. Security was trying to create a big deal over the Duc case, make it seem like I'm a criminal. They don't like me, so they convinced Duc to complain against me.

So I have been here more than a year, and it has been a waste of time. I want to go to America and study and make a future. While I stay here, there is always the temptation to get into trouble. Because of my problem with Duc, people think I'm a tough guy. I'm afraid somebody might want to fight me to show he is tougher than me. If I am attacked, I might not be able to be patient, I have to defend myself.

Postscript: *Tuan Den finally left the PRPC in April of 1992 for Dallas, Texas. His last few months in the PRPC did not go completely smoothly. He was involved in a brawl with Charlie, his former close friend and cellmate in Balanga. Out of anguish from this incident, Charlie sliced off the tip of his own pinky.*

Shortly before Tuan Den left, his friendship with Raymond—his former close friend, cellmate, and teacher, as well as the interpreter for this interview— went sour. Tuan Den had suspected Raymond of double-crossing him and threatened him several times. Raymond, correctly believing that he was on the verge of going to America, was very uneasy about this, not wanting to get into any trouble that might delay him.

Raymond and Tuan Den finally received their call to go to America, within days of each other. A few days before his departure, I visited Raymond at his billet. To my surprise, Tuan Den and Charlie were there too, and all three were once again the best of friends. Also surprising was the improvement in Tuan Den's English. He was doing his best to communicate without Vietnamese translation. The times Raymond did have to translate, Tuan Den listened with extreme attention, trying to pick out the new words and phrases.

Tuan Den told me that he was through with getting in trouble, and he wanted to learn English and make a new life for himself in Texas.

Shortly after getting settled in Dallas, Tuan Den received a visit from the Dallas police, who somehow had heard of his troubles in the PRPC. It was a checkup visit. They wanted to meet him and to let Tuan Den know that they knew about him.

Tuan Den was shocked by the number of homeless on the streets and resolved to stay out of trouble and not wind up like them. He found work and housing in Dallas, but soon moved on to New York, and finally to Pennsylvania, where he is learning to be a tailor.

Tung Joe Nguyen and Julie Nguyen

"I consider Vietnamese as my family, as my people too, but they don't think of me the same way. They always think of me as a stranger, uneducated, with an uneducated mother ... all stereotypes."

While I was in Misawa, Japan, writing this book from the data I collected in the Philippines, Captain Nguyen, an American of Vietnamese descent stationed at the nearby American air force base, was kind enough to check my work and correct my spelling of Vietnamese words. At our first meeting, he asked me if I would be interested in interviewing two more Amerasians. "Sure," I said, "but where?" "One works with me in Supply," was his response, "and his wife is also Amerasian." He gave me the number of Joe and Julie Nguyen (no relation to Captain Nguyen). I called them that same evening and made an appointment to meet them the next day. They would be the only Amerasians I interviewed outside of the Philippine Refugee Processing Center.

Joe Nguyen peruses my map of Ho Chi Minh City with amazement. "Oh, they even have maps now," he laughs. "When I lived there they recycled the paper so many times it was brown. You could barely see the pencil marks on it when you wrote."

The oldest of the three children of an American businessman and a Vietnamese woman, Joe stayed behind with his mother when the Seventh Day Adventists slipped his younger brother and sister out of Vietnam just weeks before the fall of Saigon. Joe's father had left Vietnam years before, remarried, and started a new family. Although he was advised by Joe's aunt that two of his children had come to the States, he made no attempt to contact them.

Joe and his mother, weary of the prejudice and discrimination accorded Amerasians and their mothers in Vietnam, thought only of getting out. Joe remembers, "We thought about leaving Vietnam constantly. My mom dreamed about it almost every night, dreaming that she was in the States with me, and then waking up in tears, realizing that we were still in Vietnam, with not enough to eat."

In 1983, that dream became a reality when they exited Vietnam via the Orderly Departure Program and settled in Rochester, New York. Seven years later, after mastering a new language and completing high school, Joe married, joined the U.S. Air Force, and was stationed on Misawa airbase in northern Japan. His bride, Julie, also a Vietnamese Amerasian, joined Joe in Misawa. Now, three years later, Airman E-4 Nguyen and his family are weeks away from transferring to a base on Okinawa, in southern Japan. "In Vietnam I always thought about going to the States," Joe, now twenty-four, reflects with irony, "And now, by the time I finish my tour in Okinawa, I will have spent more time in Japan than in America."

At about five feet, ten inches and slimly built, the Western features which marked Joe as an outsider in the land of his birth predominate. Julie, with a bit more of Asia in her appearance, is a blend of East and West. We are in their tiny apartment, outside the gate of Misawa airbase in Japan. Kimberly, their eighteen-month-old daughter, toddles around the place as I speak to her mom and dad, occasionally stopping to fiddle with my tape recorder or bounce on the knee of one of her parents.

Joe: My father was a civilian. My mom says that he was the chairman of a company over there in Vietnam. I forget the company, but they were dealing with refrigerators, freezers, fans, stuff like that. He is from California.

From what my mom told me, her and my dad were getting the paperwork done so they could get married. Before it could get finished, he had to go back to the United States, so the papers never became official. When me and my brother and sister were born, we all have American names, but they're not in our birth certificates because my mom and dad were not legally married. My dad left Vietnam in '72 or '73, and he never contacted us again, nothing at all.

My mom says she was seventeen when they met, that must be in 1967, and I was born in 1968. I have only vague memories of him. In '75, my mom had all these pictures, but we had no idea at the time what the Viet Cong would do. A lot of rumor was going on. If they find out that you married to an American and have American born kids, they would kill you, kill the kids, and all that. My mom took out everything, all the paperwork, all the pictures of us and him together, and burned it all, so no one would find out.

Right before the VC came, my mom's church said that they could take some kids to the United States. It was a very big church, the Seventh Day

Adventists, and they also had a big hospital next to it. They took my brother and sister as "patients." I talked to them about it *[ten years later in the States]*. My brother was too young at the time, but my sister remembers that they wrapped both of them up like mummies, claiming that they were burn victims and that they had to be evacuated to the States to be treated. That's how they escaped to the United States. My mother lost touch with them, but afterwards she still went to the church and asked them to contact the States to find where her son and daughter were at. They told her a little bit, but they didn't want to tell her everything. They said that they are still alive, they live with foster parents, and that's about it. I have no idea why they would not tell her more.

I have an aunt, she went to the States before 1975. Her husband and my dad were good friends. My mom contacted her, trying to find out about my brother and sister. My aunt finally wrote back and said, "I have knowledge of your husband. He lives in California, he has a wife and kids." My aunt asked her husband to tell my dad about my brother and sister being in America. My dad said, "I know that they are over here now, but there is nothing I can do for them. I have my own family to take care of now." And that was the end of that.

When Saigon fell, there was chaos. I remember outside, there were a bunch of houses next to my mother's, and we all had painted flags on our doors, the old flag, the yellow one with four red stripes. As soon as they *[the North Vietnamese]* came in, I remember looking out the door, and I see them runnin' into the next house across the street from us, guns and everything. This scared me, and my mom told me to stay inside the house, not to go out. They ordered us to paint over our flags, and a couple of days later I go out in the street and I see tanks and VC coming through and people waving at them, all that. Not too long after that they ordered us to move out of the house. All the houses, they were taking them all.

They say that we no longer could stay at those houses, and they gave us two choices. They would give us land, and we could become part of a group, and we would live together, and work the land *[in one of the New Economic Zones]*, or we could go ahead and sell our house, buy our land, and work it on our own. So my mother went ahead and sold the house, took the money, and bought land in another place, in Long Thanh. It's basically jungle. We went there with my mom's boyfriend. He had been in the South Vietnamese army before.

My mom hired people to cut trees down, pull up roots, and prepare the land for growing vegetables. My mom's boyfriend, he started drinking there, every day, constantly. After a while he couldn't manage anything. We were paying ten or fifteen people by the hour to work the land, but actually, they just came out there to sit there until the day's over and collect money. My mom has high blood pressure. She was too ill to look after them, and her boyfriend was too busy drinking all day long. The land was on a hill, so any fertilizer and stuff that did get put down, the rain washed away. We stayed there about three years. We lost a lot of money and nothing was growing. Finally, in 1979, we gave up and headed back to Saigon.

Because we had moved to Long Thanh, we no longer had documents permitting us to legally stay in Saigon. We couldn't collect any rice or anything from the government. We have to live on our own, and my mother has to go to the government office to beg for permission to stay there. They usually give you a week or two, or maybe a month. Then you have to go back and beg them for more time, or you have to move out of there before they arrest you. So we have to move back and forth, back and forth, all over the place. I can't go to school because I don't have the documents for Saigon. We just moved from one place to the next until '83, when we left Vietnam.

When we left Long Than, we went over to this house, where the brother of my mom's boyfriend lived. It's just a burned-out house, only a few walls left, and they put a little roof over part of it. We begged them to let us stay near there. They said okay, and my mother went out and bought dry coconut leaf, and made a roof using one of walls. Pretty soon, those people ganged up on us. They called my mom a prostitute, a whore, just because she had been with an American guy and had American kids. That's why Amerasians are called "children of the unwanted." Even the neighbors said stuff like that, and finally it drove my mom away. My mother's boyfriend tried to stick up for her, but his brother beat him up and kicked him out. At that time, my mom's boyfriend was trying to quit drinking, but he became a drug addict instead. My mom tells me he was a very nice guy when they met, but in Long Thanh he started drinking and then in Saigon he got hooked on drugs. From that time, he didn't stay with us no longer. He just moved around, went anywhere he wanted, didn't come home. One or two months later he would come back, steal whatever we have in our house and sell it, so he can buy more drugs. This continued even until the day we left Saigon.

Me and my mom we went over to this church—the church that took my brother and sister to the States in '75. They told my mom we could stay there and take care of the place. We stayed for a while and left. We kept movin' back and forth.

As an Amerasian, I wasn't being treated very fairly when I was in Saigon. My mom, she cooked stuff for me to sell on the street. I had a little table and chair so I could sit there and sell. Little kids that lived nearby, they would come over and harass me. They would pick on me and throw

Tung Joe Nguyen in uniform (courtesy of Joe Nguyen)

rocks at me . . . even when I was in my own place, in the church. I remember one time, I was about twelve or thirteen. It was in the afternoon. My mom was out, and I was sittin' outside in the yard, layin' under the tree. All of a sudden a big rock fell on my head, and I had blood all over me. I ran all over the place. Those kinds of things always went on. When they saw me walking down the street, they would make fun of me, call me *My lai [Amerasian]* and throw rocks at me or hit me.

The parents will see their kids abusing Amerasians, and they just stand there and look at it, and nothing will pass their mind. You know, they think that that's the daughter or son of a hooker, a whore, a prostitute, so it's right for them to get hit. I remember one time, going to a movie and walking home by myself at night. I was probably thirteen at that time. There was a whole bunch of kids hidden out in the bushes, and they just ran out on the street, beat me up, and took off. I was just standing there, I didn't know what was going on. They probably knew I would be coming home and were hiding there purposely, waiting for me to get there so they could beat me up. That's their game, going around, finding us, teasing us, and beating up on us. And the parents don't do anything about it. That's how they treat us.

Before we moved out of Saigon to Long Thanh, I went to school up to fourth grade. When we moved to Long Thanh, I tried to go to school there, but they said, "No, you can't go, you don't have any paper work, plus, you're 'My lai,' you're half–American." After we moved out of there back to Saigon, my mom went to the school, begging them to let me in. They say, "No, he can't go to school, he don't have any paper work, plus he's too old for school, plus he's 'My lai.'" So I had no choice but to work all day, selling food on the street.

I had only one or two friends. With Amerasians, we don't have a chance to talk to each other because we are so busy working. Just seeing them, I recognize that they are Amerasian. They have blonde hair and stuff like that, but I have no time to come over and talk, so we never have a chance to become friends. I see plenty of Amerasians walking around, and they also being picked on just like I am. Every day people bothered me. Every time I would see a new kid, someone who didn't know me, it didn't matter where it was at, he would be there laughing at me, teasing me, calling me "My lai." It continued for years, it never stopped. I didn't like to go near other kids. They just kept calling me that, so I didn't associate with them at all. A few Vietnamese kids around my neighborhood, first they were teasing me, but then they get to know me and become my friends, and those are the only people I played with, when I had time.

We thought about leaving Vietnam constantly. My mom dreamed about it almost every night, dreaming that she was in the States with me, and then waking up in tears, realizing that we were still in Vietnam, with not enough to eat, trying to make ends meet. She tried to figure out a way to go, but we had no money. Only rich people could afford to leave by boat, because you have to pay x amount of money to leave, and even then it's not guaranteed that you gonna go. We knew some people that kept on trying for ten, fifteen times, losing all the money that they had, and they still couldn't get out. So there was no hope for us, we just sat there, and all she could do is dream that one day we could leave.

I had two Vietnamese brothers, but they're both dead now. They were from my mom's Vietnamese boyfriend. When we lived in that burned-out house, my mom was pregnant. We lived very far from the hospital. When she went into labor, my stepdad was not home, and she asked a neighbor to take her to the hospital. Before she could get there, somebody delivered her right out there on the street, and they used dirty scissors to cut the cord. The baby got infected, and he died at six days old. The other one was born about a year later, in '77. He died in '80 or '81, from drowning.

About 1983, my mother found out about the Amerasian Program, that if you are Amerasian and you can prove it, there is a chance for you to go to the States. So she filled out applications, and it helped her knowing a lot of English. She was talking to a lot of people, running all over the place, and we finally were accepted. We were, my mom told me, in the second group of Amerasians that left Vietnam.

My mom's younger brother had a son, but he couldn't afford to care for him. He couldn't feed him and couldn't send him to school. He tried to give the kid to my grandmother, but she didn't want him. Now, my mom still had the birth certificate of my drowned brother, so she said, "Here's a chance, let's see if it works." She put in the paperwork for him using my dead brother's birth certificate. We convinced the Vietnamese that he was my younger brother. There was no way for them to prove that he wasn't. He's pure blooded Vietnamese, just like my brother, and he was actually born the same year, 1977. So he came over with us, and he's in America now, living with my mother and calling her "mom."

We came over to America, to Rochester, New York, on April first, April Fools' Day. The next day, we had a snowstorm, which is very unusual for that area in April. That was my first snow experience. We went outside and played in the snow, the whole family, including my mom, because she never saw snow before either.

I remember, in Vietnam, when we went to the farm at Long Thanh. At night, I'm sittin' there with my stepdad, and he's trying to teach me the times table. That's the only thing I knew, the times table. I couldn't do anything else except that until I studied in the States. When we got to there, I was fourteen years old, goin' on fifteen, and my mom was tryin' to get me into the school. They say I have to take this test, but I couldn't do it. I couldn't read, I couldn't write. They gave me the basic math like subtraction, addition, multiplication, division. I could do the addition and subtraction, and the multiplication, because I knew the times table, but very basic, like two times four. Anything complicated like four times thirty, I couldn't do, because I didn't have the basic knowledge. Division, well, I was clueless on that, I just didn't know how to do it. So they said, "Well, he's fourteen, goin' on fifteen, and he doesn't know anything about math, we'll put him in the seventh grade."

I couldn't speak a word of English, nothing at all. They put me into this school where I was the only Vietnamese. They put me in a class to try to teach me English, but I had no idea what they are talking about. I stayed in seventh grade for just two months, because we got to the States in April, and we get out of school in June. So the following year they just pushed me up to eighth grade.

One day this man saw me playing in the street. He was the Boy Scout master, and he came over to ask me if I wanted to join the Boy Scouts. I couldn't speak any English at the time, so he went upstairs and talked to my mom and said he's interested in putting me into the Boy Scouts. She said, "Well, he don't know any English." So he came over my house every day and sat there teaching me one thing at a time. He would point at something and say, "What's this called?" and that's how I started learning English. He is like a father to me because he taught me everything I know—English, math, reading, writing, everything. Every time I had problems in school, he would be there till midnight, one in the morning, to help me. And I was able to go all the way through high school.

About a year or so after we got to the States, my mom made contact with the foster parents of my brother and sister, and they were nice enough to bring them over to Rochester to meet us. My brother's foster family was in Washington, my sister's was in Virginia. The man who taught me English, I call him my "uncle," he telephoned them and arranged for us to meet them on the road.

They both came on the same day, in the same car. We parked on the interstate and waited for them. We sat there for a while, and then this big van pulled up, and the two of them walked out. I looked at them, and I said, "That's my sister, that's my brother," and they looked at me and did the same thing. I mean, we knew instantly, as soon as they walked out of the van. My mom cried all day long, everybody cried.

We went to our house, but first we went to a park where we could play around. Now when I think about it, it was kind of foolish. We didn't even sit around and talk to each other, sayin' "How you doing?" We just held each other and walked around the park, goin' on all the rides, just the three of us. My mom and their stepparents are the only ones who really talked.

That's the only time I saw my sister. My brother, he calls my mom all the time. He's in the marines now, but when he was going to college he used to drive up and visit us. My sister, she don't contact my mom that much. Once in a while she calls, and that's it.

I was dating this girl, almost since the time we came to the States. She was a full-blooded Vietnamese, she came over with her brother and sister. She was the youngest in the family, and they keep tellin' her not to see me because I'm Amerasian. They put me down, they put my mom down. They say that we are nothing, that she deserves better.

After I graduated high school, we went to the same college, Rochester Institute of Technology. I was studying micro-electronic engineering, and she was studying electrical engineering. There was too much fighting going on between her and her family about me. They were saying that my family is low, that my mom been with an American guy and stuff like that. They assume that if a woman has an American child she must have been working in the bar. The fact is that my mom lived with my dad for three or four years and had three kids with him, but they don't want to look at that. They just say that she has an American, a mixed-blood boy, and that's all they need to know. So my girlfriend was always fighting with her family, and we keep fighting between ourselves all the time. There was just no way to take the pressure, and finally, we broke up and I left school.

I told my mother that I quit school, and she yelled at me a bit, but I told her that I would go back again, this time to a different school. I made an application to go to the University of Buffalo, and they accepted me. I got a job, just waiting for the fall to start school. One day I was looking through a pile of junk mail, and I saw this letter. It said, "If you want to learn about the military, just check here." I was kind of bored at the time, so I said, "Well, let me learn a little about the air force," and I checked it and sent it in. About a week later, a recruiter called and told me to come out to the office to talk to him, and that's when I got lured into enlisting. They persuaded me, and I kept on going along with them until the day I raised my hand and was sworn in, and that's when I realized, "Man, I'm in the military." I called my mom from Buffalo, and said, "Mom, I'm in the military." She almost passed out, she didn't know anything about it. At the time I was still waiting for school, that was May, and school was supposed to start in September.

Julie also lived in Rochester, with her brother and sisters and her parents. Her brothers and sisters are Amerasian too, and her older brother, he was my best friend. He used to come over all the time. I met them when they first came to America. I was in school, and I already knew a lot of English, so I became a translator. Every time there was a new Vietnamese kid coming to the school, I was picked to help them out, to go to their house and translate, to bring them to classes, stuff like that. So I knew Julie for five or six years, and I always thought of her as my little sister. I never thought that she would be my wife. But after I broke up with my other girl friend, our families started talking, and they fixed us up together. Pretty soon we fell in love and got married. And she came out here to be with me.

I regret now that I don't have a chance to go back to school, because now I have a wife and kid, but if I was not in the military there would be no way for me to support them. So, I'm kind of sad that I'm not in school, but I'm kind of happy that I'm in the military, because now I can take care of them.

In the air force, I work in Supply, I do paperwork there. After you join the military, you put down your preference for where you want to go. They have all kinds of bases, overseas and Stateside. I wanted to go overseas, and I put down Japan as my first choice. I been here three years, and I love it. I get along with everybody, including the Japanese. People are so tight here, because we work in a very close environment. Everybody knows each other, everyone helps each other. That's why I like staying overseas.

Tung Joe and Julie Nguyen

I'm Amerasian, you know, but I'm no different then anybody. For me, living as an American is more like a family then living in Vietnam. I consider Vietnamese as my family, as my people too, but they don't think of me the same way. They always think of me as a stranger, uneducated, with an uneducated mother . . . all stereotypes. So I'm kinda glad that I went to the States, to be who I am today, because if I didn't go to the States, I don't know what I would be right now.

Julie Nguyen, now twenty-three, came to America in 1985, passing through the Philippine Refugee Processing Center. She arrived in America speaking no English, and unlike Joe, learned very little of the language in her five years there. She explains, "I was sixteen when I came over, and they put me in ninth grade.

There was an ESL program, but I didn't learn. The teacher would be trying to teach us English, but each group, Lao, Cambodian, and Vietnamese would stay in their own circle, talking their own language, so I was always talking in Vietnamese." Ironically, in Japan, where she has lived for three years, she has found more opportunity to use English and has progressed to where she can easily hold a conversation in her new language. As we speak, when she can't find a word, Joe fills in for her.

Julie: My real mother asked my stepdad if she could come to my house and visit me. I was about nine, we lived in Ho Chi Minh City. I didn't know who she was. She sat down and cut my nails, and she cry a lot. And I ask her why she cry, and she say, "It's nothing, I just remember something sad." I say, "Don't worry, you don't have to cry," but she just can't stop. She visited for about an hour, then she was gone.

One day she come to my school and she want to talk to me. She says, "I want to visit you, I want to hug you, that's all." Another day, my family, they hit me, they yell at me a lot and I tell the lady, "I want to go with you. You don't hit me, you don't yell at me." So she took me with her for one week. It was like heaven, nothing happened *[nobody beat me]*. Then one day my *[step]*mom and my *[step]*dad come over, a lot of people come and take me away. I cry, "I don't want to go home, I don't want to go home. I want to stay with you." My *[step]*dad is hitting her and beating her, and she runs to me and says, "One day when you are grown up I find you," and she runs away. My *[step]*dad chased her, but he didn't get her. They take me home, and my stepmom carries me like Joe carries our daughter *[Joe is holding Kimberly over his shoulder]*. She told the people around, "It was her daughter, but she gave her to me, and now she came and took her away again, she didn't tell me nothing." I remember, I say to myself, "Huh. I am adopted. I am not her daughter." I cry a lot, and I know that other woman is really my mother.

A lot of times she comes to visit me, and she gives me money, and she wants me to go with her, but I can't go with her, because I am afraid that my *[step]*dad could find me anywhere. She comes to visit me when I am older and work in my *[step]*dad's beauty shop. She would come see me, but she would hide, so my *[step]*dad couldn't see her.

My real mother didn't have any other children, just me. She says that she miss me, she want me to come with her. One day, when I was fifteen, she comes with her friend, and she asks me to go with her. She says, "Now you grown up, you know everything *[that I am your real mother]*, you come with me."

I say, "No, I can't go with you *[Julie is in tears]*. My stepparents, they feed me, they raise me, and now that I grown up I run away? I can't do that." I say, "Maybe one year, we go to America. I write you, I send you money, please, just give me your address." But she says, "I live anywhere, not one place. I move from one place to the next, I have no address." So when I went to America, we lost contact.

Joe: When Julie said that she was going to the States, her mom didn't believe her. She said that there is no way for you to go there. So Julie left before they saw each other again, and she never got a place to write her mom. Now there is no way for her to locate her mother.

Julie: I have trouble with my *[step]*dad two years ago. He says my mom sold me, not give me for adoption . . . sold me . . . *[Julie becomes extremely emotional while recalling this.]*

Joe: Yeah, he wrote us a letter. When I joined the service, and I wanted to marry her, my family and hers got together and sat there and planned the wedding. Her *[step]*mother had died four years before, and her stepdad met another lady, who also had an Amerasian daughter. So they had four Amerasians living in the house, and two of them got married before us, in that same year. Somehow it came up that we couldn't get married because he don't want three of them to get married in the same year. He wanted us to wait until the following year. I didn't agree with that, and neither did my mom. I had to leave for Japan with the military, and there was no way I could come back from there to get married with her.

So they were fighting and arguing, my family and her family. My mom wants us to get married now, and they say wait until next year. Her *[step]*-dad lost control. He took her upstairs and started beating on her. Her brother and I had left to go to the movies. When we left everything was going well, so we thought everything was fine. Meanwhile, back at home, her *[step]*father is beating her with his fists, and all the guests are downstairs. My mom ran upstairs and tried to break it up and told Julie to come home with her. Her stepdad told her that she had a choice, either to go with me or break up with me and stay home with them. That's when she told her stepdad, "I'm sorry, but I choose him." And he kicked her out of the house. He threw all of her stuff outside, and her sister took her to a friend's house.

She called me at home telling me that her *[step]*dad kicked her out, and I picked her up and brought her to my house, and we got married that same week. I left for Japan, and she stayed with my mom for seven weeks before joining me. When she was in my mom's house, her stepdad wrote her a six-page letter explaining her life story, everything. He said that when she was a newborn, they went to the hospital and bought her. Her mom wanted money. He even gave the price that he bought her for. That's how she found out that her real mom sold her and didn't give her away, but we don't know if that is true or not. We think that her *[step]*dad was just trying to hurt her emotionally, trying to tell her that he owns her, and that he felt betrayed that she left home and went with me. We think it was all written intentionally to hurt her.

Julie: My real mom, she didn't say "bought," she said, "I didn't have the money to feed you, to take care of you. That's why I give you away." And I got mad, I say, "Why, why you give me away? Even if you don't have the money, why you give me away?" She said, "I thought this family be good for you. They have a lot of money, they can feed you, that's why I gave you to them. I didn't know that they would abuse you."

In Vietnam, I went to school up to the fourth grade. I didn't have any close friends. Amerasians don't have that. In my neighborhood, people see me and laugh, they do mean things to me. They throw stones at me, they say such bad things. They call me "American," so I know I'm half–American, but I don't know who my father is. My sister and brother are Amerasian too. My stepmother said she married American and that we are her children, but from different fathers, and that's why me and my sister and my brother are not the same looking. But now we know that's not true.

My sister, she really was the child of my *[step]* dad's sister. Because my stepdad's sister in Vietnam wrote him in America and said, "Why you don't give my daughter back so I can go to America?" So now she knows that she is adopted, but before she didn't know.

My stepparents love my brother a lot. Like when they give us a sweet, they give my brother a whole cookie, and me and my sister a quarter, or something like that.

Joe: Her sister and her kind of share the same circumstances. The way she was telling me, when they have food they just give it to the brother, and whatever is left over, that he don't want, they share between the two of them. Everything is the same way. He comes first, and they get the leftovers. Everything is for him, and the girls have to do everything the family wants—cooking, cleaning, go and make money—but the boy can go and do anything he wants. So, they think that he is the real son of the mother, because of the way she treats him.

Julie: If I did something just a little bad or broke something, they yell for one or two days and hit me.

Joe: She has all kinds of scars, on the head, on the hands, from being beaten. They physically abused the two of them, her and her sister, since they were little kids, and up to the day we were married, they were still abusing her. When we were married, she was still in high school. I took her into school and went to thank one of her teachers for teaching her English. That was the first time he met me, and he said, "Take care of her, because I know her family hit her, abused her. She comes to school with black eyes and bruises, everything." She was fifteen or sixteen years old, going to school with bruises on her arm, on her face, and everywhere else. And when the teacher asked where she got them, she would say, "Oh, I fell, oh, I hurt myself." But actually he knew that the parents were abusing her, but he could not prove it.

She didn't want to tell me this because she is so afraid. She thinks if she tells somebody she will probably be beaten more, and there is more danger for her than there is help, so she keeps her mouth shut. Her *[step]* dad was fistfighting her, beating her with elbows, fists, and kicking her. Even her older brother hit her.

But it was that letter her stepdad wrote, that's what really hurt her. She thought that they adopted her because they loved her, and then when they told her that they bought her... Well, she thought of them as parents, of him as a dad. That they would say something like that to make her feel bad, well that hurt her. That's what hurt her the most.

Julie: He cut my hair, he slapped my face. I hate them, but I still love them. I don't know why, I still think of them.

Manivong

"How could I know what the government's
policy towards Amerasians would be in the
future? This is why I decided to go to America."

*Manivong is his Khmer name, and he is from the Mekong delta area of
Vietnam. This region was once part of Cambodia, and is home to a large population of ethnic Cambodians known as Khmer Krom. Manivong's mother belonged
to this ethnic group; his father was an American soldier from Milwaukee, who
gave him the name Robert. Like many Khmer Krom, Manivong has a Vietnamese name as well, Tran Xuan Thanh.*

*Manivong spent eight years as a Buddhist monk, leaving the order in 1989
to marry. He is literate in the Sanskrit-based Khmer script, but not in Vietnamese
or English, though he speaks Vietnamese fluently. We converse through an interpreter.*

*He shows me some baby photos. In one, he is with his baby-sitter, seated in
a rattan stroller. Another shot is of him as a toddler, posing near a living room
bar. There are a number of snapshots of Manivong in the temple, wearing the
flowing orange robes of his order.*

*His most prized photo is a five-by-seven of his father, blonde, crewcut, peer-
ing through a pair of horn rimmed glasses. The resemblance he bears to his son
is unmistakable; Manivong's father was about the same age at the time the photo
was taken as his son is now. Superimposed over the heart area is a small image
of Manivong's late mother. On the flip side is written a Milwaukee address, and
the inscription:*

> *To Sapim, you are the number one girl of my life. I love you and want you so
> much*
>> *Love always,*
>> *Lt. Ballman (Batman)*

I WAS BORN in a small village in Hau Giang, in the Mekong Delta
region, and I lived there all my life. Like most of the people in my village,
I am Khmer, as is my wife.

70

According to what my grandparents told me, my mother went from Hau Giang to Bien Hoa to learn how to be a seamstress. She met my father there, and they got married. My father was in the air force *[according to his documents, Manivong's father was in the army]*. He left Vietnam in 1970. I was born before he left, and he named me Robert.

My mother was suffering from cancer at the time my father was to leave Vietnam. He wanted her to go to America for treatment, but she would not leave Vietnam and her parents. My father returned to America without her.

When my father got the news of my mother's death in 1971, he came back to Vietnam and made a funeral ceremony for her, in accordance with Buddhist tradition. He wanted to take me back to America with him, but my grandparents wouldn't let me leave. My father wrote to my grandparents until 1975, but I have not heard from him since then.

I lived with my grandparents in a small hut made of coconut leaves. I went to school for a very short time, but I had to stop. It's very difficult for Amerasians to stay in school. Within a few years the Communists had taken over, and both my grandparents died. I was on my own.

I went to live at the Khmer Buddhist temple. At this time, the local authorities were restless, and the townspeople were afraid that the Communists would destroy the temple if an Amerasian novice stayed there. A monk in the temple tried to protect me. He told the people that I was an orphan and needed help. But after one month, I had to leave the pagoda.

For a few years I worked tending water buffalo for people in the village. Many other Amerasians in the town had a similar situation, no homes, working odd jobs to survive. I had no house. At night I slept in the cemetery, sometimes on top of the flat concrete slabs they build over the grave. *[I ask if Manivong if he was afraid, as many Khmer and Vietnamese are, of ghosts and spirits. He laughs and says he was not.]*

I entered the temple again about two years later, when I was about twelve. This time they accepted me, because the attitude of the local authorities had changed a little, and there was no longer a problem for an Amerasian to stay there. In my province, there are one hundred and eighteen temples, and I visited many of them. I studied in the temple, Vietnamese and Khmer language, Pali *[the language of the Buddhist prayers]*, and Buddhism. I also worked in the field and in the garden.

I felt comfortable in the temple, free in spirit. I felt that since I was a monk, no one would disturb me. But I could not be at ease because government attitudes often changed. How could I know what the government's policy towards Amerasians would be in the future? This is why I decided to go to America.

In Vietnam I could not have real freedom, I could not change my life for the better. In the temple, I was accepted by the other monks. There was

Manivong in his neighborhood of the Philippine Refugee Processing Center

no problem that I was Amerasian, but outside, it was different, there was discrimination. When I went out, I often told people that I was a different race, Chinese for example. This made it easier.

When I get to America, I want to go to school. I hope to be an inventor, to invent electronic things, but now I worry that I won't even be able to afford to pay rent. I am a free case. I have no one to sponsor me in the United States, but I want to go and live in Wisconsin. That is where my father is from. I wrote him sixteen registered letters from Vietnam. I think someone received them because they were not sent back, but I never got a reply. I believe he is still alive, and I will find him.

My

"I hit the streets, and survived by begging...."

The monsoon in Bataan usually runs its course by the end of September. On this October eighth, however, the skies have opened with a vengeance, turning the road leading to the PRPC jail into a muddy quagmire. Inside the detention facility, refugees are incarcerated for the usual variety of crimes and infractions: unauthorized transfer of billet, gambling, frustrated homicide. My is in for the most common offenses, violation of the refugee camp liquor ban and "slight physical injury." In plain language, he got drunk and got into a fight.

This is not My's first time in detention. He spent four years in a labor camp in Vietnam. My feels that the flimsy charges of theft and "moving without the proper documents" that sent him there would not have merited this sentence had he not been Amerasian.

My's legs and left arm are a mass of scars from self-inflicted knife wounds. His left forearm is unmarked, but above the elbow, the scars are uncountable, one leading into the next, forming a solid mass of tissue which almost encircles the biceps. His legs are almost completely covered with scar tissue from razor slashes. This carnage was done under the influence of "pills," at a time when My was "depressed and suffering."

My interpreter, himself an Amerasian, knows My from Vietnam. He is, in fact, the one who made out My's application for the Orderly Departure Program. He informs me that My disappeared before his interview, going back to the province in order to bring his family to Ho Chi Minh City to register for ODP as well. This necessitated starting the application process over again from the beginning.

My knows nothing of his biological parents, having been abandoned at a market in Da Nang as an infant and picked up there by the woman who was to become his stepmother. His fair skin and Western features, though, give testament to his heredity; he is obviously Amerasian.

My, twenty-one, is in the PRPC with his stepmother and her family. His girlfriend and baby son are still in Vietnam.

73

I DON'T REALLY KNOW where I come from or who my parents are. I was abandoned at the Da Nang market when I was a newborn and picked up there by a lady who had a stall selling fabric. She says that I was about three days old when she found me.

She is here in camp with me now, her sister and her nephew, and my black Amerasian stepsister and her husband and child.

This lady picked me up and took me home, and I stayed with her and her family. She was good to me, but her sister, my aunt, and my aunt's husband, they hated me. They were jealous that my stepmother loved me. They despised me because I was Amerasian. They made my life miserable, and finally I ran away when I was still pretty young.

I hit the streets and survived by begging and odd jobs—selling cigarettes, soft drinks. I would sleep at the market, I was just a street kid. I guess it was about three years after I left my stepmother's house that I heard that she was sick, so I went back home to see her.

I stayed there for a while to spend time with her, but I got into some trouble with my uncle. He called the police and claimed that I had stolen some things from my stepmother. He also complained that I had left the house without permission. You know, in Vietnam you can't transfer from one place to another without informing the local authorities. It is a crime against the Communist government's rules. The police came to arrest me. My stepmother defended me. She told them that I had not stolen anything, that I had not done anything wrong, but they took me away anyway. They hate Amerasians.

They brought me out to the provincial jail for about six months, and then they sent me out to a labor camp and it was four years before they let me out. I had to work, but they also let me study. First year I studied in the day and worked in the afternoon and evening. The second year I worked in the day and studied in the evening. They taught me how to read and write in Vietnamese, how to do some math, and their history, about how the Communists defeated the Americans and the French.

Most of the work I did was farm work. You know, all the guards are Vietnamese, and they don't like Amerasians. The worst work, the hardest jobs, the heaviest loads, they save for the Amerasians. Everyone is part of a work team, and each team has the team leader. The team leaders, they also don't like Amerasians, and they discriminate against them.

When I was about about eighteen, they released me, and I went back to my stepmother's place in Da Nang. I was on probation. I was supposed to stay there, not go out, not move around. But after two months I left. I just was fed up with the people around there, always talking down on me because I am Amerasian, looking down on me, thinking they are better than me.

So I went down to Saigon and was sleeping in the bus station and selling some soft drinks to make a little money when I met this woman. Her idea was that I should marry her, and she would help me make the papers to go to the United States. See, this way she could go too. So I said okay, and we tried that. But when we made the application, the local officials questioned my residence. They said that it was not correct, and they wouldn't complete the paperwork. So, I was out of there and on the street again.

At that point I went back to my stepmother's house and asked to borrow some money to buy some tools. She gave it to me, and I set up a little stall on the street, fixing bicycles. At night I slept in front of a shop that sold firewood. After a while I was working for the owner of the firewood place, delivering loads of wood in a pedicab. I was still living on the street. I couldn't sleep in my stepmother's house. I still couldn't get along with my aunt.

In '89 I saw a lot of Amerasians were going to America, and people were asking me, "Hey, why don't you do that?" I went back to Saigon, down to Amerasian Park. I stayed there in the park, and I applied to go to America through the Amerasian program. But I went back to Da Nang, and I missed my interview and had to apply all over again.

I came back to Saigon again, and my family waited in Da Nang. I was waiting for the interview for the second time, but I fell in love with a Vietnamese girl, and she became pregnant. My family and I were interviewed and accepted, but my girlfriend was three months pregnant, and I refused to go at that time. I didn't want to leave her. So I missed the flight here and had to wait again. I couldn't take her with me because all the paperwork had been completed already. She is still in Vietnam with my son.

I got in some trouble a few weeks ago, that's why I am here in the monkey house. I was down by the stream near neighborhood four, drinking with some friends. Later, when I was back in the neighborhood, I got into a fight with four Khmer Amerasians. Security came, and they ran away. The security guards said that I smelled of liquor, so they arrested me. So they put me in here for violation of the liquor ban, for one week. One week passed, and I asked about getting released. Now they tell me that I am also charged with fighting and have to stay here in the monkey house longer. When I get out of jail this time, I am just going to stay home and go to school. I'm not going to hang out with friends anymore.

It's not easy here. They let me out in the morning to do work credit and in the afternoon to study English. After class, I have to come back to the lock-up. My girlfriend from neighborhood ten brought me some rice, but they say that I came back from school late, and they never gave it to me.

You want to know about these scars on my arms and legs? Well, in Vietnam I was suffering and depressed, and I would take some pills and

My

take a razor blade and just cut myself. I was just feeling sad and disappointed. But I haven't done this for a year now.

When I get to the States, I'm going to try and bring my girlfriend and son over from Vietnam. I want to be with her, I don't want to stay with my stepmother's family.

I don't know what nationality I am. I'm Amerasian. I don't want to live with Vietnamese in America. I don't want to live with Amerasians either. They know me too well already. I just want to live in a place where there are no Vietnamese.

I'd like to get some vocational training in America, maybe learn how to fix motorcycles. Yes, that's what I'd like to do, motorcycle repair.

Kerry

"While I was in the hospital, Vietnam
fell to the Communists, and we were
trapped. We never got back to my father."

*Mr. Thanh, a young Vietnamese refugee who had been acting as my inter-
preter, informed me that there was an Amerasian in his neighborhood who had
been born in the United States and carried an American passport.*

*I went with him to check it out and met Kerry, a twenty-year-old white
Amerasian. Kerry, speaking not a word of English, produced a sheaf of papers,
including xeroxes of his birth certificate, U.S passport, his and his mother's U.S.
army medical cards, as well as an original resident alien card issued to his mother,
Thu Thi Sturgess.*

*His documents show that he was born in Fort Sill, Oklahoma, on June 30,
1971. He and his mother lived there for several years with Kerry's American
father, who was stationed on the base.*

*In 1975 Kerry and his mother returned to Vietnam for a visit. Although they
held return air tickets to the United States, the Communist takeover left them
trapped.*

*Kerry's wife is in the PRPC with him, as is his mother, Thu Thi Sturgess.
Sturgess is hearing and speech impaired, but her son seems to communicate easily
with her.*

MY FATHER WAS an American soldier in Vietnam. He married my
mother there and brought her back to the United States. That's where I was
born and lived until I was about three years old. In 1975, my mother took
me back to Vietnam, just for a trip, but things went wrong, and we were
never able to return to the United States.

My mother is deaf, and she can barely speak. The neighbors cannot
understand her, but I lived with her all my life, and I understand what she
says. This is the story she told me, of how we got caught in Vietnam:

My father was stationed in Da Nang. My mother sold beer and soft drinks on the base there. They met, fell in love, and got married. When my father took my mother to America, she was already pregnant with me. I was born there, in Oklahoma, in 1971.

My father usually went to work in the morning and came home late at night. One time my mother was waiting for him to come home. It was very late. She looked out the window and saw my father kissing another woman. When she saw that, she took off her wedding ring and threw it out the window. She resolved to become a Buddhist nun and shaved off all her hair, in the tradition of women entering the Buddhist order. She demanded to go back to Vietnam.

Now, my father was very sorry, he didn't want us to go. My mother insisted, and they compromised. The plan was that she and I would go for a short time and then return to the States. My father bought a wig for my mother, and he bought us round-trip tickets from America to Vietnam. Since she was living in the United States as an alien, she needed papers to reenter the United States. My father got those for her.

We were supposed to stay in Vietnam for two months, visit relatives, and come back to Oklahoma. But I got very sick in Vietnam, and I was in the hospital for two months, and we missed our plane back to America. While I was in the hospital, Vietnam fell to the Communists, and we were trapped. We never got back to my father.

We received two money orders from my father, and then we didn't hear from him anymore. How could my mother contact him? She cannot hear or speak. She cannot read or write, not even Vietnamese. So there is nothing she could do.

I was only four years old when the Communists came. But I remember at that time, my mother wept every day.

I didn't go to school in Vietnam. I didn't have any Vietnamese documents, and the government would not accept my American papers. I can barely read and write Vietnamese. When I was about ten, I got a job on a boat that delivered blocks of ice to restaurants and shops.

My mother remarried, with a Vietnamese man. She didn't have any more children, but he had many from his first wife, and they came to live with him and my mother. So I left home and mostly slept on the boat. I would go back to see my mother once in a while, maybe every seven or eight months. These were my happiest times. When my stepfather died, I came to see her more often.

I had very few friends. I was working on the boat. I couldn't go to school, and many people didn't like me because I was part American. When I was a boy, many people would taunt me. Some even hit me. They called me "American, son of the imperialists." They shouted, "Go home to America."

A few years ago I met a Vietnamese woman. She was living in America

Kerry

but came back to Vietnam for a visit. This is the card she gave me. *[It says, "Jake Bloom, commercial pilot." There is a U.S. address.]* She asked about my situation, and I told her that I was born in America and was trying to get back there. She asked me to give her my original documents and told me that she would bring them to America and help me go to the United States. She said she would come back to Vietnam in about eight months. We waited the eight months, but she didn't return. We were worried, so I went with my wife and my mother, and we applied for the Orderly Departure Program. In about a year, the woman came back, and she took me to the U.S. office in charge of the Amerasian cases. I was accepted to go, but only me, not my mother or my wife. I would not leave them, I refused to go alone. We reapplied, and eventually I was accepted along with my mother and wife.

I never understood about that woman, who she was or why she tried to help me.

The Orderly Departure Program told me that because I was born in the United States, I am an American citizen, and I have the right to go directly to America. When we left Vietnam, they first took us to Thailand. When we got there, they told us that because I was over eighteen, I would have to go to the Philippines to study first. We were very disappointed, we left Vietnam thinking that we were going straight to America.

In Vietnam I worked very hard and I could never go to school. Here, in the PRPC, I can study English, and the work is not very hard, so it is better here than in Vietnam, but still I am anxious to go to America. I want to find my father, I will be so happy if I can see him. I hope he can help me to continue studying. We have many things to talk about.

Nguyen Thi Ngoc Thuy

"All children of Americans were
considered children of the enemy."

*At first glance, I take Thuy for Cambodian. It is her dusky complexion and
the full turn of her cheeks. She is sitting outside the neighborhood five market,
a black umbrella shielding her from the sun. Spread in front of her on a plastic
tarp is a bewildering array of goods for sale: old Walkmans, used clothing,
English-Vietnamese dictionaries, ancient clothes irons that run on charcoal
embers.*

*I try out a few words of my limited Khmer on her, and she answers in same.
After a few sentences, we both run out of language, and Thuy laughingly breaks
into English.*

*Thuy did spend a short time in Cambodia, where she picked up the few
Khmer phrases she used in answering me, but her copper-toned skin and thick
wavy hair come from her black GI father. Her mother is Vietnamese. I was not
the first to mistake Thuy's ethnicity. In Cambodia, even the Khmer people
thought she was one of them.*

*Although she hardly spent a day in school in Vietnam, Thuy has acquired
some skill in the English language. She is quite outgoing and is not afraid to make
a mistake. Although we generally spoke through an interpreter, she would try to
understand my questions in English and take a crack at answering them directly.
When the language became too complex, she would turn to the translator for
assistance.*

*She is in the PRPC with her husband and three children. The youngest, she
says, she found abandoned on a bridge in Ho Chi Minh City. Thuy, now thirty,
was herself an abandoned child, left with an often callous caretaker when her
mother married a Vietnamese man. After enduring years of ill treatment, she left
for Saigon, where she spent most of her life, living on the street.*

*One evening, as we sit in her billet, Thuy hands me a tiny black and white
photo. At five years old, her slender child's frame belies the stocky lady she would
become. Her mother sits by her, clad in the traditional Vietnamese* ao dai. *The
woman and the child both stare stiffly at the camera. The photo, sepia from age,*

has the antique quality of heirloom pictures one sees in lockets or in tiny filigreed silver frames. Thuy recounts how, after the fall of South Vietnam, she traced her mother to a village in Thuan Hai province. Despite a happy beginning, their reunion ended in conflict, brought on by the refusal of her mother's husband to accept her. In spite of Thuy's pain at this second rejection, the two women reunited and made amends just weeks before Thuy left Vietnam in December of 1991. "Even though she abandoned me," Thuy says, "even with all the problems that we had, she is still my mother."

I WAS BORN in Phan Thiet, in Thuan Hai province. I never saw my father. My mother told me that he went to America when she was three months pregnant. She said my father's name was Mickey, and she was washing dishes at a bar where she met him. That's all I know about him.

When I was little, my mother washed dishes at Minh Mang restaurant near Phan Thiet. After that she worked as a vendor. She left me with a lady, a sort of baby-sitter, who watched me while she went out to earn money.

When I was still young, maybe seven or eight years old, my mother gave me away to the baby-sitter. That lady became like my stepmother. She told me that my grandmother was angry at my mother for marrying a foreigner, my father, and that's why she left me. My mother came to visit me, but only two times. Then she didn't come no more. After that, she married a Vietnamese, and she didn't want me anymore. It was many years before I saw her again.

I was very sad when she left, but I was confused. I was young when I went to live with my stepfamily, and I didn't really understand if they were my real family or not. Some neighbors told me that I was adopted, but I could not understand.

I never went to school. My stepmother had three children, and she made me take care of them. I received little affection from that family. My stepfather didn't abuse me, but my stepmother tormented me. She hated me because I was black. She thought I was dumb. She called me stupid, and she beat me. One time she hung me upside down. When I was about as old as this girl *[Thuy points to an eight-year-old child]*, she made me strip to the skin and stand outside in the hot sun. Sometimes I would hide under the bed and wait until she left before I came out to eat.

She was so unkind. One day a beggar passed my house, and I gave her a can of rice. That made my stepmother furious. Another time I shared some food with a neighbor. My stepmother beat me for that.

We lived in Phan Thiet town, near the sea, in a big house with a well outside. My stepfather was a fisherman. I worked by carrying the fish and drying it in the sun. Then my stepmother took them to sell.

My stepfather died when I was about ten. He dove under the sea to spear fish. There was a compressor on the boat, with a hose that supplied

Thuy at five years old with her mother (courtesy of Nguyen Thi Ngoc Thuy)

him with air underwater. The compressor broke, and he could not get air. He never came up.

My stepmother hired many men to search for the body of her husband. They tried for one week, but they couldn't find him. The family was Buddhist, but there was no ceremony because there was no body.

When I was twelve, I heard from a neighbor that my real mother was living in Saigon, so I left my stepmother's house and got on a bus for Saigon. I had no money, so I tried to avoid paying the fare by means of various tricks. For example, when they came to collect my fare, I would point to someone in the back of the bus and say that she was my mother and would pay for me. When this didn't work, I would get off the bus and wait for another and try the same thing. In this way, I boarded several buses and finally made my way to Saigon. Of course, I didn't find my mother.

I went over to Ba Chieu market and begged for scraps. I slept at the market with some other beggars. After about a week, I went over to Quach Thi Trang Park and began shining shoes. I worked with a group of Amerasians — two boys and four girls, all black, like me. They have all gone to America already. We slept in the bus station, or if it was not raining, we sometimes slept in the park. You know at that time, the black and white Amerasian stayed separately, not like now. Now they mix very freely, but then white Amerasians didn't want to make friends with me.

This group taught me how to shine shoes. It's not difficult. I tell the customer to put his foot up on the shoeshine box, I put on some polish. I have a long cloth. I hold an end of the cloth in each hand, and then I buff the shoe, like this. *[Thuy demonstrates a vigorous shoeshine motion.]* I got three dong for a pair of shoes. Some days I would do five pairs, other days only two pairs. We pooled our money in the group, that's how we lived. I also worked as a dishwasher in a boardinghouse and as a newspaper seller.

I would take a bath and wash my clothes at the public faucet. One time, I washed my clothes and hung them up on a fence near a gas station. I sat down to keep my eye on them. But I got sleepy, and as much as I tried, I couldn't help dozing off. When I woke up, my clothes weren't there. I ran up and down the street looking for them, but it was too late. They were gone. *[Thuy laughs at the memory.]*

There were gangs on the street. Sometimes bad things would happen, but nobody bothered me. After I lived on the street a while, I knew my way around. I think maybe I had a look about me, and people left me alone.

When I was fourteen, the Communists came to Saigon. I was selling newspapers on Le Lai Street at that time. All the Americans had left Saigon. All children of Americans were considered children of the enemy. We could not find work or a place to live. It was very difficult. I was afraid, and I felt lonely. I began to think, even though I had been mistreated when I was a girl in Phan Thiet, wasn't it my homeland? So I got on a bus and went back there, back to my home province, Phan Thiet.

When I got to my stepmother's house, I saw that there were new owners. The neighbors told me that my stepmother had died of hemorrhagic fever. I was sad, despite the way she had treated me. Some neighbors told me that my real mother was living in a small village, not too far from Phan Thiet. I took a bus there. It is a poor farming village. When I found my mother's house, we recognized each other immediately. It was almost like telepathy. We just held each other and cried, overcome with emotion. We were so happy that we could not talk.

I stayed in my mother's house for two days. It is a small thatch hut with a dirt floor, like most of the houses in the village. After that, she took me to a friend's house, where I waited while my mother discussed the situation with her husband. I didn't think he was very happy that I had come.

After a week I moved back to my mother's house. I stayed there for three months. We got along well for the first month, but after that my mother and her husband started arguing. He didn't want me to live in their house, and he always walked around with a cold face. Finally, my mother and I had an argument. She told me, "You are stubborn, because of your mixed blood." I became angry. I told her, "If I were white and beautiful, you would never have left me." My mother didn't say anything, she just cried. Soon after that I left my mother's house. I just slipped out without telling anyone. I did not want to disturb the harmony of her house or disrupt her marriage.

When I back to Saigon, I was afraid that the government would send me to the New Economic Zone. Some friends of mine heard that it was easy to make money in Cambodia, so they decided to go there. I went along with them. We crossed the border at Dinh Xuong village, Dong Thap province. Because I was black, they didn't question me. They thought that I was Khmer from one of the border villages. These people often cross back and forth, so I walked right across. My Vietnamese friends had to sneak around, but I walked right through because I'm black like a Khmer.

We took the bus to Prey Veng city. I set up a stand near the Buddhist temple frying bananas and selling them. At night, I slept at the market. In a few months, I began to do general buying and selling. I bought from Vietnamese and sold to Vietnamese and Khmer.

The Khmer liked me better than the other Vietnamese because my color was more like theirs. They would say that my skin is like a Khmer, but my face is different. I went to sell at the market with Vietnamese who were born in Cambodia and spoke the language fluently, but the people used to think that I was the Cambodian because of my color, and I was the one they would talk to. This was different than Vietnam, where they hate my black skin.

Cambodia was much better for business than Vietnam. There were not so many rules and regulations, and the Khmer people are very kind. Many Vietnamese do business in the market, and nobody bothers them. I always was honest with the Khmer, and they were good to me in return. Many times they invited me to their homes, to eat together.

I left Cambodia, just when many Vietnamese soldiers were coming in. A lot of Vietnamese were leaving at this time, and there were stories of terrible things happening to the Khmer, but especially to the Vietnamese. I was afraid that Pol Pot would kill me. It was said that the Khmer Rouge cut Khmer into three pieces, but mutilated Vietnamese into seven pieces. Why the difference, I don't know. There were Khmer Rouge in the hills, and even in the town. Some people in town, you don't know that they are secretly Khmer Rouge, and at night they kill you.

When I got back to Saigon from Cambodia, I started sleeping on Le Lai Street, by the Le Lai Restaurant. There were many people sleeping out there, many Amerasians. One day, the owner of the restaurant, a Chinese guy, asked me if I wanted a job. He gave me food and clothing and a place to stay, and he said he would protect me if I had trouble on the street. Sometimes he let me sleep in the restaurant. Sometimes I worked in the day and slept out on the street. I worked there for a year, I worked very hard. One night the owner came to me when I was sleeping. He told me that if I didn't sleep with him, he would throw me out on the street again. He was around thirty, I was only about seventeen. I had nothing, so what could I do? I let him have his way *[Thuy is weeping at the memory]*. I hated it, but what choice did I have? After a few months, I became pregnant. When I was three months pregnant, his wife confronted me and put me out.

So I was seventeen and pregnant, no home. I just wandered around, finding work as a dishwasher in little food stalls, sleeping on the street.

When the time came to have my baby, I couldn't get to the hospital. I gave birth on the street, right on the sidewalk. Some strangers, some passersby helped me. After the birth, I kneeled on the street with my baby in my pants, the cord still attached. I was too weak to hold the baby. I tried to get a taxi to take me to the hospital, but none would stop. Finally, after two hours, one did, and I got to the hospital. My baby was healthy, but my legs, my knees, have always given me trouble since then, pain from the knees to the ankle.

After my baby was born, I started selling ice tea in Quach Thi Trang Park near Ben Thanh market. One man stopped at my stand and bought ice tea from me every day, on his way to hairdressing school. He became my boyfriend, and now he is my husband. We lived together on the street.

At this time, the VC came and rounded up all the vendors. They told us that if we didn't voluntarily go to the New Economic Zones, they would send us there. They told us that if we went voluntarily, there would be a

Nguyen Thi Ngoc Thuy, husband and friends outside her "home" on the sidewalk in Vietnam

house and a job for us. That's what they said. So we made a paper to "voluntarily" go to the New Economic Zone.

We had no choice over where to go. They just sent us to Cay Truong 2 in Song Be province. We lived on newly cleared land on the edge of the jungle and mountains.

We built a hut out of palm thatch, and that's where we stayed. I cleared land, dug holes, planted rice and vegetables. All labor, all hard. We planted manioc. We didn't get paid for our work, but we sold part of the vegetables we grew for a little cash.

I made a little stove out of three stones. They gave us some rice a few times a week. I had to borrow pots to cook in. I was voted in as a leader for distribution of goods, but there wasn't much to distribute. Rice was lacking, we had to eat manioc.

Some of the cadres there teased me. "You are American," they said. "Why don't you go back to America?" I said, " I planted the rice, now I want to harvest." But I never did. It was too hard to live there. It was difficult to get water, food was scarce. One day we went to the market in a nearby village, as if we were going to buy supplies. When we got there, we boarded a bus for Saigon.

We got to Saigon and just continued to live on the street, wandering around. I sold fruits like mango and banana on the street in front of Independence Palace. My husband couldn't find a job as a hairdresser, but

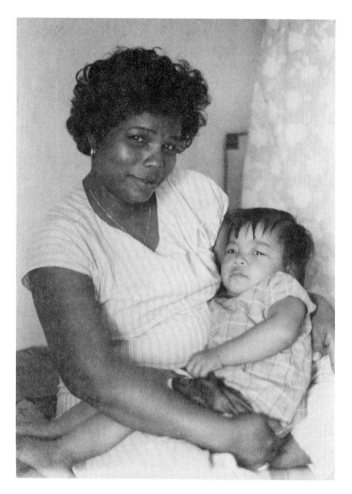

Thuy and her son

he got some work as a bricklayer. We had no ID card, no household certificate, so nobody could rent a house to us. My whole life in Saigon, I stayed on the street. *[Thuy shows me a picture of herself, her husband and some other people sitting on mats on the sidewalk. There are some makeshift enclosures in the background. Thuy points to one ... "That's my house."]*

Sometimes it would rain, the water would come inside. We would have to stand up and hold the babies. My oldest one would stand under an overhang in front of a house. This is how we lived.

At times the police would come and tell me to move my things. Where could I go? But if I didn't move them, they just take them all away and I never see them again, so I have to move.

My husband never knew his real family, he was an orphan. Many people tell him that he looks French, but since he never knew his parents, he doesn't know for sure. He was raised by a stepfamily in Dong Thap province.

In 1988 I was pregnant, and my husband wanted to visit his family. I went with him. They hated me, they wouldn't talk to me. They said to my husband, "Why did you get a black wife? You are white."

It's worse in Vietnam for blacks than whites. The Vietnamese hate blacks. That's why I don't want to live with Vietnamese in America. Vietnamese don't like me. They always make me feel inferior. Even when I was a girl, seven or eight, people didn't want to make friends with me. That's when I knew I was not the same as them.

I applied for the Orderly Departure Program in August of 1989, and in December of '91 I got here. I never paid any bribes, I was very lucky. Many people have to pay bribes, sometimes more than $1000. Just before we left for the Philippines, we stayed at the Amerasian center in Dam Sen. I went back to Phan Thiet province and got my mother, and I brought her to Saigon. She stayed with us for a week. Even though she abandoned me, even with all the problems that we had, she is still my mother. That's what I told her. *[Thuy shows me a color shot of herself with her husband and daughter, standing in back of her mother, a seated fiftyish woman. Everyone seems happy.]*

I hope that my husband can get a job in the United States, maybe as a hairdresser. Maybe I can be a laundry woman or do ironing, something like that. What I would really like is to be a saleslady — sell watches and cassette players, something like that. I just want to support my kids. I want my children to go to school. But I am worried. We learned that in America everything is run by machine. How can I work? I never went to school.

Postscript: *A week before her departure for the States, I visit Thuy in her billet in neighborhood six. She is rummaging through a cardboard box for a book of photos. When she locates it, she lays it on the table for me to peruse and walks off to start a pot of rice for dinner.*

I open the overleaf, and roaches pour out onto the table. They continue in a rude stream of various sizes and maturities. Empty brown casings of roach eggs hang on the plastic housings of the photos.

In the neighborhoods, insects dominate. So many people live so close together, with no food storage facilities and inadequate trash disposal, that roaches are impossible to control. The evenings, especially, belong to them. They patrol the walls, the bed platform, boxes and bags, like an army.

Thuy returns with a broom, laughing. She bangs the photo album on the table, and the exodus increases. The broom pushes the retreating army onto the floor and out the door of the billet.

Thuy with her mother, son, and husband in Vietnam, 1991 (courtesy of Nguyen Thi Ngoc Thuy)

Top: **Thuy selling at the PRPC market.** ***Bottom:*** **Thuy, husband, and son at PRPC departure area on the day of their departure for the United States.**

Thuy is happiest at her buy and sell business. She pulls out a cardboard-display of ersatz gold rings, the latest movers in her market enterprise. "I buy three pesos [twelve cents]," she comments happily, "and sell five. I sell many."

Despite her natural optimism, she has the same jitters that every refugee experiences as their departure to the States moves closer. "What can I do?" she asks. "I don't speak English. All I know is buy and sell."

I describe the nature of the American flea market and tell her that many immigrants open booths there. She visibly brightens. "I like that," she repeats several times. "Yes that's what I want."

Thuy and her family left the PRPC for Memphis, Tennessee, on July 8, 1992.

Phan Vinh Phuc

"In a social situation people might whisper to me discreetly, 'Are you French Vietnamese or are you Amerasian?' I would say, 'No, I'm pure Vietnamese, it's just the way I look'."

Phuc works as an assistant teacher. It's basically an interpreter's job given to refugees who "test out," score at the top end of the English exam given to all new arrivals at the Philippine Refugee Processing Center. He is a twenty-four-year-old white Amerasian.

In his face, American and Vietnamese gene pools blend smoothly. His hair and eyes are brown, rather than the black common to Vietnamese, but Vietnam is in the cut of his cheekbones and nose. In Vietnam, he was sometimes able to "pass for Vietnamese," and sidestep the onus that American blood carries. In school however, his parentage was known. Phuc didn't let the barbs of his classmates keep him from an education. "Many Amerasians drop out of school because of the taunts of the classmates," Phuc says in fluid English. "When my classmates teased me, it motivated me to try harder, to do better than them . . . and I did."

I AM FROM Ho Chi Minh City. When I was young, I lived with my mother and Vietnamese stepfather. One of my earliest and most painful memories is of them quarreling and of my stepfather beating my mother. I must have been four or five. I remember that I was very upset. I couldn't stand to see it, and I ran out of the house. At that time he left us, and he got another wife. He took my half-sister with him, and I rarely saw her after that.

My mother told me that before 1975 my stepfather worked in a company, I think the name was MRC or MRK. That company makes the highways and sidewalks and bridges in Saigon. He had an American friend, and sometimes he brought his friend to come home. I don't know what

93

happened between that American man and my mother, but that man is my father.

The idea of my mother is not the same as the idea of me. I want to know about my father, but I feel shy about it, because when I do ask, she says, "You don't talk about that." Sometimes we have a quarrel, and I go out. So all I know is that my father worked for the MRK company, and he wore a hardhat at work.

My mother never remarried. We lived together, only the two of us. In '75 the VC came, and she was scared. We heard the sound of guns and hid under the bed. We put bags of rice around to shield us, but we didn't have any problem.

When I was young I didn't know I was American. One day I went to my aunt's house to eat lunch, and one of my cousins said to me, "You have an American father." It happened so quickly, and then her mother shut her mouth and told me, "No problem, no problem, don't believe her." But at that time I am old enough to understand what she says, and I feel sad. I go into the toilet, I look in the mirror, and I cry by myself.

In my neighborhood, I didn't experience much discrimination. Most of the people were of a higher class, and they didn't insult me to my face. What they said behind my back, I don't know.

I went to school for sixteen years. In elementary school, some kids bothered me, but it wasn't too serious. Sometimes they called me "Fox" after a character in an American movie or made some jokes about me. I didn't stay with anybody so much. I just studied and went back home. In high school if there are some Soviet or Czech people come to visit the school, my classmates say, "Oh, there's your father, that's your father. Look, there's Phuc's father." I just smile, I don't say nothing.

Many Amerasians drop out of school because of the taunts of their classmates. When my classmates teased me, it motivated me to try harder, to do better than them . . . and I did. I was a loner, but I did very well in school, and my teachers liked me. They would supply me with materials when I didn't have any, and that made me feel good.

Most of the hurt I felt came from my family. My aunts loved me, but their sons insulted me all the time. My second and third cousins were cruel. They tell me, "You're a bastard, you don't have any father" and things like that. I just say to them, "Who are you? You don't pay for my life, so you have no right to criticize." They would smile a sly, nasty smile and go away. I will never forget the look on their faces. Coming from my family, this hurt me very much, and many times when I was alone I would cry over this. I spent much time alone rather than face these difficulties.

Since I don't look American too much, I would try to pass as Vietnamese. Sometimes I would go somewhere, and in a social situation people might whisper to me discreetly, "Are you French Vietnamese or are you

Phan Vinh Phuc

Amerasian? I would say, "No, I'm pure Vietnamese, it's just the way I look," and they would say "Oh, sorry, forget about that, no problem." I was shy about being Amerasian, and that was one way I could avoid the problem.

My mother works as a clerk in a bank. She worked there before '75, and she still works there now. Before '75, the bank was called Tin Nghia Bank, but the Communist government renamed it Saigon Cong Tuong Bank *[Industrial Trading Bank]*. Sometimes if I visited her there, somebody might say, "Phuc, you look Amerasian. Are you?" I wouldn't answer, and my mother would just smile, but not affirm it. Since I look almost Vietnamese, and I have the name of my Vietnamese stepfather, I sidestepped the issue.

Before I came here, I was a student in the College of Architecture at the university in Ho Chi Minh City. In the university there are special dispensations given to sons and daughters of government officials. For example, say you need a score of twenty to get in. The Communist official's children get three points extra automatically, so they only need to score seventeen. I think they even have separate classes, because I never saw any in my courses.

The cost for the officials' children is very low, but for the rest of us it is very expensive. For three years, my mother supported my studies. But in the third year of my studies, my mothered quarreled with me. She said she could no longer afford the high cost of sending me to school. Finally, she agreed to pay one more year, and then I would have to look for another way to get money. So I completed four years of the five-year course. My relatives knew that we needed money for me to finish school, but nobody wanted to help. Some even avoided my mother's house so they wouldn't be asked to chip in. My uncle, who is a teacher, passed my house every day to work and never stopped in.

Anyway, even after finishing school, there is little work available, and what exists is given to the children of the government officials. This is one of the reasons I left Vietnam.

The Communists make your life very difficult. We had to get a permit to travel anywhere. This permit had to be stamped ten, even twelve times — a tremendous hassle. Until '87, when the Communists loosened up a little, there were occasional house checks. They would come in the house and look around for people hiding, subversive materials, I don't know what. Government officials could call you to their office for any reason, and you had to report immediately.

Between '78 and '80, we prepared to leave Vietnam by boat, but the plans fell through and we didn't go. I was very young, I don't know what happened. After high school, I thought of escaping, but we were hearing terrible stories of people lost at sea, attacks by pirates, things like that. My mother said better to apply for the Orderly Departure Program and wait.

I have a Vietnamese girlfriend in Vietnam, but her family doesn't accept me. They are like all Vietnamese, they look down on the Amerasian. They don't say nothing to me, but I see when a Vietnamese friend comes to their house, they treat him much better than me.

They are afraid people will look down on them if their daughter marries an Amerasian. I asked my girlfriend, "Can I go to your family and tell them we want to marry?" She said, "No, they will not accept you." Before I left Vietnam, I asked her to marry me and we would go America together. She said, "No, you go, and we will see. After a few years, if you can come back and we still feel the same, maybe we can marry." But I think she will not wait for me.

My girlfriend's parents, I see how they look at Vietnamese who go to America and then come back to Vietnam. They look at them very high. I hope maybe when I come back to Vietnam they will look at me that way.

Postscript: *By the time he left the PRPC in July of '92, Phuc had a new girlfriend, an Amerasian named Lan. Phuc was resettled in Rochester, New York. Within a month, Phuc moved to Chicago to join Lan, who had resettled there.*

Hung

"I never had a father's love, only a
mother's, and that was not enough for me."

*On a bleak afternoon in July, I sat in a billet in neighborhood six, waiting
for a break in the weather. It was not to come soon. The monsoon rains had locked
into Bataan with a vengeance and would not relinquish their grip for several
months.*

*Outside in the downpour, a young black Amerasian navigated his way
home. I caught a glimpse of him as he came in out of the weather and entered
the billet next door, wearing only gym shorts and flip-flops. Self-inflicted burns
and slashmarks are common among Amerasians, but never had I seen them to
this extent. The young man's torso, arms, and legs had been terribly mutilated.
Raised lines of scar tissue overlay his body, one slash criss-crossing into the next.
Tattooed ladies danced across his belly. I walked under the dripping overhang
that runs the length of each row of billets and onto the tiny concrete slab fronting
his living area. I introduced myself through my interpreter, and we shook hands,
a bit awkwardly. Hung laughed; this may have been his first handshake. He had
just arrived in the PRPC, and shaking hands is not a Vietnamese custom. His
mood was light and upbeat, he smiled easily and frequently. We arranged to meet
again the following afternoon.*

*My interpreter and I arrived in his billet at 2 A.M. the next day. Hung was
nowhere to be found. His mother sat cross-legged on her wooden bedframe, a row
of cards spread out between her and another Vietnamese woman. Fortunes were
being divined, Hung's mother's specialty. Judging from the number of clients
waiting patiently in the cramped billet, business was good.*

*Twenty minutes later Hung arrived, wearing a checked pair of pajamas, his
feet covered with mud. He had been out playing soccer. When he saw us, he
pounded his forehead with a fist. "I forgot," he said sheepishly.*

*A hint of the country of his upbringing rests in Hung's cheekbones and eyes.
Otherwise, his appearance is that of a young black man. Although in high spirits
when we first met, Hung was subdued, even somber during our interviews. Like*

98

many in the PRPC, he has left family behind. He worries about his wife and child
in Vietnam; foremost in his thoughts is how to bring them to America once he
arrives there. When he mentions them, his eyes swell with tears.

I AM FROM Ho Chi Minh city, from Nguyen Cong Tru Street, near the
Thai Binh market. My mother was married to a Vietnamese husband and
already had one baby when she met an American man. She was working
at the Hung Dao hotel. That's where it happened. She became pregnant
with his baby. That's me. I was born in 1968. I don't know anything about
my father except what I told you.

My mother's Vietnamese husband managed a troupe of performers
called *Tuoi Tre [young age]*. They had magicians, singers, acrobats. My
mother and him still kept on living together after I was born. They stayed
together until 1980, when they divorced. They had three more kids but my
Vietnamese stepfather didn't want me around, the son of another man.

My mother sent me to my maternal aunt for a few years and then she
brought me back to her house. I was young, I didn't understand anything
but when I got back to my mother's house I could see that my stepfather
didn't love me. He only loved his own children.... My skin is different
from theirs.

I only went to school up to second grade. The students don't like black
skin, they hate it. They like to play with the fair-skinned people. They never
let me forget I was black and that I had no father. They always called me
names and made me ashamed, so I stopped going.

You ask me about my scars. All my life people despised me, they called
me a "bastard," a "nigger." I didn't care about myself. I wanted to die. So
I took a razor and slashed myself all over. People see my scars and they
think, "Oh, he's a tough guy, he's a troublemaker." They judge me. But
it's not like that, I just wanted to die. I tried to kill myself four times. All
my life has been sad. I never had a father's love, only a mother's, and that
was not enough for me.

It is very common that when a young man reaches seventeen or eighteen years, the government takes him into the military. The Amerasian and
Chinese cannot carry arms, so they must do labor for the government instead.

The authorities asked me to join with the fire prevention team and also
a security team that helped in the arrest of illegal street vendors and confiscated their goods. I was against that. I refused to join in the harassment
of vendors. I wouldn't do it. One day the authorities came to my house
and told me to go to the police station. When they call you, you have to
go. I went down there, and they arrested me. When the authorities ask you
to participate in their schemes, and you refuse, they send you to Duyen Hai
district, to the "State Farm for Agricultural and Industrial Education and

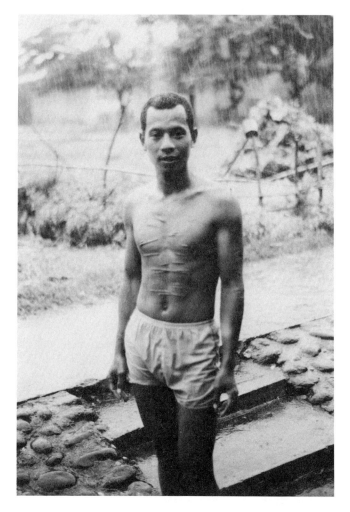

Hung outside his billet in the PRPC

Labor" to do the "duty of building the defense economy." What a joke. All those grand words are fancy lies. It is nothing but a forced labor camp. President Nguyen Van Thieu said, "Don't listen to the words of the Communists, watch their actions."

Duyen Hai is on a kind of a peninsula. One side is facing the ocean, and one side has a river. It's difficult to escape, but not impossible. Who do they send there? Young people they don't like vendors, homeless people, prostitutes, criminals, people they suspect of committing a crime or anybody who opposes them.

We are forced to labor there. We had to dig canals to channel the sea water into fields. These became shallow salt ponds, where we harvest the salt. The work is very hard, a lot of digging.

I said it was not impossible to escape, and I did, after only about twenty days. I swam across the river at night. I made it back to my home in Ho Chi Minh City, but because I was sent to Duyen Hai, my name had been rubbed out of my household register. Without that, you cannot legally live in a place, so I was illegal in my own home, in my own family's house. What could I do? I had nowhere else to go. I tried to lay low and keep away from the authorities. I got some work helping a fish merchant, carrying ice from the factory to the ice trucks. You see this? *[Hung pulls a flap of skin on the right side of his neck, almost under his chin, and shows a long scar.]* I fell down carrying a chunk of ice and a sliver went right into my neck.

A year or so after I got out of Duyen Hai, I was drinking with some friends. I was feeling low, thinking about how miserable my life was, how the government hated Americans and children of Americans, like me. The more I drank, the more outraged I became, and then I did a stupid thing. I went with a friend to a place outside the police station. It was nighttime. We yelled out things like "Down with the Communists," stuff like that, and ran away. About a week later the police came and picked me up. They said I had been identified as the one yelling counter-revolutionary slogans, and they arrested me. They sent me up to Buon Me Thuot, to Dak Minh prison camp. I was supposed to be there for forty-eight months.

This camp is not for political prisoners. There are other ones for that, like Han Thanh. Dak Minh is a prison camp for criminals. I was the only Amerasian there at that time.

The camp is surrounded by very thick forest, and the work there is mostly cutting wood, planting trees, and building some structures . . . like huts for us to sleep in. You can't grow rice up there, only manioc or sweet potato. We got up at five, no breakfast, and went out to work. Sometimes we had to walk a kilometer to get to the worksite, sometimes six or seven. You better work. If you don't, or if you tell them you're sick and they don't buy your story, they might make you stand in the stream up to your neck, sometimes all afternoon. Dak Minh is in the mountains, that water is cold.

For lunch we get some rice and not much else, not even fish sauce or salt. Sometimes we try to find some leaves we can eat in the forest, but if the guards catch you, they'll beat you. And we don't get any tobacco. We try to scrounge the butts the guards throw away when they are not looking. When we get back to the camp, we have just a short time for dinner. We have to be in our huts by five-thirty. If you are not, you get punished. If you break their rules, they might put you in the metal box. *[Often made from metal storage containers left by the Americans, the metal box can be burning hot in the day, freezing at night.]*

We sleep in huts, about twenty or thirty prisoners to a hut. The huts are pretty flimsy. We sleep on big bamboo pallets, and at night they chain our legs to an iron bar. If you are a good worker or they like you, you might get to go in a hut where they don't chain you at night. I worked hard there, and eventually I wound up sleeping in a hut where my legs were not chained.

That's when I made my escape. Even if you get out of the camp, the forests are dense, and it's easy to get lost there. You must be brave to try it. If the guards catch you, they string your thumbs together, behind your back, one hand over the shoulder, and the other behind your waist, and they'll beat you. And there is the metal box. . .

There are guards on watch at night, but you have to wait until they are not paying attention, or even dozing. This is what we did . . . and we made a break.

We were in the jungle for several days. We ate some wild fruit—but not much, because nobody knew what was poisonous and what was safe— and we prayed. Eventually we got out of the jungle and made our way to the town of Ban Me Thuot. From there, I got back to Ho Chi Minh City.

My family made the paper to go to the United States in 1982 but we had to wait almost ten years. That's how it is. We had no money to pay bribes. We will go to my cousin in America. He was living in Chicago, but he moved. I think he is in Washington now.

My main concern is my family. I left my wife and son in Vietnam. My wife was an abandoned child, and she moved around a lot. She doesn't have household registration or any documents, not even a birth certificate. We lived together and had one son. When he was born, I got the birth certificate for my son, but my wife has no papers and we didn't have enough money to bribe the authorities to make any for her. So I had to leave her and my son behind, and that's all I can think about. She is living in my mother's house in Ho Chi Minh City. The house is under my mother's name, and now that my mother is here, I worry that the government will confiscate it and force my wife and son out on the street.

I can't tell you any more about my story. I will not be able to hold back my tears. I cannot remember . . . I only think about my wife and son. How can I go back to Vietnam to visit them? I think I must wait for a long time, and I miss them very much.

Va

"John Lennon is my idol."

Va is a slight, fair Amerasian. He speaks English well, and, surprisingly, is exceedingly well versed on American pop and rock culture and is a big fan of rock music. I loaned him several music cassettes after the interview.

As we spoke, Va seemed quite tense, almost overwrought, his composure often on the verge of dissipating. After the interview, I was to discover the cause of Va's tension. Va's "mother" has been accused of having been a broker of Amerasians in Vietnam, of finding Amerasians for Vietnamese who wish to claim them as family and thus achieve eligibility for resettlement in the United States. While the charges are being looked into, the Joint Voluntary Agency, which has the responsibility of facilitating refugee resettlement from the PRPC, has placed Va's "family" on hold, and their departure from the PRPC and subsequent resettlement in America has been indefinitely delayed. Va himself, it turns out, was bought by this family, and is of no relation to them, but is nonetheless affected by the hold. He was originally scheduled to leave five months ago, but must now wait, with no indication of when he will be allowed to depart for America. "I live without hope," he says mournfully.

WHEN I WAS a boy, I didn't know that I was half–American, but when I got older, some children in the neighborhood were very mean. They bothered me, they called me, "half-breed, half-breed." They even dragged me down. They always use the bad word with me, some even had bad manner with me. I don't pay attention to them, I just try to go to school and do my work, and I don't give a damn. But when I growing up, I just hated it.

The Vietnam always call me "Amerasian, Amerasian." When I go out, and in my school they all call me that, and I don't like it. When I make a mistake, they say, "You do that because you're Amerasian. You're not the same as Vietnamese people. Your father fought against the Vietnamese government." They tell me, "You are not the same blood as me. You have to go back [to America]." I don't like that, I hate it.

The Vietnamese hate Americans, but they want to go to America. All they think about is how they can go to America, and they have to use Amerasians to go. They just think about how they can get what they want. It is the same in any society, when people want something, they will do anything to get it.

[Va asks me where I grew up, and I tell him New York.] New York . . . many famous people want to live there so they won't be recognized. I know John Lennon lived there, he was killed in 1980. I read a book about him, he is my idol. In my mind, he is a genius. I listen to the Beatles, songs like "Imagine," "All My Lovin'," "Woman," . . . I like "Woman" very much. Do you know why John Lennon was deported from America? They say it was because of drugs, but that was just an excuse. I believe he really was deported because he opposed the Vietnam War. I know Elvis Presley too, the king of rock. I like Led Zeppelin, Deep Purple, and Sting, from England. Not many Vietnamese listen to that. Most listen to Bony M. and Modern Talking.

I can play the guitar, but just a little. I hear the American music, and they play very well. When I play it sounds so bad, so I stopped.

I also have to read books because I don't want people to look down on me. I read books by Danielle Steel, Sidney Sheldon, and a book by Donald Trump, the billionaire. I would like to do business. I just like society. I don't like nature *[biology]*, I don't like chemistry, I just like history and psychology, and poetry. I write poems in Vietnamese, I really like poetry.

Pha

"All my life people have despised me because
I am black. Will it be that way in America too?"

Pha sits on her bedframe, holding two of her three children on her lap. The older has a bad eye, the result of an extended illness. As we speak, her mood is one of melancholy and resignation.

She had no schooling in Vietnam and can neither read nor write. Although she has completed ten weeks of English training in the PRPC, she never ventures to use it, deferring instead to the interpreter.

When we finish the interview, Pha hesitantly directs a question to me through the interpreter. "All my life people have despised me because I am black," she says. "Will it be that way in America too?"

I WAS BORN in Long An twenty-nine years ago. I lived with my mother, my grandmother, and some cousins. I have no brothers or sisters. I never knew my father. I had a picture of him, but when I went to interview for the Amerasian program in Saigon, they took it. I cannot remember his name. It is a long name, and I forgot it. My mother never told me anything about him.

My mother was a bar girl. That's where she met my father, in a bar. She had some other pictures of him, with his address written on the back, but my mother died in 1980, and I don't know what happened to those photos.

I didn't go to school, I was embarrassed of my skin. I started to go in Long Anh, but the students always insulted me, called me "black girl." People always talked bad about me because I was black.

There were many Amerasians in Long An, but I was not friends with any. You know, in Vietnam, Amerasians are not friends with each other. Black Amerasians are embarrassed of the way they look. They don't like to play together.

My family didn't love me, they didn't love my mother. They looked

Pha

down us. Before '75, it was not so bad, but after '75, the family didn't want
to keep me at home. They were scared of the VC, they wanted to send me
away where nobody could see me. Around 1977 the government told
mothers of Amerasians to come to a meeting. Some they let go home, some
they sent to jail. My mother was afraid at this time, and she was arguing
with my grandmother, so we left for Ho Chi Minh City.

We stayed in Ho Chi Minh with no ID papers, and soon the government forced us to go to the New Economic Zone at Dong Ban, in Tay Ninh
Province. There was nothing there but mountains, trees, and a few huts,
no market at all. For that we had to go to the nearest town. My mother worked

Pha and her children

clearing land for rice fields. She cut down the trees and cut up the wood, and I would carry the wood out. We worked every day, Saturday, Sunday, we didn't take holidays. And that has been my life even until now.

I grew up strong and could work hard. I was able to earn a living, and the police knew this. Many times they came around, and I had to pay them off or else they made trouble for me.

My mother died in 1980. We couldn't pay for a doctor, there was nothing we could do. I thought then that she drank some bad water, but I believe that she just worked herself to death.

Near Dong Ban there were some other Amerasians, but they all have gone to the United States now. Of course I wanted to go before, but I had to wait until I could get the money to bribe the officials. Some friends helped me by giving me the money, and I am very grateful to them.

Life here in the PRPC is okay, better than Vietnam. I learned a little English, and we get enough food. In Vietnam I always worked hard, but sometimes we had no food. I was never happy there, even on a big holiday like New Year's I was sad. I remember the hard times, like when I was pregnant and broke, and nobody would help me. It's not as hard for the white Amerasians. If they have money, they can go to school. But black Amerasians, even if they have money, they can't go to high school. The government doesn't let them. I heard that, I don't know why that is.

In America I'd like to be a farmer, to plant rice. That's what I did in Vietnam, and that's all I know. I want to work, I must work. My husband is handicapped, one leg is no good. He was born like that. I worry that it will be hard for him to find a job.

My family is going to California. Our sponsor is a friend from Tay Ninh who went to America two years ago. I want to live with Americans, not Vietnamese. I have American skin. In Vietnam everyone called me American because of my color. So I want to learn American language and customs. I don't want to stay with Vietnamese anymore.

I'm sorry, I can't talk anymore... It makes me too sad.

Mai Linh

"They say, 'You black, you can't sit down with
my children.' So that's why I didn't go to school."

*"When you goin' back to the world [to America]?" Mai Linh wanted to
know. I paused, startled. This twenty-five-year-old black Amerasian would continue to surprise me with snippets of GI slang. Taunted by her Vietnamese classmates and their parents on her first day of grammar school, she left and never
went back. She cannot read or write in any language, but she learned to speak
English, first from her mother, then from an ex–ARVN officer. Mai Linh loves
to surprise with the unexpected colloquialism: "It blows my mind, they [Viet-
namese] so stuck-up."*

*We met in October of 1991, shortly after Mai Linh's arrival in the PRPC,
and spoke at length in English without the aid of an interpreter. The conversation
turned consistently to her plight as a black Amerasian woman in largely homogeneous Vietnam. At these points, with her emotions close to the surface, her eyes
would take on a distracted look and her speech became jumbled, almost in-
coherent.*

*Months later, in March, we met again. She had taken up jogging, and her
frame, chunky in October, had turned lean and muscled. Although she appeared
more relaxed, the averted gaze and mumbled speech would return when she recalled
the painful past.*

*Mai Linh is one of the numerous so called "gold cases" in the PRPC. The
family who on Mai Linh's documents appears as her own, actually is of no
relation to her. She took their family name and claimed them as kin to enable
them to immigrate to America with her. Generally, in exchange for this service,
an Amerasian or her real family receives a quantity of gold, and the bogus family pays the requisite bribes to Vietnamese officials for the processing of documents. Mai Linh declined to go into the details of her own particular arrangement.*

*She requested that she be referred to as Mai Linh in her narrative, as she
was in Vietnam.*

YOU CAN CALL me Mai Linh. I'm from Cam Ranh. My card says I'm twenty-two, but I'm really twenty-five. When we made the paper to come here, we changed my age.

When I was young, I lived with my mother, only the two of us. My mother never got married after my father left. I don't have no brothers, don't have no sisters. My mother, she liked me to go to study. She made the paper to let me go to school, but when I went there, the people, they were calling me "black, black." I got very angry, so I leave. I come back home and tell my mama I didn't go. She say, "Why not?" and she make me go back again.

So I go back to school, and a man and woman over there, they slap me. They say, "You black, you can't sit down with my children." So that's why I didn't go to school [Mai Linh is sobbing heavily]. This is my country...

My mother want me to go to school, and I trust my mother, but I never go to school no more. I just hide, I go out and play with my friend. She looks like you, white. About eleven o'clock I go home, and my mother says, "Mai Linh, you go to school?" I say, "Yes," but she looks at my schoolbook, and she sees I didn't go, and she slaps me. Then I tell her, "I never go to school no more." She says, "Why?" I say, "You crazy. I go to school, some people slap me, they slap my friend. They say they don't want no black, they don't want no white American." So I tear up that paper [school registration], and I never go to school no more.

They be Vietnamese who slapped me. It blows my mind, they so stuck up. Another time, one Vietnamese girl, she talks bad to me and my friend Hue. She say, "I don't like black girl, I don't like white girl, because their father American, because their mother be bad, be a whore." So I slap her. The police come, and they say, "How come you slap this girl?" And I say, "Because she talk bad to us." So the police put us in jail for one week, and I can't get home. I don't like no Vietnamese, I hate them. I like to be friend with black Amerasian or white, like you. I don't like no Vietnamese.

My mother was from Saigon. She was part Indian. She not Vietnamese, her father was Indian. She had long, beautiful hair. She go to Cam Ranh to work in the E.M. [Enlisted Man's] club. Her father say, "You don't go, you stay in Saigon," but she don't listen.

In Cam Ranh she lived together with one "soul brother," black. That man be my father. They stay together ten months, then he say that he go to Pleiku. He tell my mother that two or three months he be back, but he don't come back. My mother didn't know what to do, because she get no letter. She wait for him, but he never come back, so my mother go to see a friend of his. That guy says, "Oh, your boyfriend go home to America already." My mother asks, "How long?" He says, "About one month ago."

Now, I don't know if my father he die or not, I don't know where he go. His name was John. He was in the army, airborne, the Thirty-third. That's all my mother told me.

Before, my mother had pictures, had a paper that say she stay with him. *[In Vietnam, it is common for unmarried couples to get an official "living together" document.]* When the VC were coming, she heard that they would look for the white baby, the black baby, the American baby. They want to know who is the woman that stay with the Americans. So my mother be scared, she burn all pictures, all papers. Because VC say he hate Americans, he don't like no girl who worked for the Americans, got baby American. He say if he sees black American or white American, he gonna kill them.

My mother used to take in clothes and wash them. That's how she made money. Sometimes I also did laundry for some people, Indian people, the same color as me, not Vietnamese people.

I learned English so well because my mother has a book and she teach me in the nighttime. And she says, "I want you to go to school and learn to read. You very stupid, you can go talk English but you don't know how to read." I tell her, "I don't need to read." And she slaps me, and I throw the book, but I don't go to school. I say, "If I want to read I have to go to school, but I don't want to go to school. Okay, I be very stupid. Everybody be smart, I be stupid, I don't worry about it. I never go back to school no more."

My best friend was not black like me, she be white. Her name is My. She go to America already. One day she come to me and says, "Mai Linh, three more days I go the world." I say, "I hope you have very good luck. When you go to America, you write your number so I can find you."

In Vietnam, I had only Amerasian friends. I don't like no Vietnamese. My mother, she work E.M. club, she get married to a black man and born me, so I don't feel that I am Vietnamese. I speak Vietnamese, because I born in Vietnam, but I don't like no Vietnamese people.

They make us feel bad, that's why you see out of many American black and white children, tens and thousands, only have ten who go to study. The Vietnamese talk bad, they beat American children, they slap them. They say, "You a black girl, you a white man, how come you don't go to America? How come you live here?" Make anybody feel bad, that's why we don't want to study.

Many Vietnamese children, they treat me no good. They throw rocks at me, they pull my hair. So I say, "Uh-uh, I don't go to school no more." Not only me, but all black and white children, it's the same. One day I see one white Amerasian, some Vietnamese they beat him up. The mother come and says, "How come you do like that?" They say, "We don't want no Amerasian here." So that's why many Amerasians they don't go to school, and that's why they be stupid, because they don't go to school.

Before, in Vietnam, I stay in my house, I be all by myself. I feel bad, angry, I do anything. I drink whiskey and take a razor and cut myself on the arms. That's how I got these scars. You think I'm crazy, but I'm not crazy. I do it to forget, but sometimes I can't forget.

My mother die when I be about ten years old. I miss her very much, so I make this tattoo. *[On Mai Linh's arm tattooed in English is "I love Kan."]* Kan, that's my mother. When my mother die, I go live with my grandmother. There one Vietnamese, he stay next door. Before the VC come, he be lieutenant in the South Vietnamese Army. So I go to that house, and he teaches me English. He wants me to go to school, to learn Vietnamese. I say no, I don't want to go because they call me "black," they make me feel bad inside. When people teach me something, I feel so good, but when I go out, people talk no good to me, I feel so bad. That's why I don't like to go out.

My grandmother, she treat me okay, and I stay there for a few years. She got children live with her, they call me sister. But this one boy there, he be about nineteen, he don't call me sister. He talk bad to me because I be black. He say bad things about my mother. He make me so mad, I slap him and I leave that house. I go down to the bus station, and five in the morning I take a bus to Saigon. I didn't say nothing, nobody knows where I go. Right now they don't know where I am, they don't know if I live or die.

Before, when my mother work the E.M. club, she have one friend. That woman live in Saigon. I go to her house and stay there about three weeks. That woman have one friend who live nearby. She sees me, and she asks me where my mother is. I don't let her know that my mother die. I tell her I don't know where my mother be. She say, "Come stay with me, we make paper and go to America together." So I say, "Okay," and I go stay with her family, and we make paper to come here.

We tell the Orderly Departure Program that she is my mother. That's why I use her family name. But I am not her child, she not born me, understand. Sometime she make me feel bad, but I keep cool, I don't say nothin'. I think, "I don't have a mother, no father, no sister, no brother. Where am I gonna go? Who will take care of me?"

So right now, okay, she take care of me, and I help her go to America. But when I get to America, I don't stay with her. When we get off the plane, she go that way, I go the other way, that's all. I can't tell you no more, because if I do, later she come in and make trouble.

Here in the PRPC I like to study, to learn to speak English very well, so when I go to America it be easier. Some girls be no good. They like to go around, to make trouble. I don't like that. I like to go study one o'clock, six o'clock go home. I study at home, then nine o'clock go to sleep.

I don't have many friends. I have one girl, she be good friend, she black

Mai Linh

like me. She come to my house, she sit down, we talk, "Okay, where you go to school, what you do, how long till you go to America?" We talk, we laugh.

I like to be friends with girls, many men be no good for sure. I see black girl, white girl, they go around too much. One girl she get pregnant, the boy don't say nothin', and she feel very sad. Maybe when I go to America, I find a man who be good, but here in the PRPC, the men are no good, there is trouble every night. Just last night, in neighborhood four and neighborhood three there were big fights. I think I better wait till I go to America, maybe find an American man.

When I get to America, first thing, I want to find my father but I don't know how. If I had a picture, maybe, but I don't. I don't know anything, even his *[last]* name, because my mother don't let me know *[Mai Linh is in tears]*. Maybe he die already.

What I wanna do in America? What I do? I go America, I have to study. Daytime I study, nighttime I get a job and go to work. That's all, what else can I do?

In America I don't want to stay with Vietnamese. I don't want no Vietnamese to be my mother, my father. If I can't find no American to be my mother or father, I stay by myself.

Postscript: *Mai Linh left the PRPC for Des Moines, Iowa, in April 1992.*

Vu

"I have never said to anyone what I said here."

Vu and I sit in a tiny kiosk at the edge of the Philippine Refugee Processing Center. The tail end of Typhoon Dinting is with us, and occasional bursts of rain punctuate our conversation. Below the kiosk lies lush paddy, smooth as the felt of a billiard table. The mountains beyond sit swathed in fog. A fringe of banana trees, cultivated by Aeta tribesmen on the lower slopes, pokes through the cloud cover.

Vu is a soft-spoken, articulate man of thirty-eight. We converse without the aid of an interpreter. When an English word eludes him, he pursues it in his Vietnamese-English dictionary. He is in the PRPC with the daughter of his adoptive parents and a nun from his church group. He listed them as his wife and mother respectively on his documents to enable them to emigrate to the United States with him.

"Looking like an American" is generally qualification enough for acceptance to America under the auspices of the Amerasian Homecoming Act. At five feet nine inches, his skin dark, his hair close cropped and curly, it was easy for Vu to meet this criterion. His father, however, was not American. As we begin our conversation, Vu hesitates when I ask what he knows of his father. His voice breaks as he tells me that his mother was raped by a "black French," a North African soldier in the French colonial army.

I WAS BORN in Thai Binh, in the north. My family moved to Da Nang in 1954, that year many Catholics went south.

I don't know if my father was French or American. I think maybe he was French. French or American, I never mind about that because my mother and my stepfather were very kind to me. I never asked my mother about that. One time, I remember my mother told me that my father was a black French, and I stopped my mother, because I couldn't take this. Because ... I cannot tell you why, it's private *[Vu's voice begins to quiver]*. My mother said that she was raped by a black French. He was my father.

In 1973, I passed my examination for my high school diploma. There was a small party, my stepfather was absent at that time. It was then that my mother said to me that she had been raped, raped by a black French, and I . . . I felt very angry. I stopped my mother, and I walked out.

My Vietnamese stepfather was in the army, so we moved a lot. From Thai Binh we moved to Da Nang, then to Nha Trang, then to a mountain town in Buon Me Thuot province. I remember it just a little. There was a small market, and from my house if I went to the market I had to go to the south, and the market was on the left. From there, we moved back to Nha Trang.

In 1963, after President Ngo Dinh Diem was killed, we moved to Saigon. From 1964 to 1975 my family lived in Saigon, in Ba Queo. We were very close. My father was a warrant officer first class in the South Vietnamese Army, he has died already. My mother is still in Vietnam. She didn't want to come with me, she said she was old to leave her country. My two half sisters in Vietnam are married, and they also don't want to leave the homeland. Their father was born in Vietnam, and I don't know how to explain their feeling. They love the motherland. I am here with my adopted sister. She is listed as my wife on my documents, but we are not really married. I also came with a sister from my church. She was a friend of my adopted mother, but here she is listed as my mother. You see, in Vietnam, I have my real parents, but I also have adopted parents. The name of my adopted father is Dinh Duc Viem, and my adopted mother is Le Thi Sao. In the beginning, I was a friend of their son. We studied in the same class in high scool. They are like foster parents to me. In the Vietnamese way, when you have great respect for someone who is like your father and mother, if you agree, they can become your foster father and mother. In Vietnam, sometime I live with my own family, and sometime I stay with my foster father and mother.

In my neighborhood, the people look at me badly, they look down on me. I was the only Amerasian living there. When I was young, I used to go around alone, play alone. I had no friends. I never spoke to my mother about my problems because I afraid she would be sad.

In the school I attend in Saigon, there were only three students like me. I am one of three. They were all black, there were no white Amerasians. Even though we were the only Amerasians, we did not stay together.

For the other two blacks, I don't know how about them, but for me, in the class, I often got something like discrimination. The classmates look at me like I am a low type of person. I was very sad, but I think I must study, study until . . . if you compare between me and them, I will be higher than they are.

In my last three years of high school, I did very well, but in the first year I could not, because the students forced me to sit in the corner of the class and taunted me. I was alone, I could not go against them. I did not dare to complain to the teacher, because when I finish the class they would beat me up.

But, the last three years of high school I have three friends. One is the son of my foster parents and the others are my classmates. They always stick up for me. They are very close with me. They always help me how to study, they always come to my house for studying, playing. This was my happiest time.

In Vietnam before 1975, I just finish my high school and went to attend college at Van Hanh University. It is the same name as the temple here in the camp, Van Hanh. It means all things are very lucky. In the university, the discrimination wasn't as bad. Of course, it was there, but I didn't think about it because I must study. All of the students have to study hard, because if you fail your class, you have to become a soldier, so there is no time for discrimination. I studied reporter *[journalism]* for about a year and three months. Then the Communists came.

When the VC come in Saigon, I remember exactly—in the morning of April 29, 1975. At that time I stayed home alone. My father and mother and younger sisters had left my house and stayed in Long Thanh. Before the VC came to Saigon, my stepfather left the army. He became a civilian. He took my mother and my sister to Long Thanh to become farmers, and I stayed in Saigon to continue my studies in college.

At the time the VC came, I thought it was all over, and I was very sad. I sat in front of my house, and I saw the VC pass my house.

In the beginning I was afraid, I feel afraid. But a few hours after I don't feel anything, because I think all is over, maybe I come to the end of my life. Because at that time I live in a compound that is used for the family of the *[South Vietnamese]* soldier only. So I thought that if the VC come in, they will cut off my head. *[Vu is laughing.]* A few days after the day the VC came into Saigon, I stop my studies. I think that they will not allow a young adult like me to go to school. They make us go to a meeting, and they tell us that the Communist way is the best in the world, and we must replace our way of life with Communism.

I just attend for three months some meeting like that, and on January 6, 1976, I become a prisoner of the Viet Cong. They arrest me because I keep in my house three grenades and two guns.

I got those weapons because I fight them at night. I, with my friend in the compound where I live, we fight with them. I use a branch of a tree and like that, and we attack them four times.

In the compound, there is a gate and it has no street light. It is very dark by night. I, and some friends who were in the marine corps of the South Vietnamese government before, we hide behind the wall and wait for the VC. Sometimes they walk along the wall, sometimes two men and sometime one man. They are so proud, they believe nobody can hurt them, nobody can knock them out. But when they pass through the gate we follow them and whack them on the back of the head, like that *[Vu swings his arms as if chopping wood]*.

They didn't know that we were there. They think that they are untouchable. So I use a branch of wood and I knock them out. One time I did it by myself, and my friend was in back of me, and three times my friend did it. They never fought with us, all the four times they fell down, and we get their weapons. So I got two A. K., my friend took one B-40, you know that one? It is a gun like a bazooka, but smaller. We also got some grenades.

One kid in the area, he was fighting with his friend. He knew that I had a grenade in my house. He came to my house and ask me to give him one grenade. I didn't give, so he told the VC government that I had their weapons.

When the VC came to my house, my mother had just come back from Long Thanh three days before. While we have our lunch, they come in and they catch me. Two of them went straight upstairs and took out the wooden box which had the guns and the grenades inside. They took me to Chi Hoa prison. From that time till February 1977, they lock me up.

I had no trial, no judge. For the first three months in Chi Hoa, they beat me. They tell me that I am the son of an American, they call me a reactionary element. They beat me with their hands and the handle of the gun. Sometimes they beat me Monday, and not Tuesday, then maybe Wednesday they beat me, and again Friday or Saturday. They hit me with the gun over here and over here, and they broke this one *[Vu points to his collarbone]*. They want to know the names of my friends, but I don't tell them anything, so they beat me more. After three months they left me alone. I was very weak at that time and could no longer walk. My legs were paralyzed from the beatings and the food. The diet in jail is very poor.

We stayed about forty to a cell, nothing to do all day but to think about home. The only time they let us out is to go to take a bath. Two times only, I had problems, once with a prisoner and once with a guard. Once the sauce of another prisoner's bottle spilled on my blanket, and I shouted at him. The dai bang *[chief prisoner, usually the toughest in the cell]* kicked me two times, once in the chest and once in the back. I couldn't do anything because he is very big. The other time we were going to the bath. My legs were very bad, and so I walked very slowly. So the Communist guard, he gets angry and he beat me. I fell on the ground and I lie for a while. I don't remember so well, but some of the prisoners helped me stand up and took me back to the cell.

They never told my family where I was. My father was looking for me from Long Thanh to Saigon. He even came to Chi Hoa, but they told him that I was not there. I wrote letters, but they never received them.

I never knew when they would release me. They didn't tell me anything. Suddenly they called me down to the office and said, "Now you are free." I wonder why I am free. I am very happy, but I don't believe it. But in the afternoon they let me out.

I got out of Chi Hoa in 1977, February. I left with my two friends who were in prison like me, and they were freed together with me. We went on the bus, and I returned to my foster mother's house. I could walk by myself, but I was still very weak at that time. I got to my foster mother's house at night, about seven o'clock in the evening. She was very surprised, she thought that maybe I was dead. She cried and she took me in and fed me. I stay in my foster mother's house about one week, and then I went to Long Thanh to the house of my stepfather and my mother.

I remained in Long Thanh with my mother and stepfather, and when my health was better I helped them to earn money. I cut wood in the forest and made charcoal. I and some friends in my neighborhood work together. In the morning we go to the forest and cut wood, and two or three P.M., we come back in the house. My stepfather at that time was old and weak. Sometimes he would go together with me, but seldom.

In a week if I earn money for two or three days, I help my father the other days. He had a garden. It was in the forest, about seven kilometers from my house. We grew corn and some kind of bean. We also planted rice, but it was not rice paddy, not flooded. We grew dry rice. My father had got the land in the old plan of the Saigon government. They gave retired soldiers land in the country. It was the policy of the government to encourage people to leave the city. The Communists didn't bother him about that land because they also liked people to leave the city and go to New Economic Zones. Since we were in the country already, we didn't have to go.

My father was forced to attend a class called Tay Nao *[Brainwashing]*. The Communists want to throw all the old ideas out of his head. The class was about three months, and after that, my father came back home and lived like anybody else, but without civil rights. Once you are a student in the brainwashing class, you don't have the same rights as other people.

After the class finished, in a month he must come one time to the Communist village office, usually on Saturday night. I don't remember exactly. I think it was for about nine or ten months, and after that the Communist man give a piece of paper of release, that they could go home. Every week the Communist made the old soldier work something like labor, planting rice, corn, something like that.

My father didn't talk about those classes. He was a quiet man. Even before 1975, he was like that. I have rarely seen him laugh. I remember when I passed my examination and got my diploma, the first diploma, I saw he was very happy, but he laughed just a little because he was very quiet. But he loved me very much. He died in 1985.

In 1978, my family became like many other families in South Vietnam, very hungry. There was no rice. I don't know, maybe the Communist government took all the rice from the south and brought it to the north. I heard that, but I don't know. We have no rice, we must eat the corn and manioc. Sometime you eat a little and you think it tastes good, but if you use it daily, all the time, it's very bad.

From '78 to '80 we had little rice. But in the end, '79 or '80, my family had some food because we planted rice and corn.

From 1980 until I came here in 1992, I worked at anything I could to make money. Sometimes I drove a lambretta in Saigon. I worked as a laborer, I took any job. I can repair radios a little, and I did that. I worked in a church. Sometimes I went into the forest and dug the roots of the bamboo tree and sold them. I did anything to support my mother and sisters.

I had to attend class, like the class of my stepfather. It was a class for young adults only, civilians, not only Amerasian, but Vietnamese also. The Communist government forces us to attend the Communist youth meetings. . . . If we don't agree to attend, they will take us to work like a farmer, to dig the ground. They will make us do forced labor.

If you say, "Now in Vietnam there is freedom," that is not true. I have seen in the building here in camp on the wall somebody wrote, "Don't hear what the Communists say, but look at what they doing." In Vietnam today it's like that.

In Vietnam many people want to use the Amerasian to get to America, to make the documents to go. Three times it happened. Two women and one man came and told me that they wanted to go to America with me. The man told me, "I will give you two taels of gold if you go to America with me," and I just give him a shake of my head. And the two women, the first one came and said if I became her husband she would give my family three taels of gold. But I feel very angry. I do like this [Vu makes a slapping motion], and I threw her out of my house. My mother was very surprised, she said, "Why did you do like that?" I didn't say anything.

I knew at that time she needed me, but when she would be finished with her dream, she wouldn't care. When she needed me, she would do anything she could, and when she finished, she would throw me out. I don't want anybody to look down on me. I am a human being.

Another woman who lives in Saigon came to my foster mother's house and said to my younger sister that if I agree with her, I will be her son [on the application for the ODP program, so they can go to America together]. But she is only about six or seven years older than me. I just laugh.

Finally, I agreed to change my papers and go to the United States because I wanted to study more. I have two brothers *[actually foster brothers from Vu's foster parents]* in the Palawan refugee camp. They say that if I come here, they will be accepted as refugees by UNHCR, so I agree to go.

Life in this camp is comfortable. It's very important for us to live here because we have the first step to know how the United States is, and we learn more English.

I will go on to study when I get to America, and I hope have a good job. I would like to become a reporter, but now my English is very bad. I must study and study.

In Vietnam, people always look at me strange because I am different. Even if I am reading a book or a newspaper, I catch people looking at me because I am a black boy. The Vietnamese look down more on the black Amerasian than the white. I don't know why, but I know it is so.

I have an inferiority complex. I have had it for years. It's very hard to explain in English. For example, I am looked down upon by the people who live around me. Little by little, day by day, it is impressed on my memory. If I am busy, working for example, I don't think about it. But when I am alone, it stays in my mind.

I worry about discrimination in America, from Americans. I have seen it in the TV, and I read about it in the newspaper. I am very worried about that. I have seen the white and the black fighting together, and one or two months ago I saw in the TV about the violence in Los Angeles. Men that live in the world must be united together, friendly.

I think that the way I talk now . . . I have never said to anyone what I said here.

Postscript: *I stopped by Vu's billet one night in August to give him a transcript of his interview. He was squatting on the floor, and his "mother" was rubbing his head. Vu explained she was a faith healer, practicing a technique taught to her by an Australian.*

I asked Vu if I could take a picture to use in the book. He thought for a moment and replied, "No, no picture. But you can use my story, that's okay."

Nguyen Tien Dung,
Mr. Loi, and Bich Dung

"Life is unjust, hatred everlasting."

Nguyen Tien Dung is in the PRPC with his elderly stepfather, Mr. Loi, and his Amerasian stepsister, Bich Dung. Bich Dung's husband and child are also here.

We first met in March of 1992 at the monkey house, the PRPC detention center. I was visiting an inmate, and Dung was doing a short stint for violation of the camp liquor ban. Now, two months later, he is back in, once again for drinking, and for vandalism. I was told by his neighbor that one night at midnight, Dung went on a drunken rampage, destroying, among other things, the door to her billet, before the blue guards, the camp security, hauled him away. Pleasant and unassuming when sober, he exhibits a penchant for destruction, particularly self-destruction, when drunk. He drinks when depressed, and he is often depressed.

Dung has practiced the almost ritual scarification common among Vietnamese Amerasians. Raised, pendant-shaped burn marks define the length of his right arm in neat, grisly rows of three. These were self-inflicted with a lit cigarette in Chi Hoa prison during a period of dejection. His right forearm has been slashed into a mass of scar tissue. Running down the right calf is a tattooed message in Vietnamese, roughly translatable as, "If your lover betrays you, be true to yourself." On the inside of the left calf, "Life is unjust, hatred everlasting."

Dung is an intensely handsome young man of nineteen. A purple dot tattooed above the bridge of his nose resembles a Hindu caste mark and endows him with an almost Indian aspect. A number of Amerasians sport this same tattoo, but it seems to be purely ornamental, devoid of any significance. Abandoned as a baby, Dung never knew his biological father, but from his own dark skin believes him to have been a black man.

We sit outside the wire fence that encloses the cellblock and watch as guards

bring out large hoses and spray down the cells. The prisoners scurry out of the lock-up;
two are Vietnamese, the other thirteen or so are Amerasian.

Dung speaks briefly to my interpreter and then fishes inside his shirt. He
pulls out a silver medallion and hands it to me. "U.S. Marine Corps" is im-
printed on one side. An eagle straddles the earth, upon which is engraved "For
Service to Corps and Country. Semper Fidelis." On the flip side is written "First
Marine Division." A diamond outline houses the number one. Inside the num-
ber, written vertically, is "Guadalcanal." On the bottom of the coin is etched
"Vietnam 1969."

As we examine the medallion, Dung's face breaks into a smile of immense
satisfaction. His index finger gestures towards the coin. "Father," he says.

Dung: I was born in Theresa hospital in Da Nang. My mother abandoned me, she refused to pick me up or feed me, so I was told. She left this
coin with the doctor. She said it belonged to my father. *[Dung hands me the*
Marine Corps medallion.]

I am here with my adoptive father. He and his wife adopted me from
the hospital. They always gave me a lot of affection, and I love them more
than if they were my real parents. I have an Amerasian stepsister. She was
also adopted, and she is here in the camp too. My stepmother is dead, she
died in 1983. This is my family. I never knew my real mother or father, all
I have of them is this coin.

My stepparents had one child, a daughter. She was killed in 1978 by
her husband. She was married to a junkie, and he used all their money to
support his habit. Finally, they were out of cash, and he tried to force her
to steal money from her mother. She refused, and he beat her to death.
Then he poured poison down her throat to make it look like suicide. Her
body was taken to the hospital, and an autopsy was done. It showed that
her spleen was ruptured, the doctors could see that she had been beaten.
The police arrested her husband, but he was only sentenced to three years
in prison. My sister was pregnant when her husband murdered her.

I went to school for five years. I was the only Amerasian in the class.
I couldn't stand the taunts, *My lai, My den [Amerasian, Black Amerasian].*
I had many fights, the Vietnamese would gang up on me and beat me up.
Eventually I couldn't take any more abuse, so I just stopped going. My
sister went to the same school, but she studied in the morning. I went in
the afternoon. People taunted her too, but she was cool-headed. "Ignore
those people," she told me, "Stay in school." I couldn't, but she did. She
went for nine years.

After I quit school, I just helped out at my stepparent's business. They
had a stall in the market that sold altars, the kind Buddhists use for worship.

When I got older, I looked for other work. I went down to the seaport
in Da Nang to try to get a job as a porter. The man told me straight out

that he wouldn't hire an Amerasian, so I wound up working at the Da Nang train station. It's not what you would call "official" work. I just waited on the platform and helped people unload crates, luggage, sacks of rice and they would pay me whatever.

By the time I was a teenager, I saw very clearly how things worked. I was discriminated against at every level. The police and the government didn't want me. People don't want to hire Amerasians, don't want to socialize with them. My family was looked down upon because they had adopted two Amerasians. So more and more, I began to dislike Vietnamese.

At seventeen, I stopped working at the train station. The work was very heavy, very hard, lifting all day. I was tired. I didn't want to do that anymore, I wanted to have fun.

One evening I was sitting in a cafe with a friend, drinking wine. A group of Vietnamese came in, and there was trouble between one of them and my friend, but I didn't really know what was happening. A brawl erupted, and the police came and took us to jail and gave us a terrible beating. They let us go, but I was furious that they beat me for no reason.

I had this tatoo made. *[On Dung's left calf is tattooed "xa hoi bat cong—thu van kiep" (life is unjust, hatred everlasting).]* When the police picked me up the next time, they saw the tattoo and this provoked them even more. They took great pleasure in beating me and taunting me. "Unjust," they said, "Well, here is some more unjust."

I was picked up and beaten many times, usually for fighting or drinking, or for no reason at all. I never really stole or committed any crimes. I just drank too much. My life was miserable, and I tried to drown my sorrows.

All the time it was the same cop who would pick me up, take me to the station, and beat me. I wanted revenge. My friend Vinh and I saved up some money and bought a gun. We planned to kill that policeman. We hid the gun in Vinh's house. Somehow, the police found out, and they went to my friend's house and arrested us. Vinh was tried and sentenced to five years. He is still in prison now. I was considered an accessory, since the gun was not in my house. I didn't receive a trial. They just sentenced me to two years hard labor.

First they took me to Tho Dan prison in Da Nang for three days. This used to be an armory, where they kept guns and bombs. After that I went to Hoa Son prison, in Quang Nam Da Nang province. After about ten days there, they shipped me off to Tien Lanh labor camp, also in Quang Nam Da Nang. Tien Lanh means Angel, and the joke was that you had to be an angel with wings to escape. This camp has both political prisoners and criminals, but they are separated, not kept in the same buildings. At work we are nearby, but in jail we are separate.

In the camp there are two lines of five buildings, each separated by about five meters. Each one was about fifty or sixty feet long and maybe thirty feet wide and held about fifty prisoners.

The *dai bang*, chief prisoner, was called Thanh Seo, because of the big scar on his face *["seo" is scar in Vietnamese]*. The guards choose the dai bang from aggressive long-stayers. They use him to keep the other prisoners in line. The people in the cell hate the dai bang, but they can't get back at him because they would be the ones to suffer, since he has the support of the guards. The guards hold the dai bang responsible for escapes and problems. He has to keep order. We even had to ask his permission to go and take a piss, so he would know that we were not trying to escape. If you didn't follow the rules of the cell, he'd beat you. You had to get up on time, go to sleep on time. There are so many rules, and you have to learn them well. When a visitor comes, the guard tests you before you can see the visitor. He might say, "What is rule number three?" and you have to recite it before you are let out to see the visitor.

Tien Lanh is a labor camp, and most of the labor is farm work—clearing land, planting rice. We worked from seven to eleven, got a small bowl of rice, and worked until five P.M. and then back to the cell. The farm was about ten kilometers from the prison. We had to form a line, with a guard at the beginning and a guard at the end, and we would walk to work. If you tried to make a break, they would shoot you. If you work slowly or try to stop for a while, they beat you with the rifle butt. If you try to escape, they fire in the air three times to alert the other guards. If they catch you, they beat you really badly, almost to death. This happened to Wo Van Thanh, an Amerasian who also came to the PRPC. He was in Tien Lanh with me. He got caught trying to escape, and they beat him savagely. He later got TB and was treated here. His departure *[from the PRPC for the U.S.]* was delayed.

After six months at Tien Lanh, I came down with malaria, a very bad case. They sent me to the hospital in Da Nang. When I was feeling better, I was able to escape from there. I made it to my house in Da Nang, and then I got to Ho Chi Minh City by train. I would hide at checkpoints, you know, *nhay tau ["to jump off the train," expression used in Vietnamese to indicate avoiding paying the fare]*. I'd leave the train at the station and get back on before the it pulled out, or I'd hide in the toilet when the conductor came around.

I went to Dam Sen, to the Amerasian center that the United States runs in Ho Chi Minh City. I couldn't get in "legally," since I had not been interviewed or accepted to go to the United States. I stayed "illegally." Many Amerasians do this.

One night I drank too much rice wine. I lost control and started shouting, "I am an Amerasian, why am I not allowed to stay here legally? Why do you try to keep me out, why do you discriminate against me?" I

Nguyen Tien Dung with his father's medallion

broke up some furniture and stuff. The police came, and I was back in prison, this time Chi Hoa prison in Saigon.

Back in prison again, I was depressed. That's when I did this *[Dung gestures towards the burn marks on his arm].*

My family had applied to go to America through the Orderly Departure Program in 1983, but nothing happened. We applied again in 1988. This time my family received a call slip to come for an interview, but they didn't know where to find me. They knew that I had gone to Saigon, and my girlfriend told them that I had been in Dam Sen. So they went to Dam Sen to look for me. The director told them that I had been sent to Chi Hoa prison, and they found me there. Shortly after, I was let out of Chi Hoa, and we went for the interview.

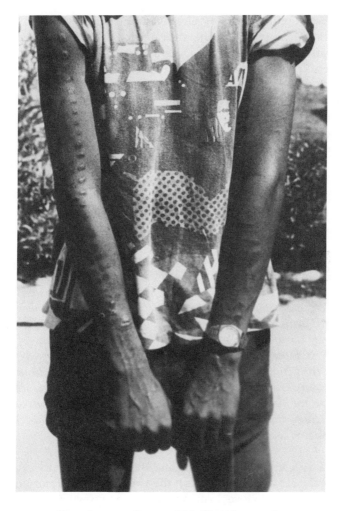

Dung's scars from self-inflicted wounds

When INS sent me to the Vietnamese doctor for an exam, he looked at my scars and said that I must be mentally ill to do that. So they put me on hold.

A month later, I had to come down and see the American doctor. He didn't say that I was crazy, but he thought that my scars were a cover up to hide needle tracks. He thought I might be a junkie, so I had to come down every month to have my blood tested, to make sure I was "clean." I had to wait months before we were able to leave Vietnam.

While I was waiting, I married my girlfriend. She is a black Amerasian, like me. We had a ceremony, but we didn't make the official documents.

We had both applied for ODP already, and we didn't want to delay our departures with more paperwork. She came to the Philippines ahead of me, and she left here for Arizona on December 9, 1991. I got to the PRPC on December 12, just three days too late to see her and my son. She delivered my baby here. We will join up again when I get to America.

I know that drinking is ruining me. This is the second time I have been thrown in the monkey house here for drunkenness and vandalism, but when I get depressed, I can't help myself.

Dung's stepfather, Mr. Loi, is a frail, silver-haired man of seventy-two. The lenses of his glasses are thick and opaque; his eyes seem distant behind them. He moves about with the aid of a cane. Despite this air of fragility, Mr. Loi speaks concisely and lucidly, sliding effortlessly between Vietnamese and French. My interpreter congratulates him on his fluency in the latter.

Mr. Loi is bemoaning the dishonesty and inefficiency of the Vietnamese bureaucracy that processes applications for the Orderly Departure Program. "It was very hard to get accepted by the ODP," he states. "If you pay them bribes, the Communist officials will do your case faster. But I had no money, so I had to go around, from this place to the other, from here to there. I made the paper in 1983 and again in 1988, and we finally left in 1991. The Communist system is completely corrupt."

With us in his billet is Dung's stepsister, Mr. Loi's adopted Amerasian daughter, Bich Dung, a diminutive woman with an extremely pleasant disposition. At twenty-one, she is almost eight months pregnant with her second child.

We sit just inside the door of their billet. A few magazine ads decorate the wall, including a blurb for "recaps and previews of your favorite soaps: 1-900-321-SOAP." Nearby is a Soviet-Vietnamese calendar.

Mr. Loi: I adopted both Dung and Bich Dung when they were about three months old. I raised them as if they were my own, according to Vietnamese custom, and I love them as if they were my own children. I am very close to them. When my wife was dying in 1983, she made me promise to always care for the children, no matter what happened, and I have. I devoted my life to them, and I never remarried.

I was born in North Vietnam, near Hanoi, in Bac Ninh province, Gia Lam district, Bac Trang village. Bac Ninh is famous for its pottery and porcelain, but my family was not involved in that. We were business people. I myself worked for British Shell company from 1950 to 1953. The director was French, so we were able to communicate. I learned French in school and can speak very well. I also worked for the tramway, the train lines.

I was born in 1919, so I was already thirty-four when I went to Da Nang in '54. I migrated under President Diem's policy of northerners going south. I had married in the north, and of course my wife came with me. We originally went to Saigon, where I applied for a job with the Ministry of Information. They posted me to Da Nang. My wife opened a stall in the market selling bicycle parts and tools. When the VC came in '75, they confiscated the shop, and she opened another one, this time selling copper altars.

Before '75, my job with the government was the family's main source of income, but after '75, I was looked on as a traitor by the new government and was denied access to any kind of employment, so I just helped my wife in her shop. When my wife died in '83, I took over the shop.

You can see by the stream of refugees leaving the country what a failure the North Vietnamese government is. They issue food cards, and if you have one, they supply you with cheap food. But these cards are only for the Communist employees. Most people, like myself, don't receive them. We have to buy at the market, and the food prices there are very high. As a former South Vietnamese official and the stepfather of two Amerasians, I had to continually suffer rumors, backbiting, and discrimination both from the government and from the neighbors. Now I am taking my children to the United States, so they, especially Bich Dung, can meet their fathers.

In '72 we adopted Bich Dung and in '73 Dung. We had a daughter of our own, and she loved her stepbrother and stepsister so much. *[Mr. Loi breaks down at this point, remembering his daughter, who was brutally murdered. We pause, and he begins again.]*

Bich Dung's mother was a friend of my wife. When she gave birth to Bich Dung, she didn't want to keep an American baby, so my wife took her. There is a lady who I knew in Vietnam who has now resettled in Massachusetts. She has some information about Bich Dung's father. He was not black, but Hispanic, and he wore a Red Cross arm band, so I suppose he must have been a medic. Bich Dung hopes that she can talk to this lady when we get to America, and perhaps her information can lead Bich Dung to her father.

We got Dung a year after Bich Dung. Somebody came over to my house and said that there was a baby out by the hospital gate. My wife went to see. She came back with a woman who was carrying a little red baby. When my real daughter saw him, she was so happy and wanted us to keep him. The woman was crying, but she left Dung. He was inside a little bamboo basket. Inside the basket were also a few toys and, wrapped in plastic, the marine medallion. That is the medal that Dung wears now.

In '75 when the Communists came, we had to make family books, so I wrote down that I had two adopted Amerasian children. They looked down upon me because of that and because I was a former employee of the South Vietnamese government. But I was already old, and they didn't give

Mr. Loi with Nguyen Thi Bich Dung and her oldest son

me too much trouble. Bich Dung didn't have too many problems. She didn't really look American, and she is so good-natured a girl.

Bich Dung: I first realized that I was Amerasian in the seventh grade, when classmates called me "My lai, My lai." In 1985 when we applied for the Amerasian program, my father first told me that I was Amerasian. I really didn't believe it. I was always small. Most Amerasians are big and tall, not like me.

Mr. Loi: Dung though, is black skinned, obviously Amerasian. They teased him with the nasty rhyme about "My lai," the one that says that the

Amerasians have twelve assholes, and if you plug up one, gas and shit comes out the others. He would fight every time they said that. He always had problems with the police, he always hated and fought them, I don't know why. When Dung was in Saigon, I got a letter from the police saying that he was in prison for breaking the light on a police car, and I had to pay three hundred thousand dong to get him out of Chi Hoa prison.

In 1990 the Communists made a plan to arrest "undesirables." They had a list at the police station, and Dung was on it. On November 20, 1990, they went from house to house, looking for people on the list. When they came to mine, they asked for Dung. He was asleep on the floor, it was the middle of the night. They pulled him in and sent him to Tien Lanh prison for five or six months. I visited him a number of times and so did his brother-in-law. It is a very hard life there. Dung came down with malaria, and they brought him back to Da Nang and gave him back to the family. We got medicine for him on the black market and treated him ourselves. Dung told you that they sent him to the hospital and he escaped, but that is not the time he escaped. When the police had him in jail waiting to be sent to Tien Lanh, he did escape, but he was caught very quickly.

Dung was very good at home. Sometimes he drank wine, but he was still good to the family. But when he moved to Saigon and lived with the Amerasians in Dam Sen Center, he became bad. There were many criminals in there, and their influence turned him bad. At home, he is still nice. He is very good with his sister and the family, but I am very sad at the problems that he has.

My family is a free case, I have no relatives in the United States. Dung has a wife there, he married her before she left Vietnam. I held a wedding in Da Nang for them. She is in Arizona now. About two months ago, she wrote Dung a letter saying she doesn't want him anymore. Something has changed in her life, but I really don't know the details. Dung hid the letter and doesn't want to talk about it. Of course he is very sad . . . she has his baby.

So Dung's wife won't sponsor us anymore. I don't know when we can leave here. Can you help us to go to America soon?

Postscript: *In July, Bich Dung gave birth to a healthy baby boy. In August, Mr. Loi and Bich Dung and her family were resettled in the United States. Although his infractions of the often onerous Philippine Refugee Processing Center rules were minor, Dung has been placed on administrative hold and was not permitted to accompany his family. Dejectedly, he waits to be allowed to join them in America.*

Loan, Be, and Dung

"Now that we are here . . . these three look
down on us and treat us like dirt. If it weren't
for us, they couldn't have gotten out of Vietnam."

*Loan, twenty-five, and Be, twenty-three, are sisters. Dung, their brother,
is twenty-two. All three are black Amerasians from the same father. Unlike most
Amerasians, they lived together with their father when they were infants, though
they can no longer remember him. The three are tall and sturdy, much larger than
the average Vietnamese. All have the dark skin of their father, though only Be
has his curly hair. Dung, the brother, is almost Indian in appearance.*

*Be is caring for her tiny newborn, just three days old, fanning him intermit-
tently against the oppressive heat and the omnipresent flies. Loan's four-year-old
daughter eyes my cassette recorder, entranced. Neighbors file in and out of their
billet in neighborhood two, curious about why an American has come to spend
so much time talking to the three siblings.*

*Carved into Dung's right arm are a series of tiny marks, roughly in the shape
of an "S." These, along with much smaller markings behind each ear, were made
by his American father, he says, so that in the event of separation his father could
identify him.*

*They have several family photos. One, of their mother, shows a very pretty
long-haired young lady standing by a living room bar and a tiny Christmas tree.
A few of the photos include their father, but he cannot be seen clearly. There is
one terribly faded black and white of him, but all that can be made out is that
he is a black man. On the back of the snapshot is written "V.N."*

*There are a few shots of their father's family from the States. One is entitled
"Eugene and his Christmas toys." It is uncertain if the young boy pictured is their
father's nephew or a son from his American wife. Their father, like many
Americans who fathered children with Vietnamese women, had a wife and child
in the United States. Along with the photos is a yellowing strip of paper upon
which is typewritten the father's name, Sgt. Robert Lowry.*

The siblings had applied to leave Vietnam in 1984, but like so many applicants unable to pay off Vietnamese officials, their applications were "lost." Frustrated with the delay and unable to pay the necessary bribes to speed up the process, they were approached by a third party who claimed he had the means to expedite their departure. All the three had to do was to claim three strangers on their documents as their spouses, affording them passage out of Vietnam. This meant leaving their real spouses behind, which they had no recourse but to do.

All is not well between the three Amerasians and their partners of convenience. Be speaks forthrightly of what the sisters consider to be the patronizing attitudes of their "husbands" and how the "husbands" look down on them now that they are out of Vietnam. Be's bogus husband happened into the billet as we spoke and eventually walked out in disgust at Be's strong words.

Loan: When I was young, we lived with my father, but I can't remember him. My mother told me that he was in the army, and he went to the United States in '72 for treatment of a heart ailment. He returned in '74 and left again in '75. We couldn't go because he had another wife and family in America.

Be: I remember that we lived with him in Vietnam, but I can't picture his face. He wrote us some letters after he went back to the States, but only my mother read them. We don't know where he is now. I want to find him, but how can we do that?

Dung: He marked me on the ears and on the arm. He told my mother that if we ever got separated, he could identify me from these marks. And those pictures he sent from the States . . . my mother told us that he said to print those pictures in a newspaper, and he would find us.

Be: We had an apartment in a four-story building in Saigon. My mother worked for the U.S. Army. That's where she met my father. In 1975, the VC came to Saigon, and they knew my mother had worked for the Americans. They demanded papers, documents, but my mother had already burned them all, all the documents my father left behind. We have only a few photos left, and I still have his ID card.

The VC took our apartment. We had no money or food and no place in Saigon to stay. My mother worried that the government would send our family to the New Economic Zone or that she would be sent to reeducation camp, so she took us to her home village, Dai Ngai village, in Long Phu district, Hau Giang province. This was the place of her mother and father, a farming village, flat with rice fields, about twenty kilometers from the main market town.

We lived in a tiny hut made of coconut leaf. We had some land, and if our harvest was good, we didn't sell it. We just paid our percentage to the government and kept the rest to eat. If the harvest was poor though, we were in trouble. We also would work for other farmers to make extra money, but there were difficulties. We were the only Amerasians in the village, and many farmers would not hire us. Life was severe, but it was better than being sent to the New Economic zone. In Hau Giang, we worked our land, and we worked for other people. In the New Economic Zone, you worked for the government, so you were not free.

Our relatives despised us because we were black. We kept away from them, but they taunted and insulted my mother. They were jealous. One time my mother was sick, and she asked my aunt for a loan of some money to buy medicine. My aunt told her, "You had an American boyfriend and plenty of money. Did you help us then? So why should I give you anything now?" After that, my mother didn't want anything to do with that aunt or our cousins. We moved to our own house, far from the rest of the family.

Loan: Before we moved to Hau Giang, we all went to school in Saigon. Be and I went about three years and Dung two years. The Vietnamese students all made fun of us because we are black. When we first got to Hau Giang, there was no school in the village. A few years after we got there, they opened a small school. We went for a short time, but again, the students teased us. They didn't want anything to do with us.

Be: Life was hard in Hau Giang, food was sometimes scarce. Even when we were children, we worked. There was very little time to play, and not many people to play with. No Amerasians lived near us. Often people would shout at us, make fun of us, not only children, even adults. We didn't say anything, we just ignored them.

Dung: Even though we are large in size, we are few in friends, so people feel free to harass us. One time there was a festival in town, and there was a boxing contest. I entered, and I knocked out my Vietnamese opponent. I guess he felt shamed, being beaten by an Amerasian, because that night he came to my house looking for me with a group of his friends. I had to run away, and luckily I was able to escape.

It was hard for me to get work. People wouldn't hire me to work in the fields if they could get Vietnamese, and there were plenty of Vietnamese available. It was easier to work as a fisherman, because there were not as many who had that skill. The village was near the end of the river, not far from the sea. I learned how to fish the river first, in a small boat, and then some friends took me to sea to learn ocean fishing. I learned to fish and pilot the boat, and I liked that better than farming. Unlike the farmers, the fishermen treated me fairly.

Be: I applied for a job at a local canteen run by the government. They told me that all positions were filled. Then they hired people who applied after me. They just didn't want to hire a black Amerasian.

Dung: At seventeen, people must do forced labor for the government. They don't pay you anything. All the men have to do this, but the government gives the Amerasians the worst jobs, the heaviest work. The Vietnamese do the easy work.

Loan and Be with their children, and their brother Dung

Whenever I used to go out, people would taunt me, but over the last two years, that hasn't happened. Amerasians are valuable now, they are a ticket to America. Now everyone wants us.

Be: We applied to leave Vietnam in 1984, but our papers were "lost." We had no money to bribe the officials, so we waited for years and nothing happened. Finally, our neighbor asked us to claim three people as our spouses, so they could go to America with us. He said that in return, he would take care of all the arrangements to get us out of Vietnam. We didn't know these people, they are no relation to us, but we did what he said. He must have paid the necessary bribes, because after that, we left Vietnam quickly. Now that we are here in the PRPC, these three look down on us and treat us like dirt. If it weren't for us, they couldn't have gotten out of Vietnam. We are the Amerasians. We are the only ones who really are supposed to be here. We don't want to stay with these people anymore. We want them to go to a separate billet, and we want to split the case, so we don't go to America together.

Our real spouses are in still in Vietnam. We had to leave them behind in order to get out of Vietnam, but we hope that we can sponsor them when we get to the United States.

[I ask about the burn marks on Dung's arm.]

Dung: These burn marks? Well, a friend teased me. He said that Amerasians were timid, that they couldn't take pain. I bet him that I could stand a burning cigarette on my skin. You can see that I won.

Loan: Our mother died two years ago this month. She started complaining of back pain, then elbow pain, and finally half her body became paralyzed. There was a small clinic nearby, and we sent her there, but there was nothing they could do. In two years she was dead.

Be: We believe in ancestor worship. Every week we get an invitation from the church to attend services, but we don't go, we keep our own religion. We feel it is most important to revere our dead relatives. *[Be shows me a picture of her family standing around her mother's gravesite, a barren mound of cracked mud. There are joss sticks and offerings of fruit.]* I hope we can make money in America to send back to have a nice gravesite made for my mother. It's the most important thing for us. That and finding our father. Maybe if we put the pictures he gave us in a magazine, he will recognize them and contact us.

When I see my father, I am afraid he will not understand me, because I speak Vietnamese. But I will ask him, "Do you love me, did you miss me, because for a long time we have not seen each other."

Phuong

"They loved the Amerasian when they
needed to leave Vietnam, but now they despise me."

*Phuong spotted me before I reached the door of her billet. She motioned for
me to wait where I was and walked out without a word to any of the people seated
inside. "I don't want them to know I'm talking to you," she told me through my
interpreter. "They'll only make trouble for me when I get back."*

*Phuong was "bought" in Vietnam by the family who now shares her billet.
As an Amerasian, she and her family qualify for resettlement in the United
States. Like so many families desperate to leave Vietnam, Phuong's "family"
sought an Amerasian who would be willing to claim them as legitimate relations. They paid the necessary bribes to Vietnamese bureaucrats and did the
requisite paper work to expedite departure via the Orderly Departure Program.
All Phuong had to do was claim them as bona fide mother, father, and siblings,
and they were accepted for immigration to the United States as the family of an
Amerasian.*

*Invariably, once a bogus family has been accepted for resettlement and no
longer needs the Amerasian, the relationship turns nasty. Phuong's case is no ex-
ception. She complains that her "family" torments her emotionally and physically.
She wants to move to another billet, but under the authoritarian and capricious
rules of the Philippine Refugee Processing Center, unauthorized change of billet
is an offence punishable by incarceration in the local rehabilitation center. So
Phuong must continue to share quarters with people who despise her.*

*Phuong is twenty-four. Her looks are decidedly Western, her hair long and
auburn, her skin fair. Like the majority of Amerasians in the PRPC, she is a
"free case." She has no relatives in the United States to sponsor her and does not
know where she will be resettled.*

MY FATHER LEFT Vietnam in 1972, so I know very little about him. I
was very young when he left. My mother told me that he had an eagle tattooed on his arm and that he was about twenty years old when they met.

He worked in an office for the army, maybe like a secretary, I don't know. He never really married my mother. They just lived together.

He wanted to take me and my mother to America in '72, but my mother's parents didn't want her to go, and she obeyed. He sent letters and money from 1972 to 1975, but after '75 we never heard from him again.

My mother was wounded. She was wounded by a grenade thrown into her house in 1968, that was before I was born. I don't know if it was political, or because she had an American husband, or if it was a robbery attempt, but she was hurt badly and had a lot of shrapnel taken out of her head. She always suffered from headaches after that, but I don't know if that was the only reason. She was a nervous woman.

I was born in Quy Nhon and stayed there till I was about eight. I went to school, but when you have white skin, it's hard. My classmates teased me, and even the teacher didn't like me. She paid no attention to me. Even if I gave a good answer, it didn't matter, she only liked the Vietnamese. You know, the teachers teach us that the Americans came to steal Vietnam, but they could not beat the Communists, that the Communists drove them away. Of course this was embarrassing for me. My brother and I were the only Amerasians in the school, and we didn't have many friends. The children always called me "American." I always wished that I could go to America.

The government often made my mother attend meetings at night. I was just a little girl, so I don't know what they were about, but I remember her going. The government confiscated her house, actually two houses. We had one in Quy Nhon and one in Pleiku. My father had bought them for her. People looked at my mother like she was a whore because she had had an American husband. Even our relatives were nasty to her, and when I was about ten, we moved out of Quy Nhon, to my aunt's house in Pleiku.

For me and my brother, Pleiku was easier that Quy Nhon. In Quy Nhon we lived in a village. In Pleiku we were in the city, there were many other Amerasians. I didn't stand out so much, I didn't feel so ashamed. We couldn't afford school, we all did farm work. Even when I was small, I worked, digging holes for planting peanuts.

My mother always suffered from tension. She was very nervous. She was always thinking about her misfortune and about the property that the Communists confiscated. She went through a period of severe headaches and died shortly after. She was only thirty-nine or forty.

After my mother's death, I remained at my aunt's house in Pleiku, helping her in the fields and hiring out as a laborer for other people. But our relationship became strained. She had given birth to children of her own, and of course she preferred them to me and my brother. So when I was about 16, I went out on my own.

I got a job washing dishes in a restaurant and saved a little bit of

Phuong

money. I met a friend of my mother's. She owned a boat and was going to escape from Vietnam. She agreed to take me and my brother. We went down to Nha Trang beach and took a small boat taxi out to the big boat. We never made it to the boat. The police stopped the taxi and arrested us. They let my little brother go, but I went to jail for a month.

In jail, I became friendly with some of the women prisoners, and they invited me to stay with them when I got out. One was the friend of the owner of a large restaurant called Thanh Thao *[The Fragrant Herb]*. The owner and I became tight friends, confidants. She told me that she had been the lover of an American colonel and had an Amerasian son from him. She also had adopted two other Amerasian children. I became the cook there at the restaurant, and she paid me a good salary. I can cook very well. You know Canh Chua, the Vietnamese soup we cook with pickle, and Ca

Kho, fish cooked in fish sauce? These were my specialties, but we cooked all kind of Vietnamese food. I worked there for four years and lived in a room in the back of the restaurant. My brother had gone back to Quy Nhon to stay with my grandparents, and I sent him some money every month. But there were some problems between the owner and the police. I think they hated her because she had three American children. Eventually, she had to close the restaurant.

When the restaurant closed, my boss gave me a third of a tael of gold in rings. I took that and some money I had saved and became a trader. I went to Buon Me Thuot and bought coffee and took it down to Saigon to sell. In Saigon I bought tobacco and rice noodles and sold that. In this way, I supported myself for several years.

When I was twenty-three or twenty-four, I heard about the Amerasian program. I decided to register, but first, I wanted to go to Quy Nhon to visit my brother. On the way, I met an old woman. She was bringing many things to her son, who was in reeducation camp in Pleiku. We became friendly, and I went with her to the camp and helped her carry her load. After, I returned with her to Saigon, and she introduced me to many people who wanted to pay me to claim them as family so they could go to America with me.

She took me to the sister of the woman I am living with now. This lady said, "Why don't you come and stay with my family?" My own plan was to go and stay in Dam Sen Amerasian Center, but this woman scared me. She told me about all the problems in Dam Sen. She said, "If you go there, the other Amerasians will make trouble for you." She also told me that I would have to pay bribes of two taels of gold to make all the papers, something that she would take care of if I stayed with her. I didn't have that money. I felt very confused about it, so in the end I agreed to join her family and we registered for the Orderly Departure Program together. When I was interviewed by INS, I told them that she was my adopted mother and that we had been together a long time.

There are six members in the family, her, her husband and four children. When we were in Vietnam being interviewed, they were very nice to me, sure. But now that we are here, they don't need me anymore. They treat me like dirt. They even tell me, "We're on our way to America already, we don't need you anymore." They insult me, berate me, the daughters even have attacked me. They loved the Amerasian when they needed to leave Vietnam, but now they despise me. I never got any money from this family when I helped them come here. They didn't do anything for me. They just used me.

I went to CFSI [*Community Family Services International*] for counseling about my problems with this family, to try to separate from them. I saw Mr. Dan, he is a Vietnamese counselor there, but he has lived in America for many years. He had bad words for me. He said, "Even an animal keeps loyal to those who feed him," but I am not an animal. He says that I should be loyal to that family. They couldn't be here without me. They used me, and now they mistreat me. Why must I be loyal to them?

He told me that the Americans made a mess out of Vietnam, but they couldn't defeat the Vietnamese. Now they feel guilty, so they are taking the Amerasians to America. But when the Amerasians get there, nobody cares about them, nobody wants them, so I had better stay with this family. He talked to me in a very degrading manner. I told him, "You depend on the Amerasians for your job, and you are paid by the American government, so who are you to criticize? If there are no Amerasians, you will not have this job."

Dan wouldn't help me, I asked Bob *[an American working in the PRPC]* for help. He is helping me move to another billet, away from that family. I asked that I be permanently separated from that family. I don't want to go to America with them.

Before I came here, when I was living in Ho Chi Minh City, I got a job in a beauty shop. I curled the hair, you know . . . permanents. There I met a man, he cut hair, and we fell in love and got married. But I married him after I made the paper to come here. Once you make the paper it's very hard to change it, to add another name. The family I am with, they said it would cost three taels of gold *[in bribes]* to add my husband's name, and we would have to wait longer to leave Vietnam. They didn't want to do it. I did not press the issue. I was afraid for my husband, afraid that the family might do something to hurt him if I made a problem, maybe even kill him. You know, it's very easy to hire a "hit man" in Vietnam, and very cheap, really.

So I am here, and my husband is still in Vietnam. I feel very sad. I miss him, and the family I came here with abuses me. How can I study, how can I learn English?

Postscript: Shortly after we spoke Phuong was given permission to transfer away from her "family" to a different billet. She immediately moved in with a friend, an Amerasian girl like herself. When I left the refugee camp in August of 1992, Phuong had not yet completed her studies, but was scheduled to be resettled in the United States in early 1993.

Hieu

"I don't want any more trouble. I want to be a good guy."

I am sitting across from Hieu in the small waiting room at the monkey house, the detention center at the Philippine Refugee Processing Center, where he is a detainee. Hieu, compact and muscular in cutoff jeans and a sleeveless "Fido Dido" T-shirt, has the light skin of his American father. He wears his brown hair long, and a key hangs from a hoop that dangles from his left earlobe, next to a pink post earring. On his left shoulder are some small tattoos of plus and minus signs and a colon. A skull and crossbones adorn the other shoulder, and a blue dragon crawls across his thigh. The scars on his arm are self-inflicted. ["These scars, I smoke and I burn myself . . . because I am very sad."] A huge slice mark runs over the heart area of his chest. It is the souvenir of a knife wound he received at seventeen while breaking up a fight in Vietnam between a teenager and an older man.

Hieu's three years in the Philippine Refugee Processing Center have been spent much the same as his previous twenty in Vietnam, largely in detention. Hieu tends to "lose it" when he drinks, and he drinks frequently. As a result of his troubles, his departure from the refugee camp for resettlement in the United States has been indefinitely delayed, and the uncle who was to be his sponsor in Texas has decided not to accept him.

Despite his total lack of schooling and his inability to read and write, Hieu has picked up quite a bit of English in the PRPC and Filipino detention centers, as well as a smattering of Tagalog. He forgoes the use of an interpreter, insisting on speaking to me directly in English. "I want to live with Americans," Hieu explains. "I want to talk only English, I don't want to talk Vietnamese anymore."

I DON'T KNOW where I was born, but I lived in Saigon City. I live with my mother and some members of my family, three young brothers and a sister. I am the only Amerasian. I never met my father. Even his photos, my mother threw them away when the Communists came. But sometime my mother tells me about him. She says that I'm like him, I look like him. My father was a soldier before, in the mountain. His name was Larry.

I didn't go to schoool in Vietnam. I want to go, but the children hurt me. They say, "You not like me, you American." I remember that. I feel hurt, I never go back anymore. Anyway, I am very poor, I have no money for school. I never learn to read and write Vietnamese. I can't read English either, only speak.

Sometimes I live with my mother in Vietnam, but lots of times I just leave home. I have a problem with my family, and I go stay with a friend. When I feel okay, I'm not angry anymore, I go back home.

I am very poor, I have no money. Some friends of mine they steal things, and they give them to me to sell. Then I start stealing myself. I snatch and run, chains, anything. I was young, fourteen or fifteen. I am not part of a gang, just me and my friend. He's Amerasian also. I steal things all around Saigon City, but the police, they pick me up many times.

Sometimes they put me in jail in Saigon, sometimes they send me to a camp outside of Saigon. There we have to work on the mountain, work very hard.

My mother is very angry. When I come home, she says, "What's wrong with you? Stay here, don't go out." But I say, "Mother, I'm very sorry, but I just got out of the monkey house, and I want to go out. I don't want to stay home."

The Vietnamese hate American children, they always say, "Leave, go home," and I want to. I don't want any Vietnamese friends, I don't care about the Vietnamese. They don't like me, so I don't like them.

I came here to the refugee camp in 1989. I'm here almost three years, and I been in jail many times, like in Vietnam. Before, I have a friend here, I know him from Vietnam. We been in the monkey house together. He invites me to have some drinks in his house. When I am very drunk, he says to me, "Now, I will box [beat] you, and what will you do?" I say, "Leave me alone, let me sleep. I don't want boxing, I don't want trouble, because I want to go America." He says to me, "You want to go to America? I make you die here in the Philippines. You never go to America, I kill you first." I think he will get my knife and kill me, and I will die here . . . so I stab him, before he can kill me. He don't die. He's not hurt too bad, but they send me to the monkey house for three months.

When I get out of the monkey house, I have another problem. You remember a few years ago there are Filipino and Vietnamese fighting in the market. That time I don't have nothing to do with it, I was only watching. The police come to my house, and they say, "You were fighting with a Filipino." I say, "No, I was only looking, not fighting." They say, "We have a picture," but they don't let me see it. So they put me in jail six months,

Hieu in the PRPC detention center, the "monkey house"

for nothing. I am in jail with two other people. They go to America already, but me, I'm still here.

So when I get out, I don't have any trouble for a long time. I'm a good guy, because I want to go to America. But I wait for the list *[for his name to appear on the departure list for the United States]* and no name. I wait and wait, and I'm very sad. One day I am drinking, and I'm very noisy, but only in my home. The neighborhood leader comes in to talk to me. I say, "I am the same as you, Vietnamese." He tells me, "No, you are not the same as me," and we start fighting. I hit him only one time, but they send me back to the monkey house again.

So I am in the monkey house, my brother comes to give me food. The police on duty, he don't want to open the door to let my brother give it to me. I say to police, "Can you let me go over there to eat? When I'm finished, I go back in the cell." He don't let me, so I get angry. I break the door, I wreck the cell. About ten police grab me and put me in the car and send me to jail in Napot *[a nearby detention facility]* for seven months.

Now I am in the monkey house again. You know here they keep me in the cell, they never let me out. Why, I don't know. They let everybody go out but me. I say, "Excuse me sir, can I go out, work outside," but he don't let me out, he is angry at me. You know at New Year all prisoners go home. Only me stay here. I don't know why.

My mother says to me, "What happens in your life, you back in the monkey house again." I say, "I know it's no good, but it's not my fault." She says, "One time okay, two times okay, but you're always in the monkey house. What is wrong with you?"

My family is so angry at me. They say they don't want to wait for me anymore. I promise, I don't want any more trouble. I want to be a good guy.

Postscript: *Four months after Hieu and I had spoken at the detention center, I was visiting a Vietnamese friend in neigborhood four of the PRPC. Her daughter walked in with an Amerasian boy of about twenty. He was very pale, obviously distraught. My friend told me that he had just come from the hospital, where his stomach had been pumped. "He tried to kill himself," my friend explained. "One Amerasian boy in neigborhood two, lives next door to him. He comes in and takes everything from his house and says he will kill him if he tells anybody. So my daughter's friend, he feels very sad, and he takes too much medicine [sleeping pills]." "Who is the boy who stole his things?" I asked. "His name is Hieu," my friend told me. "He is very mean. They call him "Hieu Loco."*

The next afternoon I went to visit Hieu in his billet, but he was not home. He had been arrested again and was once more doing time in the detention center.

Charlie

"Everywhere I went, people looked down on me."

I first met Charlie at the PRPC jail, commonly referred to as the "monkey house." As we began to speak, a group of about twenty Amerasians arrived at the entrance, accompanying a new detainee, a white Amerasian being brought in for carrying a deadly weapon, "troublemaking," and "fighting." Charlie viewed the commotion dispassionately; he had seen it all before.

Tall and lanky, his movements loose and almost laconic, there is little of Asia in Charlie's appearance. His hair is brown, his complexion light; the genes of his white American father clearly predominate. He sports two gold studs in one ear and arms crisscrossed with burn scars self-inflicted with a cigarette during a fit of depression. "USA" is tattooed about six inches above his left wrist, and on one leg a tattooed hand brandishes a pistol. Another hand is coming up to grab it, as if to restrain the shooter or, possibly, to aim the gun. Beneath this image is a Vietnamese sentence, roughly translatable as "The rice bowl in prison will see me again." The implication is that trouble is Charlie's fate. (See photos pp. 44 and 45.)

Whether by destiny or design, the tatooed phrase is eerily apropos. Separated from his parents, terrorized by his aunt's vindictive husband, and out on his own early in life, he entered an alternating cycle of petty crime and incarceration. This cycle remains unbroken in the PRPC. He was serving the tail end of a five-month sentence for fighting and troublemaking when we first spoke, just one in a continuing series of imprisonments since he entered the PRPC about three years ago.

In a recent incident when he was drunk and upset with a friend, Charlie took a knife and sliced off the tip of his own pinky. Alcohol abuse has certainly been a factor in his troubles.

Charlie's background is one of hard times. Nguyet, a forty-seven-year-old Vietnamese womam, herself a refugee and a mother of an Amerasian daughter, knew Charlie's mother and had this to say about his background:

> *Charlie's mother work bar same as me, work many bars . . . Melody, Rosie's, Hi-Y, New York, Merrily. Many GI's come, navy, air force too, all Americans.*

Charlie's mother gets an American husband, he be army, and she born Charlie. Charlie's mother and father go to Kampuchea. Charlie be very young, he stay with mother's sister in Saigon. Mother's sister, she leaves Saigon and gets married. Her husband don't like Charlie, beats him all the time, so Charlie, he runs away. Charlie's mother and father come back to Saigon. They don't see mother's sister, don't see Charlie. They look everywhere but cannot find. Father says, "VC come soon, we cannot stay here," and they go back to America without Charlie.

Charlie arrived in the PRPC alone in 1989. He had expected to leave for America within six months of his arrival, but as a result of his numerous arrests, he has long been on "hold," an administrative limbo which effectively removes him from the pool of refugees continuing on to the United States. Whether this hold will be temporary or permanent is uncertain.

Our meetings, in which he spoke about himself, took place intermittently over the course of about ten months from late 1991 until mid-1992. The venues shifted from the monkey house, to Charlie's spartan billet to the PRPC hospital, corresponding to the rapidly changing phases in Charlie's unstable existence. He requested that I keep his real first name in the narrative, on the chance that his mother or father might read it and recognize him. Charlie attributes many of the problems that have entangled him to Vietnamese rejection of Amerasians, beginning for him, with the abuse he suffered at the hands of his aunt's husband. He puts it simply: "Everywhere I went, people looked down on me."

I WAS BORN in Saigon, but I moved to Tay Ninh with my aunt when I was about eight. I really don't remember much about Saigon from my childhood days. The only memory that sticks in my mind is of black American soldiers riding around in Jeeps. I was afraid of them. I guess that's why I remember them.

We were sent to the New Economic Zone in the Chau Thanh area of Tay Ninh province. We were very poor, and my aunt had to work very hard, but soon after we got there my aunt fell in love with the Communist village chief, a former guerrilla soldier. We moved into his house, a thatch hut with a dirt floor. His position made life easier for my aunt, but very difficult for me. He was a former guerrilla soldier, and he hated me, hated my American blood. He beat me, he tormented me with pliers. He even threw me down a well and almost drowned me. My aunt didn't say anything, she was afraid of him.

I never knew my mother, only my aunt. I don't know if my aunt was really my blood aunt or not. Sometimes she told me she was my aunt. Sometimes she said that she found me in a garbage can, so how can I know? When I grew up, I went back to Saigon to the place I lived with my aunt. I wanted to find my real mother. The old people living there told me that I had two siblings, both Amerasian. My parents got them and took them to America, but I was left behind. That's all I know.

I ran away from my aunt and her husband when I was still a young boy. A girl in another village took pity on me and let me stay in her hut. She became what we call *chi tinh than,* my "mental sister." By that I mean she instructed me in the way of life, because she had more experience than me.

We lived in a small village about four kilometers from Tay Ninh town. She was a prostitute, she worked in town, on Cay Me Street in the first ward of Tay Ninh. She would take customers up to a rented room there.

As a prostitute, she had very low status in the village. So did I, since I was the only Amerasian. I was never accepted there, I had no friends. I never went to school in Vietnam, not even one day. I just played by myself in the house. People used to insult me when I went out. They called me "My lai, My lai" *[Amerasian].* I didn't do anything, I just stayed away from them.

When I was about fifteen, my mental sister was arrested for prostitution, and I was alone. She was sent to Cay Cay labor camp, about a hundred kilometers away, but still in Tay Ninh. I had no money to visit her, but I got work for one of the rich men in the village, taking care of water buffalo, and was able to save a little bit of money.

I watched over eight buffalo. I got up early, before the sun rose. I would let the buffalo graze, but I watched them carefully, so that they didn't eat the crop. If they ate any, the owner would beat me. So anytime they started to eat the crop, I would hit them to try to make them move. But sometime they wouldn't listen, and they would get into the fields, and the owner would let me have it.

After working with the buffalo for a year, I made enough money to go and visit my mental sister. But when I got to Cay Cay labor camp, I found out she was dead. They forced her to do hard labor, and she had very little to eat. She had no relatives to send her money for food.

I went back to Tay Ninh, just slept out on the street in any place that looked okay. I picked up plastic bags and bottles and sold them to earn some money. When I got enough, I bought bread and sold it in the bus station. But there were problems, there are many other people picking up plastic bags and selling bread and cigarettes, and they don't like competition. They don't like a new boy. Also, I had a problem with the son of one of the village vice-chiefs. His family lived near the bus station, and he often came down with his friends to bother me. They taunted me, called me "son of the enemy," and beat me up. Sometimes they stole the little money I had. His family was very powerful, so what could I do?

I made a plan. I had a friend with a motorbike. I asked him to wait for me outside the station. When the chief's son came, I stabbed him and fled on the back of the motorbike. I left Tay Ninh and made my way to Ho Chi Minh City.

I went to the Ba Chieu area of Ho Chi Minh City, where I had a cousin. I stayed in his house a long time. My cousin's mother-in-law didn't like me. She complained that I didn't work, only ate. It was true. I was poor, I had nothing to give them. I had no job, they had to support me, to buy me food. I tried to find work. I tried to work as a mason, but I was too weak, I just couldn't do it. With no job, I just stayed at home and eventually they threw me out.

I went over to Ba Chieu market and I begged for scraps, for leftovers, and slept on the street across from the market. Just like in Tay Ninh, there was a lot of competition. The beggars who were already working that area didn't want me there, at least not the Vietnamese. The other Amerasians were friendly.

At first I was begging, then I began to steal. I would steal fish and vegetables and sell them and get money to buy rice. I was hungry. I became part of a gang. There were only two Amerasians in the gang, me and another white guy, and we worked together. We would wait until someone wasn't paying attention, and then we would steal their goods, their fish or vegetables. Sometimes while they were unloading a truck or car, and they weren't looking, I would be able to pick something up.

We divided up what we made stealing fish and vegetables, but if we stole other things we kept it all. I began to steal chains and watches from people, from passengers on buses and pedicabs. When the people were not paying attention, I would tear off their chain or watch and run. They yelled and screamed, but I would get away.

Anyway, I got away until one time I snatched a chain, and a plain-clothes cop was right there and he nabbed me. He arrested me, and I was sent to Mac Dinh Chi prison. We just call it Mac prison. It's near the center of Saigon, near the presidential palace.

The cells can be very crowded there, as many as fifty prisoners. Other times there are only seven or eight to a cell. Some of the prisoners are pretty young. I guess I was about sixteen or seventeen at that time, and some were younger than me. Newcomers have to wash the floor and massage the older prisoners, the leaders. If you follow the orders of the *dai bang*, the head prisoner, then the older prisoners leave you alone.

It was not too bad in prison because I got up and slept anytime I wanted. All the rules were up to the dai bang. After I did what he wanted, swept the floor or something like that, they left me alone. I could do what I wanted, but I never got to leave the cell. I had no money to bribe the guards to let me work outside. If you have money, you can pay the guards to let you work out of the cell as a cook, a cleaner, something like that. But I had nothing to give them, so I just stayed in the cell.

The police would interrogate me. They wanted to know who my partners were, who worked with me. They questioned me every two weeks or so, and gave me a pencil and paper to write my story. I can't write, so I just spoke and a friend in the cell wrote what I said. I had to do this many times, over and over, and each time they took my story they would compare it to the ones I had written before and ask questions about it. Then I had to write it again. This went on for a long time. Finally, they couldn't find any of the people I had written about, and they became angry. That's when the beatings began. They tied me down and beat me with rubber hoses and demanded to know the real names of my partners. Three times a day they beat me. After the beating, you can't eat anything, just drink salt water, which helps you. They beat me for two days, and I couldn't take anymore. I had to tell them about my partners, my friends.

After I had been in for more than a year, a good friend of mine, a man ten years older than me, whom I call my "older brother," paid off the prison authorities, and they let me go.

I got out of prison and was right back on the street again, stealing. How else could I get money? I needed to eat. I was working with a partner, another Amerasian. We were on a motorbike, and he grabbed the chain of an overseas Vietnamese, a thick gold chain. My partner lost his balance and fell off the bike. People screamed and he was caught, but I got away.

So I had to leave Saigon. I was afraid that my friend would tell the police where I was. I was really scared. If the police beat my friend, he would give my name, and I didn't want to go back to jail. I had to get away, far away from Saigon.

I dyed my hair black so no one could tell that I was an Amerasian and went down to Hoa Hung train station in Saigon. I headed north, to Thanh Hoa, near Hanoi. The family of a good friend lived up there. I didn't pay for the train. I jumped on the train after it left the station, and I jumped off before the next station. I would walk around the station and get on another train. In this way I avoided ID checks and paying.

Life in the north is different than in Saigon. It is harder there. People are poorer. They wear slippers, not shoes. The clothes are poor, not the same as Saigon, and I never saw any Amerasians there. I couldn't find my friend's family in Thanh Hoa, so I got a tiny room and I stayed there for a short while. I didn't know what to do. I was afraid to go back to Saigon so soon after my friend's arrest, but I was afraid to stay too long in Thanh Hoa. People might recognize my southern accent, know that I was not from there. Then I'd be in trouble again.

I heard that life was easier in Cambodia. I had some friends who went over there. They said it was easier to make money there, and it was possible to escape through Cambodia to Thailand and from there go on to the United States.

I left Thanh Hoa and went back south to the Go Dau district of Tay Ninh province, on the Khmer border. There is a police checkpoint there.

I avoided that. There are guards patrolling along the border. I watched the patrols, and when it was clear I entered the forest and crossed the border.

I first went to Bao Wat, a small town near the border. There were some Vietnamese people that I knew living there, and I looked for them. I helped them selling things at the market, clothes, and food. Some of the Vietnamese told me that in Svay City *[probably Svay Rieng]* I could find work, and arrange to escape into Thailand, so I went there.

Svay is a pretty big town. A friend of mine was living there, a neighbor from Ba Chieu. I borrowed his bike, pedalled into the countryside, and bought chickens from the farmers. I sold them in town. It was easy to earn money. There were many Vietnamese there, and Amerasians too. Life was better there than in Vietnam.

My idea though, was not to stay in Cambodia, but to get to Thailand, and from there to America. Many Vietnamese escape this way, and I joined a group of them with my friend from Ba Chieu. We had a plan and a guide. One night I took a bicycle rickshaw to a prearranged meeting place, about seven kilometers out of town, where I was supposed to join the group. The police stopped my rickshaw. They saw that I was Vietnamese, and my Khmer was not good enough to use to talk to them. They took me to a checkpoint, and arrested me. I had no documents, no ID. You need special documents to live in Cambodia.

Charlie relates being sent to, and eventually escaping from, Cay Cay prison in Tay Ninh. After his escape, he was given shelter and work by a farmer. I expressed surprise that the farmer would take the risk of aiding an escaped convict. A Vietnamese associate of mine, himself a former reeducation camp prisoner, concurred, explaining that people living near a reeducation camp know full well the consequences of harboring an escapee. The young Vietnamese man interpreting for Charlie, however, felt that sheltering an escapee was not unusual, given the disdain of the South Vietnamese for the Communist government and its skewed system of justice. He mentioned that his own sister had aided escapees and that his brother, escaping from police custody stemming from an unsuccessful attempt to flee Vietnam by boat, had been hidden by complete strangers. Unfortunately, that same brother was shot and killed by police in a subsequent attempt to leave Vietnam by sea.

So they sent me back to Tay Ninh, to P4 prison. I was charged with attempting to escape from Vietnam. I stayed there waiting for my "trial." Remember I told you that I stabbed the son of a village chief in Tay Ninh years before? I wounded him, but he didn't die. Anyway, one of the prison guards recognized me and they decided to get even. A group of them took me into a room and worked me over good, beat me till I lost consciousness. Then they poured water over my head to bring me to and beat me some more. I stayed in P4 prison four months. Then they sentenced me to three years in Cay Cay labor camp, the same place my mental sister had gone to and died in.

In Cay Cay, there are cattle to watch, land to work, and a brick factory. They make you work in one of these places, according to your skill. If you are a farmer, you work the farm, a bricklayer, you lay brick, etc. You get two bowls of rice with salt each day, no vegetables. Every Sunday they gather the prisoners for political instruction about Ho Chi Minh's policy, the Communist policy, and Communist life. I didn't pay attention to that.

They made me work as a farmer. I got up at five o'clock, then we did exercise until six. Then we went to the farm to work until five, with a one-hour break for lunch at about twelve, everyday the same, rain or shine. If you stop or take a break, the guards beat you with their rifle butt. We were always hungry, always. Work all day and so little to eat.

Cay Cay prison is in a very remote area. It's in a compound surrounded by a barbed wire fence. On one side is a river that borders Cambodia. Another side is a school for army recruits. Another side has a fence heavily manned by police. The rest is thick forest.

When I was there only one month, I decided to try to escape. I saw others try, and I paid attention and learned from their experiences. I saw that prisoners who tried to escape through the police line were shot. It would be very difficult to escape through the army school. Prisoners who tried to escape across the river into Cambodia were often caught. I knew that those who tried to escape through the dense forest sometimes got lost and died of starvation, but I eventually decided to try that route.

I made a plan to escape with two former South Vietnamese government officials. In Cay Cay prison, the political prisoners are separated from the common criminals, and I don't know why they were in with the criminals. Maybe they had already been reeducated and rearrested for something else. I don't know. I didn't know them very well since we were working outside all day in different areas, and when we got back to the cell we were exhausted. There were many other prisoners around. It was hard to speak privately, so we had no time for small talk. When we spoke with each other, it was about escape. The older of the two officials made the plan and was our leader.

We each had cans to pee in at night. In the morning, we had to dump the contents in a trough over by the barbed wire fence at the outer perimeter of the camp. Instead of emptying the piss there, we dumped it against the wall of our cell. The cell stank so bad anyway that you couldn't even notice. We tried to do this when the other prisoners were sleeping.

Every morning we took the cans to the trough and pretended to dump out the urine there. Since the trough was near the barbed wire fence, if the guard wasn't looking, we would twist the strands of wire near to where it attached to the wooden post. We did this for months, emptying our urine against the wall of the cell, and when we were near the fence quickly working the strands of the barbed wire back and forth with our hands. After months the cell's wall, made of cheap cement and badly constructed, became weakened, and the barbed wire at the fence post was worn through where we had repeatedly twisted it.

One night I was awakened by a small pinch on the leg. It was the signal that this night was the night for escape. We took a spoon and began scraping at the spot on the wall where we had repeatedly dumped our urine. It was soft and gave way easily. When we had scraped away a quantity of cement, we were able to break off some of the block inside. In about two hours we had a hole big enough to crawl through.

I was the first one through. There were a lot of individual cell buildings spread over on the prison grounds, and I weaved through them, using them for cover. I heard shooting behind me. I made it to the barbed wire fence and got through the weakened area we had made. Other prisoners who were not in on the escape didn't know that there was a hole in the fence. They tried to climb over and were picked off by the police.

I ran through the farm fields and into the forest. It was a dark, rainy night. My adrenalin was pumping, I had just been that close to death and escaped. I ran and ran, I never looked back. I was separated from my two partners, and I don't know if they made it or not.

The forest was very thick and wide. I had some manioc and sweet potato that I hid and brought with me in the escape, but that was all.

I made my way into the forest and eventually stopped, climbed a tree, and spent the night there. Then I began to walk. I found some wild fruit and ate that, and when I found clear water, I would drink it, just like wood cutters do. I really didn't know where I was going. Sometimes I would climb a tall tree, and when I could see the prison camp, I just kept on going in the opposite direction.

I walked for days, and finally I came to a clearing and a thatch house. It was a small farm. I told the farmer that I had escaped from prison. How could I hide it? I had a prison haircut and clothes. He let me stay and work for him for a while, taking care of his cows. I stayed with him until my hair grew in. When it was time to leave, he let me have a little money, and I went to the road and got a bus to Saigon.

When I was in prison, some of the other Amerasian prisoners got visitors. Through them we heard of Amerasians being accepted to go to the United States. So after my escape, when I got to Saigon, I applied to go to the United States through the Orderly Departure Program. Meanwhile, I got a job helping a bricklayer and slept on the street.

When ODP accepted me, I moved to the Amerasian center in Dam Sen. ODP sent me for a medical exam in Cho Ray hospital. The Vietnamese

psychiatrist said I was suffering from mental illness, but this is just a way
to extort a bribe. They expect you to give them money, and then they will
say you are okay. I have heard of many cases like this. I didn't have any
money to give him, so I waited in Dam Sen for six months, and I was called
for an examination in Cho Quan hospital. This doctor was American. He
said, "Who said that you have mental illness? You seem okay." I told him
that the Vietnamese doctor in Cho Ray did that because he wanted money.
So he cleared me, and soon after, I left to come here to the Philippines.

*Charlie came to the PRPC expecting to be on his way to the United States
after completion of his five months of schooling, but just as in Vietnam, his life
became mired in incidents of petty crimes, rule violations, and imprisonment.
Probably most serious among these was his arrest and subsequent imprisonment
for his alleged part in the stabbing of Duc, a Vietnamese petty criminal who has
himself spent years on administrative hold in camp due to his own legal difficulties
and has done time in both Philippine and PRPC jails. Four Amerasians, including Charlie, were arrested in connection with Duc's stabbing and charged
with attempted homicide, "frustrated murder" under Philippine law, frustrated
because Duc recovered from his wounds. The suspects spent five months in a
Philippine prison in Balanga, the capitol of Bataan province, before Duc reluc-
tantly dropped charges. Raymond and Tuan Den, two of the Amerasians arrested with Charlie in connection with the stabbing, also discuss the incident in
their respective narratives in this book. Their accounts corroborate Charlie's
claim of innocence.*

Like many Amerasians, I came to the PRPC alone. I was depressed
and lonely. The day before I was supposed to begin ESL class, I was drinking in neighborhood three. The blue guards came and arrested me. They
took me in and beat me. I can still remember the guard who arrested me,
his name was "Karate." He is still working here in neighborhood six.
*["Karate" is the nickname of a notorious Filipino guard at the PRPC detention
center, who has since been transferred to another post within the PRPC. He is
well known for his ability to injure a prisoner with blows that damage the internal
organs but leave few marks on the body.]*
After the police worked me over, they put me in a cell in the monkey
house. Duc was the dai bang there, but I didn't know anything about him
then. He seemed very friendly with the police. They spoke together, but it
was in English so I couldn't understand. He had been in the Philippine jail
at Napot for three years and then sent back to the PRPC.
Duc had the keys to all the cells. Why the police gave him the keys,
I don't know, but he came into my cell and beat me badly, really badly. He
hurt me inside. I vomited blood, shit and pissed blood, after he got through
with me. He was the dai bang, so there was nothing I could do; but I kept
revenge inside my heart, and I never forgot the beating.

After I was released from jail, I asked some of my friends to keep an eye on Duc, to let me know when he was going to be let out. Three months later I found out he was going to be released and there was going to be a party for him in neighborhood nine. I planned my revenge, to go there with a friend, Minh, and stab Duc for what he had done to me.

I went to Duc's billet in neighborhood nine. When I got there, he had already been stabbed by Tuan Den. I didn't know Tuan Den at that time, but I learned that him and Raymond had heard about the things Duc was doing to Amerasians in the monkey house and had planned to "take care of him." So Tuan Den stabbed him, and by the time I got there it was all over.

Three months later I was arrested. The blue guards *[PRPC security guards]* came to my ESL class and told me to get in the car. They drove me directly to Balanga. They never told me why or where we were going. They just took me out to Balanga jail. I'm not sure why they arrested me but I think that Duc's friends saw me there and identified me as part of Tuan Den's group. But that is not correct, I had nothing to do with them. I had planned to stab Duc, that's true, but Tuan Den did it before I got there. Duc has many enemies.

Tuan Den was arrested first, then Raymond, then Minh, then me . . . all separately. I spent five months in prison, and then Duc dropped the charges and we were released.

I came back to camp and finished my ESL class, but JVA put me on hold, and my departure for America was delayed. So I just waited, nothing to do, just hang around. There was a black girl living nearby, an orphan. I had heard that a black Amerasian guy was bothering her, coming by and beating her. One day I saw him knocking her around in her billet, and I stopped him. There was a fight, and I wound up back in the monkey house *[PRPC jail]* for a month.

When I got out, I was still on hold, nothing to do but wait, wait till they would let me go to the United States. I became more and more despondent.

One day I was down by the stream in neighborhood four, and a Vietnamese threw a stone at me. I had been waiting for such a long time already, and I was so depressed that I became furious. I was seething, but I didn't do anything about it then. I went to see him in his billet later. I asked, "Why did you throw that rock at me?" He said, "Why, what are you going to do about it?" He started cursing me, and I punched him in the mouth and knocked out a few of his teeth. And I was back in the monkey house again, this time for six months.

Tuan Den, the black Amerasian who was in prison with Charlie in connection with Duc's stabbing, had become Charlie's close friend. However, shortly after Charlie's last release from the monkey house, they had a falling out, caused in part, like so many of Charlie's woes, by alcohol.

Tuan Den and I were depressed, we were tired of waiting around here. We were sitting around, drinking, both of us were drunk. We got into an argument, and we decided to settle it by fighting it out. We were both drunk. I said, "Let's go out to the mountain and fight there, where we won't get into any trouble, and nobody will stop us." Tuan Den said okay, and we both got clubs. I turned around and started walking towards the mountain as we had agreed, when he hit me from behind and ran away. I was drunk and upset, and I swore that I would never trust in another friend again. In anguish, I took a knife and sliced off the tip of my pinky.

I just hope I can get out of here soon and go to the United States. I'd like to study and work when I get there, but I have no skills, so I know that I must start at a low position. I can't even read or write, though sister Margarita used to come to the monkey house and teach me a little. I hope I can become fluent in English and work at a job where I can move up and make enough to survive. I would like to join the army, like my father.

I don't want to live with Vietnamese in the United States. They have always meant trouble for me. The fewer Vietnamese the better.

Postscript: *On a blistering day in May, an Amerasian teenager came to see me outside my office with a lament, "Charlie, he in hospital, die soon, die soon." In the peculiar twists that language takes when being learned, "die soon" in PRPC vernacular has been transmuted to "dead already." When I arrived in the drab surgery ward of the PRPC hospital, however, Charlie was quite alive, though looking dismal as death while a bevy of Amerasian visitors comforted him. He had been slashed four times with a "bolo," a Filipino machete, and had been brought here to have his wounds stitched. Although bloody, they were not serious.*

Despite his condition, he gesticulated angrily when describing the incident that had put him in the hospital. His irate movements stretched the I.V. drip line stuck into his left arm, and his description revealed the deep disdain with which South Vietnamese generally regard people from the north of their country. "I was walking past the market when this northerner, this Communist, ran out and attacked me. I don't know why. I didn't do anything."

The doctor who had sewn Charlie up supplied me with details. Ngoc, a refugee from North Vietnam who has been detained for years in the camp on suspicion of being a Communist, has a gold business near the market. A group of bandits held him up and relieved him of sixty thousand pesos [approximately $3000] and an unspecified quantity of gold. When the robbers fled, Ngoc grabbed a bolo and ran out after them. He came upon Charlie, whom he accuses of acting as the lookout for the bandits. In the ensuing scuffle, Ngoc slashed Charlie four times, and he himself suffered minor wounds in the fray.

Ngoc had offered to drop charges in return for the cash and gold, but Charlie refused to cooperate, insisting he had no part in the robbery and was merely passing by when Ngoc attacked him with the bolo.

The following day I came by the hospital again, but Charlie had been sent home, still protesting his innocence. Several days later he was brought to the monkey house, and then, along with another suspect in the robbery, to Napot jail, a small Philippine facility a few kilometers from the PRPC. The charge was larceny.

Three months later Charlie was back in camp, rail thin and very pale. The gold and cash had not been recovered, but charges had not been filed in Philippine court, and seemingly the affair had played itself out to no conclusion. Charlie had been released, but was still on hold, and once again was living alone in his billet, with nothing to do but wait.

MOTHERS AND CHILDREN

That year, everybody, all Vietnam, had American
children, and some people threw their babies away.
Some people told their children, "Go out."

> Mai, mother of an Amerasian son

School in Vietnam hurts a child who has an
American parent.... They learn that they are the
children of the army of the enemy.

> Tuyet, mother of an Amerasian daughter

Hoa and Loan

"The man come, he say, 'What are you drinking?'
I say, 'Saigon tea,' and I sit together with him."

"Yeah, drink Saigon tea, many, many." Hoa is laughing, and her class-mates join in. A number of the fifteen students in this ESL class are, like Hoa, veterans of the GI bars in Vietnam, where they earned commissions for coaxing the troops to buy them the watery concoction known as "Saigon tea."

Later that week, when we meet in her billet for the first of numerous inter-view sessions, Hoa is more circumspect. She requests that I not use her real name, but refer to her as "Hoa," as she was called in the Vung Tau bars. She asks that we leave the billet to speak, preferring that the neighbors not know about her past, nor of the "gold" arrangement made with the "husband" of Loan, her black Amer-asian daughter. This man, in exchange for the marriage of convenience to an Amerasian which provided him a ticket to the United States, paid the bribes necessary to expedite the family's departure from Vietnam. Hoa and Loan had little choice but to accept this bogus suitor. Lacking the funds with which to grease the wheels of Vietnamese officialdom, their application to leave Vietnam had been languishing for seven years in a bureaucratic limbo.

For the last fifteen of Hoa's forty-three years, she has been homeless. Sent to prison camp for two years and denied identification documents upon her re-lease, she supported her two Amerasian children and ailing mother through meager commerce, buying and selling rice. When the police confiscated her goods, she turned to prostitution to get the capital to begin again. Lacking the means to secure housing, her family slept on the street. Her children grew up there, and her mother died there. The billet in the PRPC is the first home her daughter Loan has known.

In a subsequent visit to their billet, I found Loan sitting at the table, studying English with a young neighbor. Hoa came inside from the back, she had been out tending her small vegetable garden. I suggested that we shoot some photos, and Loan walked upstairs to put on a fresh blouse. Once she had left, Hoa fretted about the color of her daughter's skin. . . . "She's very dark, isn't she?"

160

Hoa is well aware of America's racial problems. "It's harder for black than white in Vietnam," she says, "I have black baby and white baby so I know. I think your country be same." She fears that the prejudice her black daughter experienced in Vietnam may continue in the United States.

Her son, Phi, scheduled to leave Vietnam with them, was delayed due to a lung problem, probably tuberculosis. He is waiting in Ho Chi Minh City, taking medication under a doctor's supervision. Hoa continuously broods over her son, "He's twenty-one, he's sick, and he have to live outside on the street again."

In the billet, on an altar on the wall, a framed picture of a middle-aged lady is surrounded by traditional Buddhist offerings of joss sticks, fruit, and flowers. "I had a friend here in the PRPC, she go to America already," Hoa explains. "I don't know her very long, maybe three or four weeks. She know I don't have money, and she send me twenty dollars. You know, my mother die one year today. I am very happy I have money so I can make the offering.

Hoa's English, learned in Vung Tau bars and from a succession of American "husbands," though not grammatically perfect, is powerfully expressive. In recalling events of profound sadness, especially the departure of Mac, her first American husband, emotion often would choke her voice, and we'd switch to another topic to let the pain subside. In relating her treatment by the government after 1975, her bitterness was evident. In one instance, I asked how a policeman could be aware that her mother was sick. Her eyes narrowed and her voice tensed with contempt. "How he don't know?" she whispered. "They know everything you do."

Hoa: I am forty-three years old. I was born in Hai Duong, near Hanoi. My father was twenty-five years older then my mother, that's what my mother told me. When I was six months old, he died. In 1954, I went to Saigon with my mother and my older brother.

I went to school only two years, but I don't like it. When I come home, my brother ask me questions about the lesson. If I don't know, he hit me, so I don't want to go to school no more. I was very stubborn, so my mother take me to help her sell at the market. I can read Vietnamese, but write not so much.

I help my mother in the market until I was about sixteen. We sell fish, rice, many things. Then I go to work in bar, Melody Bar, in Vung Tau. I have a friend, she live behind my house, she go to Vung Tau to work. She say she make *bu cu* money. She say she only sit in bar for drink with man, and she don't do nothing. So I go and work bar together with her.

I never tell my mother nothing. I just left the house and didn't come back. I couldn't tell her that I was going to work bar, she be ashamed. She looked for me in too many places, she never know where I go. At the bar, so many people come, everybody is happy. I liked that. I didn't think about my mother, I was too young, I didn't understand.

The customers were all American GI's. They buy the girls Saigon tea, and they drink whiskey or something like that. If one Saigon tea be . . . how much . . . I forget, sixty dong maybe, I get forty. Saigon tea is tea and *titi* whiskey. Sometime, if I drink too many I get drunk. That's no good, I don't like that. Some don't care what I drink, but some men they taste the tea. If there is no whiskey, they don't pay, because tea is free in the bar. So they put in whiskey, and sometime I get drunk.

Saturday, Sunday, I drink many, many Saigon tea, because too many people come to Vung Tau then. They work all week and Saturday take holiday, and they have much money and buy me many Saigon tea.

You know, I work bar about two years before I have boyfriend. I be a "cherry" girl, I sit down and drink Saigon tea. I don't go in the back, I don't do nothing. I don't go home with the man. Some girls, if they want to go, they go, but I just drink Saigon tea. Too many "cherry girls" before, they go to school in the daytime, nighttime they work bar, talk to GI, don't go to bed with the men. It's not the same now. Every night you have to sleep with the man. Before, many girls, they just talk. If the man want to go home with us, we say, "No, cannot go," and we bring him to another girl that does that. I be "cherry girl" then, just sixteen or eighteen, and I never have no man.

In the bar we wear mini dress, very sexy, but we don't do nothing. We just sit and talk. Some men know that, some don't know. If it be first time you see me, maybe you don't ask me to sleep with you. Maybe three or four times you come, then you ask me. I say, "If you want to sleep with girl, I take you to another girl. She go sleep with you, but not me, I cannot." You ask me why, I say, "I cannot because I never sleep with a man. Just sit down and talk, okay; but for love, I cannot do."

There were many bars in Vung Tau. In my bar, mostly white men come, but some bars it was mostly black. I go to work at five-thirty. The man come, he say, "What are you drinking?" I say, "Saigon tea," and I sit together with him. Then he ask, "What's your name, how old are you, how long you work here, you have boyfriend?" something like that. When I first went to work, I didn't know how to speak English. My friend tells me what to say, but I forget all the time. The first day I be very nervous, scared. I don't know nothing, I just laugh. But everyday I listen, and I learn a little.

I come five-thirty and stay till eleven-thirty or twelve. Every two weeks I get paid one time, but only for the Saigon tea that the men order for me, not salary. Still, the money's good. Sometime a man gives me money, a tip, just for talking with him. The bar knows that I don't sleep with the man, so they don't get the money that he give me. I keep that all. When you sleep with man, he buys a ticket, and then the bar gets money.

The girls all have to go to the doctor one week, one time. Even though I don't sleep with the men, I have to go. Everybody has to go. The police come to bar all the time. If you have ID to work in bar, you have to have it with you when you work. The bar pays the police to stay open. I don't know how much. If they give money, the police don't check bar every day. If they don't give, the police come, make trouble, check bar all the time, and arrest the girls.

I'm still a "cherry girl" when I go live with Mac. He be the first man I go home with, first man I sleep with. Too many men come, they want to live with me, but I don't like it, I be scared. I don't know how come, but I be scared. You know, every day too many people come to bar. I sit down with too many people for sure, but only for friend, not for love.

Mac, he come to bar many time. I was about eighteen, he was twenty-six, I think. He's a white man, he be in the navy. He work on a ship, and when ship goes he must go too, but when the ship comes back, he changes clothes and comes right over to bar to see me. He tell me he have wife and baby in America. He tell me true, but I love him. I love him so much and I go live with him.

My mother never knew what I do. Very long time she don't see me, maybe two years. Then one man, he live behind my mother in Saigon, he sees me at beach with a GI. He don't say anything to me. I don't see him but he sees me. When I go home, he follows me, so he know my house, where I live. He goes and tells my mother, and my mother comes see me in Vung Tau, and she cry too much. She very angry because I go to work with man, with GI. And she see that I'm living with a GI, she don't like that. But the next day, she feel a little better, not so angry, because she sees Mac's a good man. He can't talk Vietnamese, but he be good, and my mother like him. He get very nervous when she come, he be shy.

So my mother goes back to Saigon. She be sad, but I stay together with Mac. I have only one boyfriend, him, and I stop working bar. I be pregnant, and I just stay home. When I work bar, I have too many boyfriends, but when I live together with a man, only one.

I stay with him one year and a half. We had a house, he pay every month. Sometime he must go on the ship, two weeks, three weeks, one month. He give me money when he go, he's very good. But he never told me when he go home to America. He knows, he's very sad, but he don't say. *[At this point, Hoa is overcome and must stop for quite some time.]*

He don't tell me nothing, he just cry all the time, he be very sad. I ask him, why he cry, but he don't say. I think he just go on boat two weeks, three weeks, and come back, same as other times. At this time I be pregnant, and I go to the hospital to have my baby son. After born my baby son, I come home. I stay home three weeks, and Mac don't come home yet. One day my baby pee in bed, so I take off the mattress, and I see a letter and money, too much money. I cannot read the letter, so I take it to one friend to read. The letter says that he's sorry that he cannot say before he go, he cannot tell me, but he must leave. He very sad, but he cannot do anything because he have wife and baby in his country. I cry so much, because he never will come back anymore. He work in navy three years already, so he's finished, he will never come back. This be the first time I live together with a man, that I love a man, and I want to die.

I went back to Saigon to see my mother, but I didn't stay there long because people they see me, they say, "Whore, have baby American, no have husband." Every day when I go out they say that. If I have Vietnamese baby [and no husband], it's not that bad, but an American baby... Everybody know that I work bar. If I don't work bar, how can I have an American baby? They don't like that. Finally, I get tired of them calling me names, so I go back to Vung Tau. In Vung Tau they don't say anything because there be too many bars there. Too many women have American babies.

I stay home and look after my baby, but I'm so depressed, I start to gamble, to play cards, and I lose all the money Mac give me. He leave me so much money, "bu cu" money, and I lost it all. I just want to die, but I have a baby, so I cannot.

I never got a letter from Mac. I had his address in America, but when VC come, I must throw away everything. I never wrote because he have wife and two babies. I don't want to make trouble for him, I don't want his wife to know about me. If his wife knows, it's no good for him, see.

Six months after Mac left, I went back to Melody Bar to work. This time I don't just drink Saigon tea. I go home with the man because I have baby already. I'm not "cherry girl" anymore. If a man want to take me home between five and eleven, he have to pay the bar . . . I forget . . . about twenty dollars. I get about twelve dollars. After eleven, he don't pay the bar, because I finish work already. I finish work, I go home, he come later. Nobody know, so I tell him to do that. Sometime a man work a long way from Vung Tau, fighting the VC. He come from the battlefield, he have so much money, so he give me a lot. Some of these men, they sleep, but they be scared, they have bad dreams. They yell, "VC come, VC come kill me." Some men, they be hurt. They have battle wounds from fighting the VC.

If I like a man, I go with him. If I don't like, I don't go. It's up to me. Only American men, never Vietnamese men. The men are very nice, they're okay, but if they drunk I don't go with them. They are not good the same as my boyfriend, but I go with them for money, not for love.

When I go back to work, I have somebody come to take care of my baby son. But when he was a little more than one year old, he drink milk and throw up, he cannot keep it down. I take him to the doctor, but after one week he die. I never know what's wrong with him. He just die.

I go back to work bar, and I meet my second husband. His name Phil, he's also a white man, about twenty-six. He be army, he works as an airplane mechanic. I meet him in the bar, and I live with him for eight months. He go America for one month and come back, then he stay another six months. I get pregnant, and his mother know I'm pregnant. She write me a letter. She wants me to write her a letter, me, not him. I don't know how to write, so I talk, and Phil write. You know, Phil be good, I like him, but I can't love anybody anymore after Mac. I be too hurt.

I have one son with Phil, and when he go to America he want to take me, but I don't want to go. You know, I hear he have many girlfriends. I hear, but I don't see, and I don't like that. I think, if I go with him to America, and he bring another girl home, what can I do? I be by myself, it's not my country. My friends talk about that, so I be scared, I don't go. I don't want my baby to see that, that his father have many girlfriends. He want to take baby to America, but I say "No, baby must stay with his mother." So he go to America, he write me many letters, ask me to go to him. His mother write me letters too, she know I have his son. But I don't go, I be afraid.

When Phil go home, I went back to work in the bar. After one year, I met another American, a black man, his name Lee. He work CID *[Criminal Investigation Division]* in Long Binh. You know CID? Sometime you go black market, and he go behind you and he get you. You do something wrong, he get you. He come to see me every Saturday, and Sunday he go back to Long Binh. He know I have baby son, but he don't care. He love my son, he bring him presents. He don't like that I leave my baby son with mama-san. He say if I don't love my baby, how can other people love my baby? He make me stay home and take care of the baby.

Lee left Vietnam in 1972. He went back to America very fast. One day, they say he have to go right away, and he go. When he left, I was pregnant with my daughter Loan.

He write me letters, and his mother write me letters too. She know I have his baby. They want me to go to America, but I don't want to go. You see, I have a baby boy with Phil, my second husband, but I don't go with him to America, so how can I go with Lee?

I had one baby boy from Mac. Then Mac go home, and I don't have any husband. Then my baby die, and I don't have baby or husband. Then with second husband, Phil, I have another baby son, he be white. Then I have daughter with Lee, the third husband. She's a black girl. If I go to America, what Lee's mother think, that I have one white son and one black daughter? What American people say? What his family think of me? So I cannot go, you see.

In 1972 the bars in Vung Tau closed, because no more GI's. But there were still Americans in Saigon and bars. I went back to Saigon and worked in a bar at Tu Do Street. Mostly Americans come to the bar, some Vietnamese too, but not too many. I worked there until '75, when the VC come.

You know, I never had a Vietnamese boyfriend. Many come and asked me to live together with them, but I don't want to. I don't like Vietnamese men. When I was thirteen years old, I live at home, and my friend live next door. Every day I see her husband hit her and hit her. I don't like that. Many Vietnamese men do that. So I go work in bar. I have GI boyfriend, they treat me very good.

In 1975 the VC come. Life is very hard. I want to be good, I want to sell something and look after my baby and my mother, but they don't let me do that, you see. If I sell something, the police come, he take my things. He don't give them back to me, and he don't give me money. Many times he do that, and what can I do? Even now in Vietnam, if I sell inside, all right, but if I sell outside, they don't like. You have to have money to give to the police. If you don't, you have problems. I don't have nothing to give to him, so he take my things. Not only me, many people's things, he take. But if you can pay him, he leave you alone.

If you can make six or seven thousand dong in one day, sometimes ten thousand, it's all right, but some days I don't make nothing. I have mother and babies, see. I have to pay for house, I have to pay someone to look after my baby. How can I pay for school, how can I give them something? So I can't pay off the police, and some days he come and take all my things. And when he take, I don't have money to buy again.

It's a little easier now than before, than in '75. I think if VC don't loosen up they be scared the people revolt against them. You know, when the VC come, they take people's houses away, and they send the people away very far, into the country [the New Economic Zones]. They say that they give you a house there, but they don't give. They say they give food, but they give only for three months, then no more. What can you do, how can you live?

The VC police, they know I have American babies. A policeman come to my house at night many times and make me go to the station, and he talk, he say listen to me. He say that I have to say that Americans come to Vietnam to take my country. He say that Americans say they want to do good, but inside they are no good, they always want to get my country. But I say, "That's not true, because I live with American and he don't do that. He don't do what you thinking. Always he be good, he help too many people." But VC say, "No, you lie." He want me to change my mind, and he gets very angry. But you see, I live with Americans, I know many Americans, they be good.

Sometime it would be only me at the station, sometime there would be many women there. I have to go there four or five times a week, seven o'clock at night. Whoever changes their mind, says "American, no good," okay, they can go home, so some people just say that so they can be left alone, so they can leave. But I can't say that. I don't care what I am, I don't want to say that because I live together with Americans. I have two American babies, so how can I say that?

They talk about Ho Chi Minh. They say he is so good because he work very hard and he don't need no money, he only want to help people. But I say, "I'm not sure, I never saw him, so how can I say anything about him?" So VC get very angry, and one night, at about two o'clock, when I was sleeping, he come to my house and take me to the monkey house [jail, reeducation camp]. He don't even tell me where they take me, and my family, they don't know where I go.

The VC tell us that we would only go to school for ten days and then go back home. That's what they say to all the women that have American husbands or work for the Americans. They say you have to change your mind, don't think about Americans no more. But when we come to the monkey house, we have to stay for three, four, five, even eight years. Yeah, ten days, that's what they say, but they take me go for more than two years.

For the first five months, they keep me in the monkey house in Saigon. They put me in a small room with many people. They give me one glass of water for a day. Sometime for three or four days, no water for shower. We are always very dirty. They want you to change, see. I never change, always I say that.

In my cell, there be almost a hundred people. Some are same as me, work with Americans, live together with Americans. Every day, morning and night the police come, and they tell us to read the book about Ho Chi Minh and talk about Ho Chi Minh. They want us to change our minds. I cannot read too well. Sometime I look, because if you don't look they hit you. Yeah, they hit, too much sometimes. He ask me question, and I don't know, and he hit me because I look with my eyes, but inside I don't look.

All day we stay in the cell. We can't see nothing, there are no windows. It's so hot it makes you crazy. Many people get sick, but they don't give no medicine. Some die. We are all so dirty. They don't care what happens to us. They think, if we dead, they happy. We are lower than dogs, they want to see us dead. They tell us, "Okay, now call the Americans to come and help you."

If you change your mind, they let you go out and work, and that's not too bad. But if you don't, they keep you inside. I don't go out, they don't let me. I don't know how come I can't say that I change my mind. I think it's because I have two American babies. If not, maybe I can say I change.

After three months, they let me write a letter, and then my mother came to see me. For many months, she was very sad because she don't know where they take me. Two months later, they sent me to labor camp. Many went, not only me. They put many people on a big truck, and it's covered, so we cannot see where they take us. We ride for many hours with no food or water.

They take us to this place, it's a prison camp. We sleep in houses, all prisoners, fifty people in one house. We work all day, and seven o'clock to nine o'clock at night we read Ho Chi Minh. Police want me to hate Americans. If he don't change my mind, he say he shoot me. He keep me there for a long time, he say. I never see my babies again, he tell me that.

We must wake up four A.M. They don't give us no food. Five o'clock we go walking to work and six o'clock start work. Twelve o'clock they give us some food. We get rice only three or four days, very bad rice, "titi" rice. The other days just manioc or sweet potato . . . no good. Five o'clock we walk back and six o'clock we get back to camp. They don't give you shoes, and you get these things, leeches all over your feet. So many leeches there and mosquitoes. I get many cuts and infections, and I get sick all the time, but I don't say nothing. If you say you sick, they say you lie, and they hit you.

Sometime we try to eat leaves in the forest, but if the guards catch you, they will beat you hard. If they get angry, they put you in a metal box. It's burning hot in the day, cold at night in there. You cannot stand, you cannot sit, only squat. Sometime they keep you in there for three days. They don't give you food or water. If you have friend in the police, he can slip "titi" water to you at night, okay, but if you don't, you die for sure. If you don't eat for three days it's all right, but if you don't have water, maybe die soon. Easy to die, many die. They never put me in there, because I didn't make them angry. When they say work, I work. They hit me sometimes. When they ask me about Ho Chi Minh, I don't remember and they hit me, but they don't put me in the box.

There are men prisoners there too, but they don't live near us. They live a long way away. Most are ex–ARVN soldiers. Some men, they work for Americans before. The VC make the men work harder than the women. Many die, too many die.

The guards are very mean. They think they are big, and we are nothing. They don't care if you die. . . . They say if you die they very happy. If a dog die, they sad, but if we die, they happy. They say like that, yeah. We don't mean nothing to them. A dog is worth more than people.

Sometime when I sleep, two o'clock, four o'clock in the morning, I hear shooting, and I know someone trying to escape. But if they don't shoot you and they find you, wow, they hit you very much, sure. Some people get away, but many they get back. They beat them so hard, very, very bad. And they take you to go in the metal box. Women, they hit not so much, but if it's a man, they beat him terrible. If he don't die now, he die later for sure because he be very hurt inside.

I try to escape one time, but they catch me. Me and three other people. Twelve o'clock at night we go, but we don't know the way. Five o'clock in the morning we wind up in the same place where we leave from. We get very lost. This happens many times. Sometime people go in the forest and two or three days later they wind up back. When you are in the jungle, you cannot see anything, you just walking.

The guards, they know the area, but we don't know. They know where the prisoners go when they escape. It's very easy for them to get you. They catch us, but my friend, she tell us, "I don't have baby, if they beat me all right; if they kill me, all right. But you have a baby, you must live." So she tell the guards that she is the one who made us go. We say, "Don't do that," but she do it anyway. So for us it's not so bad, but for her, the guards beat her very bad. They hit her so much, and I worry that she die. She don't die, but when they let me go home, they still keep her there in the prison camp.

My mother in Saigon, she get very sick. My babies, they don't have nothing to eat, no house to live. The guard he call me and tell me that I can go home, but he say that when my mother is finish sick, I have to go back to monkey house again.

[I ask how the police could know that her mother was sick.]

The police that took me to the monkey house, he know. How he don't know? The police in Vietnam, they know everything you do. They tell me I have to go back to jail when my mother finish being sick, but she don't finish. She never get well, and I never go back. But when I leave monkey house, the police don't give me no paper to live in Saigon, so I always be afraid.

I go back to Saigon, and I try to sell things, but I don't have money to buy rice to sell. If you have money, you can buy and then sell. But if you don't have money, you cannot. So what can I do? I have to go sleep with Vietnamese man to get money. I don't have no house. I don't have no money to pay for a house, so I go out and live on the street with my mother and my two babies.

See, before, when I be young, I come to Saigon from Hanoi with my mother. We don't have house. We live with my aunt, my mother's younger sister. Later, when I be working, I have so much money, she love my baby very much. I am the only one to make money, and I look after all my family, twenty-two people. But when I go to the monkey house for two years, I don't have money, and my aunt speak no good to my baby. She don't want an American baby in the house, she afraid of trouble with the VC. My mother took my babies to see me in jail. They very skinny. My mother say

that she don't want to live with my aunt anymore, so she went out to live
on the street. When I have money, my aunt, she love my babies. When I
go to jail and I'm broke, she throws them out on the street.

From 1976, till I came here to PRPC, I live on the street. Not many
people there, just me and my family. If it rains, we go to a house of a friend
and wait. Rain stop, we go back on the street. We sleep on the street, cook
on the street. My mother got sick, she go blind. She was sick for five years.
She lay down on the street, died on the street too. No good, my life.

You know, my brother, he's married, he live far from Saigon. When
my mother get sick, she wants him. She can't see anymore, she's blind, but
she wants to touch him, hear his voice. Six years my mother don't see him,
she says, "Please go get him." So I borrow money and send my son to get
him. My brother come, but he stay only two days, then he go back. The
next week my mother die. After my mother die, I don't say anything to him.
I never see him again because I feel very angry at him. All the time my
mother be sick, he never look after her. Only I take care of her. He's no
good, I don't like him.

When I work bar, and I born baby son, my mother come to see me.
My brother don't come because I have baby, but no husband. He don't like
that I work bar, he say I be whore. So one year, I have so much money, I
go to see him, but he still be angry. He don't want to see me. I don't care,
he's no good.

We live on the street, my family. There was water not too far away.
I wash up there and bring my babies to wash. I cook on the street. We sleep
on the street. Sometime at night, a man see my daughter sleeping, he come
up and bother her, touch her. My daughter get very upset and she cry.

I sell fish to make money, I make love to man for money, but I never
have enough money. But still, I send my babies to school, I want my babies
to go to school. My daughter went to school six years, my boy eight years.
My son is white, he don't have too many problems. Some he have, but not
too many. My daughter, she black, and she have trouble. My daughter had
fights three or four times. They say, "You black, you dirty." She not dirty,
but they say that, and she be angry, you know. I tell her if you don't say
nothing, it's all right. You keep in school, it's good for you. So many times,
she don't want to go because someone say something to her, and she be shy.
But I say, go back to school. She study only six years, then she has to work,
get money. When my mother get sick, I can't do anything, I have to take
care of her. So my babies have to go to work and can't finish school.

My children went looking for jobs, but people see they are American,
and they don't let them work. Finally they get jobs. My son Phi, he go to
work as a porter. My daughter makes handles for teapots in a small factory.
The work be very hard, and the money very little, maybe six thousand dong
one day. She get sick all the time, and we have no money for doctor.

Phi couldn't come with us to the PRPC. He got sick a month before I left. He smoke too much. One week before we come here, he go to doctor. The doctor says he's sick, his lungs are bad. He have to stay in Vietnam and take medicine. Every day he go to the Orderly Departure Program doctor, but don't pay money. I hope he will finish taking medicine and come here soon.

He's twenty-one, he's sick, and he have to live outside on the street again. He can't go to the Amerasian center in Dam Sen because that's only for people who live far from Saigon. If you are from Saigon, you cannot live there.

Now my son can't work nothing. Before he work very hard, he can lift sixty kilos, even a hundred kilos. But now he don't work, he can't. Sometime I can't sleep, I can't study. I think about my baby, sick, with no money, living on the street.

I never got married again *[after the Americans left Vietnam]*. I be very scared. What if I have Vietnamese husband and I have more children? What they think of my black baby girl? You see, if you love me, you must love my baby. I don't want to make no problem for my baby. If I have no husband, it's all right.

It's harder for black than white in Vietnam. I have black baby and white baby, so I know. I think your country be same. Before, when I go work bar, if too many blacks come to American bar, no whites come. If too many whites come, the blacks don't come. They go to a different bar. I think in your country be same.

I had black husband and white husband. I think they be same, good men. My black husband, he know I have *[white]* baby son, right? He still live with me, it don't mean nothing. He love my baby so much. When he come, every Saturday, he bring many things for baby. He's good man. He see I have a white baby, but he love me and my baby too. If he don't like my baby, I don't live with him.

My two American babies, they had many problems before, but now no. Before, Vietnamese say, "You go back to America, you dirty American, go back to America. You lose the war already, go back." They say like that many times to my daughter, 'cause she is black. My son is white, not so many problems. Now Amerasian children can go America, so Vietnamese like Amerasians. Before, nobody likes Amerasian babies. Now everybody wants to stay with Amerasian so they can go to America too.

My daughter is black, but not so dark. Her father, Lee, had a black father, but his mother was white. One day here in the PRPC, she come home from school very sad, she don't eat. I say how come you don't eat. She say she upset because teacher tell her that America same as Vietnam, they don't like black people. She think that when she go to America, things change. She don't hear "black, black" anymore. But no, teacher say America be same as Vietnam, people think that black is no good. Now she worry that American people won't like her because she is black, just like in Vietnam.

Before, she say to me, "How come you have black husband, why couldn't you have white husband, so my skin not be black?" When she say like that, I feel very sad because I love my daughter very much.

In 1984, I make the paper for my family to go to America through ODP. But they *[Vietnamese government officials]* make me wait for a long time because I don't have any money to pay bribe. My daughter, she work so hard, but she only make six thousand dong a day. My mother, she's sick, we live on the street, no money for a house. In 1990, we be waiting six or seven years already. A man come, he tell me, "I know someone who can help you pay money to go to America." I wait seven years already, so I say okay. So one man, he come, he pay the money for bribe, and we write on our papers that he is my daughter's husband. But he's really not, he just pay the money so we say that.

So he come here with us, and he live here with us, but he's not really my daughter's husband. When we go to America we will not stay together.

My daughter wants to go to America very quick because she don't like living in the house with this man. She knows he have money, but he don't want to buy anything for the house. She don't like to look at him. When he be home, she goes out. When we eat, we never eat together. She don't like him, she don't like to look his face.

The food they give us here is very bad. Sometime I cannot eat it, it makes me sick. But when we have to buy something, he say he don't have any money, and my daughter be very angry.

Here in the PRPC, we go to school every day, but sometime in school I can't think. I worry about my son in Vietnam. I worry about what I do in the United States. I don't know where I go in America, I don't know what I do in your country. I just don't know. When I get there, if I can, I go to work. I just want to have a job, make money and live together with my children, take care of them. If I have a job, any job, it's all right.

Loan is Hoa's nineteen-year-old black Amerasian daughter. Her complexion is "cafe con leche," her long hair thick and curly, pulled back and held with a barrette. She is painfully shy and soft spoken, and I hesitated to tape our conversations until we had developed an easy rapport.

Loan told her story with the aid of an interpreter. There were moments of painful remembrance: her extreme poverty, her mother being taken away with no word. The edge of these memories sometimes overcame her, and I would back away at reopening unhealed wounds.

As in the case of other interviews I conducted with mothers and their children, in certain areas Loan and Hoa's stories did not completely coincide. One such area involves her mother Hoa's release from labor camp. Hoa maintains that she was given a temporary release because her own mother was ill and unable to care for Hoa's children. Loan, on the other hand, relates an almost supernatural tale of her mother escaping from the camp, one which she says was told to her Hoa herself. When I inquired about the discrepancy, Hoa told me that her daughter was very young when she returned from prison and had confused the story of Hoa's release with the details of her unsuccessful escape attempt. Hoa did, however, confirm the supernatural aspects of the near escape. Vietnamese in general have an abiding belief in the spirit realm and often attribute unusual or inexplicable occurrences to mystical intervention. My Vietnamese interpreter found nothing unusual in Loan's story of a one-legged apparition aiding her mother to pass through the gates of the prison camp; he only said that it "gave him the goose bumps."

Loan: I first realized that I was not Vietnamese when I was about seven, when I first went to school. Some people would call me names and taunt me because of my dark skin and American blood, but others treated me kindly. I always tried to be respectful to everyone, even the people who made fun of me, but my brother would fight if anyone called him *My lai* [Amerasian].

I was always very polite to my teachers. They knew that we were very poor and lived on the street, and they let me study in grammar school, even when I had no money. In secondary school, we were not able to do that. When we had no money, I could not study there. We were so poor, I felt embarrassed making friends, socializing with people. I was ashamed of our poverty.

I never lived in a house until I came here. I spent my whole life on the street. We lived by the steps of an apartment building on Ngo Gia Tu street in Ho Chi Minh City, my mother, my brother, my old grandmother, and me. My aunt, she was my grandmother's sister, had an apartment in the building. I would shower and get water there. My aunt had more than ten children, so the apartment was very crowded. She was a drinker. When she didn't drink she was okay, but when she got drunk she became very mean, and there would be arguments. There was always trouble between her and my mother. One time my mother brought my grandmother, who was blind, to the apartment to shower. My aunt was drunk, and she yelled, "Get that blind woman out of my apartment. You are bringing me bad luck." We waited for my aunt to fall asleep, and then we went back to get water to wash my grandmother. When my aunt was sober, she was all right to us, but when she was drunk, she was terrible, and she was drunk a lot. My mother would help pay for the electricity when she could, when she had work; but when she had no work she could not do that. We all had to scrape together the money any way we could.

It rains from May to October. If it started to rain while we slept, we would have to wake up, gather our belongings, and stand under an overhang. We'd put mats on our heads to keep off the rain and wait for it to stop. Then we would clean off our spot on the street as best we could and try to go back to sleep. If it rained in the day, we would go to the aunt's house, but at night we had to wait it out on the street. If it rained all night, we had to stand under the overhang all night. If it was just rain, it was not so bad, but if there was wind as well, we would get soaked. There was nothing we could do.

When things were okay between my mother and my aunt, we could cook in my aunt's apartment. But when they were arguing, we had to cook on the street. We were so poor, sometimes we had no rice, nothing to cook. Most of the people in my aunt's apartment building knew us, and sometimes they would help us out with some food. They knew what our situation was. But sometimes bad people would steal food or our things when we were on the street. We lived on the street so long that eventually we got used to it.

In 1982 my mother went to prison camp. One time she received a summons to go to the police station, and she didn't come back. They didn't tell us where she was, for months we didn't know. I was just a young girl then. *[Loan begins to weep at the memory of these difficult times, and we pause until she is able to go on.]* We just stayed in Saigon, my grandmother and my brother and me.

After a few years, my mother escaped from the labor camp. This is the story she told me. There was a man with one leg who died in the labor camp. Sometimes he would appear, and he had the power to make the prisoners invisible. They could pass through the gates and not be seen by the guards. So my mother saw this apparition, and she was able to pass through the gates without being seen by the guards. My mother and her friend were running through the forest, and they stopped to rest. They got separated from the rest of the group. All of a sudden there was a loud noise, and they didn't know what had happened. They never saw the people in the front again. My mother and her friend prayed very hard, you have to pray in that forest because it is populated by many ghosts, ghosts of prisoners killed while trying to escape. You have to propitiate the spirits. Maybe the people in front of my mother did not pray hard enough, because nobody knows what happened to them.

When my mother was sent to labor camp, they rubbed her name out of the family book. Without that, you cannot legally live or work in Saigon, so she was very scared about being arrested again, and she tried to be very careful. She tried to work buying and selling, but it was hard to make any money.

I worked in a small place that made aluminum handles for tea kettles. I carried sacks of handles up a ladder to the second floor of the house and used a machine to smooth the handles. It was very hard work, and the money was bad. I worked seven to eleven-thirty in the morning and one to four in the afternoon. Saturday was a half day. The boss was okay, but his wife was out of her mind. She was the one who paid us, and sometimes she would go into a rage, and we couldn't get paid. We would have to come back later to get our salary. Sometime the owner would be short and we wouldn't get paid on time, though he always eventually made good. After three years I quit, the pay was just too low. Just after I quit, the place went out of business, and they had to sell off all their tools and machines.

We made our application in 1984 to come to America. The government lost it, and we made it again in 1990. This man, who is here as my "husband," came to us and said, "You have been waiting a long time to go to America. I can help you go faster if you take me with you. I will bribe the officials to let us go quickly."

He gave some gold to my family in Vietnam, and he paid the bribe and took care of everything. After that, we were able to leave Vietnam very quickly. So we got married, but just for him to come to America and pay the bribes to the Vietnamese officials. He is not really my husband.

My grandmother was sick, and in 1991 she died on the patch of street where we lived. We made a service on the street. She was buried in Ba Giao cemetery. *[Loan takes out some photos of her grandmother's funeral and describes them.]* My mother wore a white cloth around her head, a sign of mourning. The women wearing a white headband with a red dot in the middle, they are nieces of the dead. Nieces and nephews wear a white headband with a red dot. The man wearing a white hat, he is the nephew, taking the place of the son who was not there. There are offerings of fruit and joss sticks. We have paper money for the dead so they have something to spend, and musicians play the *dan gao [a Vietnamese stringed instrument]*.

Sometimes I feel depressed here. I have no money. I am eager to work, but there is nothing to do. I worry about what my life will be in America. I don't want to wind up on the street like in Vietnam.

Postscript: *Loan and Hoa left the PRPC for Houston on a gray humid day in July. Her family was sponsored by a local resettlement agency. For them, as for all the refugees, departure was a time of mixed feelings. It had been eight years since Hoa first applied to leave Vietnam to go to the States; she had waited a long time. Now that America loomed so close, however, it seemed terrifying.*

The PRPC departure area was crowded that day. A group of Amerasian kids were sprawled on the cement floor of the waiting shed, playing cards. Clusters of families and friends formed small enclaves, talking, crying, saying goodbye. I found Hoa with a group of her friends. They had been waiting for me to come to snap some photos.

Hoa was preoccupied. "What I do in your country?" she asked. "I can't read, I can't write, I never go to school. What I do there, how I get money? I will work anything to take care of my babies, but what can I do?" Her main concern was not to wind up on the street again.

Hoa told me that her son Phi was scheduled to arrive in the PRPC in a few weeks. Her sons's welfare was another worry, and one over which she had no control.

Names were being called for the refugees to have their predeparture physicals. Hoa and her daughter lined up, and we said our good-byes. "When I get to Houston, I find somebody write letter for me. I write you for sure," she assured me, but I haven't heard from her since.

Lan and Trung

"I hope that the first American I meet is my daddy."

"'If I see my father one time, that's enough, then I can die.' That's what he says." Lan is speaking about her son Trung's consuming passion. "He wants to find his father," she continues. "But he won't let me see him. He says he wants his father to remember the beautiful young girl he fell in love with, not the old lady I am now."

The "old lady" is a graceful and attractive woman of forty-four. Her English, virtually unused since her days as a secretary with the Civilian Personnel Office at the First Marine Division base in Da Nang, is still remarkably functional and descriptive; she rarely falters as we speak. Lan is not her real name, but the nickname by which Peter, Trung's father, called her, and she requested that I use it in her narrative.

We met in her billet for three consecutive evenings in the days before she was to leave the Philippine Refugee Processing Center for the United States. The Philippines was experiencing one of its frequent power shortages, and we often spoke by the smokey flame of a kerosene lamp, blindly swatting at the ubiquitous mosquitoes. Trung was frequently present, sitting on the floor next to his mother's stool, straining to catch any familiar word in the language of his father. Occasionally he would enter the conversation, and Lan would translate his Vietnamese into English.

Lan asked that I not record our conversation, and for two evenings, I obligingly took down her words in a small blue notebook. The final day of our conversations, in sympathy with the frustrations of note taking in the dim light, she graciously agreed to let me tape her story.

If you look carefully along the bridge of his nose, you might discern a slight Asian cast to Trung's features. Otherwise, his appearance is that of a handsome Caucasian in his early twenties. The ostracization he felt as a result of his white skin and round eyes has intensified his desire to search for his American father. Trung was conceived through a relationship his mother had with Peter, an

177

American soldier, at a time when her marriage to a Vietnamese army officer had dissolved. Shortly after Trung's birth, Lan and her husband reunited, and they have remained together, although Lan characterizes their marriage as "without love." They came to the PRPC along with two of their three children and Trung.

Lan's husband accepted Trung as his son, and he is the only father Trung has ever known, but Lan comments, "For Trung, it is not enough. More than anything he wants to know his American father."

Lan: I am really forty-three, but I appear a year older on my documents. I had to change them in order to get a job with the U.S. marines.

In 1965 my father died in an auto accident. That same year I went to see my uncle in Da Nang during the summer vacation. My uncle's friend took me over to an agency in order to apply for a job with the Americans. I made an appointment for the test, and then I went back to Hue, my hometown, to ask my mother's permission. She agreed, and I got the job and went to work as a secretary for the Civilian Personnel Corps at the First Marine Division base at Da Nang.

Hue is beautiful, the most beautiful city in Vietnam. Many of Vietnam's presidents are from there, like President Diem, and many kings were born there. I would have loved to stay there, but work was in Da Nang, so I had to go, and my whole family moved with me.

We stayed with my uncle for a year, and then with the salary I made at the base I bought a small house for my family. My mother went back to Hue and sold our family house. After three years, I got a promotion, and I bought a bigger house. Our life was good, I received a high salary. I worked as a secretary for the marines. When they pulled out in 1971, the army came, and I worked as a secretary for them. When they left in '72, I went to work for MACV *[Military Assistance Command, Vietnam]*.

Most of the military men I worked with were officers. They got along very well with the Vietnamese, they really knew how to treat them. First I thought that these men were very intelligent, but now I realize they must have had special training on how to act with Asian people.

In my job, I went around a lot. I went to the the Finance Department to pick up payroll, to the Civilian Personnel Office, many places. Sometimes I went out to the villages and hamlets as part of the Civil Affairs Program. We would hand out medicines, see the hamlet chief, go to celebrations. The captain and the colonel would go, and I would go along as the translator. The CO's driver, Peter Stephen Elwood *[not a real name]*, drove me to all these places. We were always together, and we got to be good friends. One day we had a bad argument. He came to my office to apologize, but it turned out to be more than an apology and that day we became lovers.

In 1970, when Peter left to go back to the United States, I was three months pregnant. When he left, he told me that he hoped the baby would be a son, and it was.

I received two letters from Peter, but I never answered them. Shortly after he left, I found out that he was married. I know his wife's name, it's Linda. I didn't want to write, I didn't want to cause Linda heartache.

I was married before I met Peter, to a Vietnamese man, and already had two children by him. He worked as a male nurse. But even before I got to know Peter, I had split with that husband. We weren't getting along, and then I heard that he had some other girlfriends. I never saw anything, but I heard about it. Little by little I got angrier and angrier, I don't know what came over me. Eventually we separated. But you know, three days after I gave birth to my Amerasian son, he came back to me and he is still with me now. He has been a good father to our children and to Trung, my Amerasian son. He is the only father Trung has ever known, but for Trung, this is not enough. Trung, more than anything, wants to know his American father.

Even though my husband is good to my children, we don't love each other. There is no feeling between us. I am Catholic, so we cannot divorce. He was Buddhist, but he became Catholic too. I know it's difficult to believe that if you don't love a man, you still must live together, even if you have no happiness, but I am Catholic, and that's what I believe. I must stay with him even if he brings me no joy, even if we argue, even if we don't love each other. He treats my children well, he treats my Amerasian son well, but between us there is nothing.

In '75 we escaped from Da Nang, in March. There were so many rockets, and the Communists dropped letters saying that they were going to take Da Nang. I had to get out because I had worked for the American military and was raising an Amerasian son.

At that time, there were rocket attacks day and night. We had to move out by a big Vietnamese military boat, evacuating many people on to Saigon. My whole family was on the boat, my husband, my children, my brothers and sisters, and my mother. On the way, the commander of the boat got the order to go back to Da Nang to pick up some more refugees, so he stopped the boat at Cam Ranh base and dropped everybody off there. Cam Ranh was under southern control and supposed to be safe.

We were there about five hours, trying to get any transportation to leave for Phan Thiet, and then on to Saigon. Before we could get out, there was a rocket attack, so many rockets. We ran away, tried to hide. But who knows, we cannot tell who are the Communists and who are the people from the south. We ran like chickens, one over the other, this way and that, looking for a place to hide. Bombs were exploding everywhere, people were dying. It was terrible, terrible. I can't even think how long it went on, I was too scared to know. I was carrying my youngest son and two of my brothers ran after me. My youngest sister ran after my mother to help her. My daughter and my oldest son ran after my brothers. When the rockets stopped, I was together with my brothers and my three of my children, but I was separated from my mother and Amerasian son. I couldn't find them anywhere, and I didn't know where my husband was. I thought they had been killed.

Two days later my husband found us. He had gotten on land transportation to Phan Thiet, and when I got there he was already there. Still, we had not found my mother or Trung, my American son, and presumed them to be dead. From Phan Thiet to Vung Tau we took a boat, a fishing boat. We had nothing. We lost everything in the bombing. But I had some gold bracelets on my arms, and I used two of them to pay for the boat.

We got to Vung Tau and stayed one night. Then we took a bus to Saigon. There we stayed with my uncle for eight months. He took care of my family, he's rich. We found out my husband's sister was living in My Tho city in Tien Giang province, and we went to live there.

One day in 1980, my aunt, she's a Catholic nun, visited my uncle in Saigon, and he told her that I was in My Tho. She came to see me, and told me that she had seen my mother and son, they were living in Phuoc Long. All this time, five years, we thought they had been killed in the bombing at Cam Ranh, and they thought we had been killed, but after Cam Ranh they had followed some neighbors to Phuoc Long and were living there.

Phuoc Long is very rural, and My Tho is a town. In Vietnam, the government doesn't allow people to transfer from the countryside to the city. If you are in the city, you can move out the countryside, but if you are outside the city, you cannot move into the city. So Trung could only come for a visit, and we would go to Phuoc Long and visit him. We were so happy to find my mother and son alive . . . after five years thinking they were dead.

After I moved to My Tho, I got a job selling material at the city market. I started to be a vendor from there, and I earned enough money to take care of the family. Then I had my own material shop for two years, but the Communists came. They say that I cannot own that shop anymore, that I have to work for them. They came to inventory all my material, and they kept it. From then, I'm just their employee, and they pay me commission for what I sell. It was that way for two years until they gave the shop back to me. My salary was very low, they just gave me ten percent commission. I don't know why they do that, take my shop away like that. They are Communists. That's why we have to stay away from them. That's why so many people were so scared, so afraid when they heard about the Communists because everything we have, everything we make, is supposed to be theirs.

I don't argue with them. Nobody can argue with them. They may kill you, they may put you in jail. I must be very careful about what I say. Because to them I am the type of person who is dangerous. They don't trust me because I am the ex–U.S. employee. They know that.

They put me in jail for ten days in 1977. They tell us we have to be honest about telling our background. So I believe that they have my records, and they already found out I work for Americans. Or, I think that maybe my neighbors told them, or if not yet, they will tell them. So I rather tell them before my neighbor does, and I said that I worked for the Americans.

So I have to be what they call . . . brainwashed. That's the word that the Vietnamese people use in that case. How long they keep you, it depends on what job you had. If I was in investigation or security or in the military, that would be different. But, I am just a civilian employee, so they keep me only ten days. Also, a woman they don't keep as long as a man.

Jail is terrible, terrible. I cannot explain to you exactly how they treat us. I hope you know what a Communist jail is. At first they use a call slip to call me to report right away to the police. I receive the call slip two o'clock in the afternoon, and I have to be there about two-fifteen. They bring me to another office, to security. I have to sit there and write down, just like my résumé, my background. I have to tell them everything. And then about two hours later, after I finish my form, they tell me to sit and wait. Then I hear the chain, and they unlock the door of some cell near there, and they call me, and they tell me to walk in. And when I walk in, there are so many women already there, with so many different troubles, reasons to be there. I just go in, and I cannot carry anything with me. That's the prison rule. You just walk in and stay there. There are about thirty females in a room like this *[about eight feet by twenty feet]*. It's too narrow for us in the hot season. We can fit in, but just like fish, one next to another. We got just rice, no other food, and about a half gallon water for a day. It's very hot, and we cannot use mosquito net. If mosquito bites us, the Communists don't worry about it, nothing happens to them. I got a cold, a bad cold because of the weather. It's too hot and dirty. I cannot tell you just how dirty it was. Really terrible. When I get out of the prison, my friend ask me how it was, I say, "Terrible, that's the only word I can use."

They got a toilet, just a temporary toilet, not by cement, just a hole, and we don't have enough water to use to clean ourselves or flush after using it. So smelly, so bad. We have to save the water for face washing and tooth brushing.

Women there had many different problems. Some of them got caught stealing, some of them, I don't know how to use the word . . . taxi girl *[prostitute]*. When we get in, we were separated in different parts of the tiny cell. Girls like taxi girls be on one side, and when I get in, the chief of all these prisoners start to question me, and they find out who I am and they put me together with the type of person like me. I don't know what they think, but they put me with the clean people. I don't know why, but they separated into so many sections in the narrow place like that. The prisoners did that themselves. They give me a mat and say, you go over here and lie down. The chief, she's the kind of person who is so mean or so strong that she can tell the people what to do. Sometimes there is an argument, and she says "Shut up! Stop!" And the people listen. It's all females in that cell, but the guard is a male, Communist police. There are women police too, but they not in that prison.

In 1978 we tried to escape from Vietnam by fishing boat. I arranged the boat through one of my friends. One of her friends owned a boat, and they were planning to get out of Vietnam, so they came to see us. They trust us because they believe I want to go, I have to go. So they came to us. It's very dangerous if they ask the wrong person, they could go to jail. They ask me, and I pay them for the transportation—two bracelets. I had four on my arm. Two I used already from Phan Thiet to Vung Tau, and two I tried to keep. They were a present from my mother. But I spent them on that trip, and we didn't make it.

Two months after I gave the bracelets, we got on the boat. Somehow the police found out about it, and they took that boat away. So the police caught us, and I had to go to jail. I was supposed to be in jail for two years, but my husband paid them off, so I got out of jail in about twenty days.

Two years later I try again. I bought my own boat, but I could not keep it because I live in the city. So I asked some friends to keep it. They lived next to the river. Somehow, I don't know how, the police got the boat. Maybe the neighbors of my friends informed, I don't know. That time the boat was in the name of my oldest son because I had a big house. If my name was on the boat, I might lose the house if the police catch the boat. So they came to my house and searched it and found my son. He went to jail for about four months, and then I paid them off and got him out of jail. My daughter and my youngest son tried again. They got caught after four and a half days. They were already out at sea, and they got caught by a patrol boat but nothing happened to them because they were too young.

The South Vietnamese, they are not Communist, but they taunt the Amerasian, I don't know why. Maybe they act that way because they know the Communists don't like us, so they try to act like they on the Communist side, so the Communists will trust them. Or maybe they just jealous because we were the American employees before. We had the good life before the Communists took over. Not too many people could get a job with the

Americans because they couldn't speak English or they weren't educated. Or maybe they didn't get a job, and then the Americans already pulled out, and it was too late. So maybe they are jealous.

Vietnamese, especially little children, sometimes they are afraid of the black Amerasians. Maybe it's because their skin is so dark and their teeth are so white that the children get scared. I don't know. But for me there is no difference between the white and black, I don't discriminate.

You know, almost ninety-nine percent of people want to get out of Vietnam, but they got no way. So after the Amerasian program started and who has Amerasian children can go to America, they hate us because they are jealous of us.

Even up to the time we came here, Trung had trouble because of his American blood. Just before we left Vietnam, on the first day of Tet *[Vietnamese New Year]*, my family was sitting down, eating dinner. My house is in front of the road, so when everyone walk by, the trucks roll by, everybody can see us. This man just comes by my house. I don't know, maybe he's drunk, and he calls to my son *du ma My lai [mother fucker Amerasian]*. He stands outside the house yelling, and my son was inside the house. It's hard to believe, but it's true.

So my son goes outside and says to the man, "Why you call me that? I don't even know you." And they start talking, and pretty soon it was an argument. Then I get nervous and I tell the man to get away from my house. Two days later he came back with another man, but my son and myself were not at home. My neighbor told him, "Get out of here or I will call the police."

A few days later they came back for the third time, during lunch hour. My Amerasian son was there, and my youngest son too. And the guy brought a man with him that is also my youngest son's friend. My youngest son is stronger than his older brother, and he says to them, "Don't bother my brother, he didn't do anything to you. In fact, he doesn't even know you, so get away from us if you want to stay my friend. If not, we will kill you." But of course, we didn't let him do that. So I stopped them, and I asked the neighbor to call the police, and the police came and took them away.

When Trung was a young boy, he asked me why he is different, and I say to him, "You just be the way you are. You are a handsome boy, they be jealous. Don't blame anyone about the way you look."

In school and on the street, my son had problems. If he went around with his friends, he had problems. But he kept everything inside, so I didn't know much about it. You know until 1989, I could not get his name in my family book, so he had to stay with his grandmother in Phouc Long, though he come to visit me a lot. I know that in Phouc Long my son had problems because he is Amerasian, but he doesn't tell me, he keeps it to himself. Only now is he telling me what went on.

Trung: When I first started school, at about six or seven years old, I realized I was not Vietnamese because of the way others treated me. Vietnamese people always looked down on me. Even when I was young, I could feel it. They don't look at me the way they look at the Vietnamese. One day some boys called me outside from my grandmother's house, I didn't know why. I went out and they just hit me in the mouth. You see the scar and the broken tooth? That guy had had a fight with a friend of mine, but not with me. But they remembered my face because I am Amerasian, so they came back to pick on me. They were afraid to fight with my friend because he had brothers, but I was alone except for my grandmother.

In school the teacher and the children would talk bad to me. The students say that I am American, I should go back to America. I don't like that. I had some Vietnamese friends, but most of my friends were other Amerasians.

I hope I can work in the United States. I will accept any kind of job. I want to continue to study English, and I want to find my father.

Lan: My Amerasian son, he really wants to see his real father. He says, "If I can just can see my father one time, that's enough, then I can die." You know that paper you gave me yesterday? *[Lan is referring to a guide for Amerasian children searching for their fathers.]* My son took it from me and went to the neighbor to have it translated, just to see if it had any information about his father. I know my son. He won't bother his father if his father doesn't want him. He just wants to see him, even just one time.

The day before our ODP interview in Vietnam, Trung told me, "I hope that the first American I meet is my daddy." You know, one time he said to me, "Mom, you must have been a lovely woman." I said, "How do you know? Now I'm old and ugly." He said, "But my father was so handsome, so you must have been lovely."

Postscript: *On the day before our final conversation, Lan found out that she and her family would be heading for Fargo, North Dakota. After her initial disappointment at being sent to such a severe climate, she found a positive aspect and had this to say:*

"I don't really want to live with Vietnamese in America because I heard that the Vietnamese that came in 1975, the ones who came early, look down on the new arrivals. In the beginning I was disappointed to be going to Fargo, North Dakota, because it's so cold, but now I think maybe it's good because there are not many Vietnamese there and maybe I can get a job easy. And this way, Vietnamese won't look down on me, and I won't feel jealous of them."

Linh and Thu

"Maybe you get married to an
American and have an easy life."

*"You know, I live with Americans for ten years. How come I can't speak
English?" Linh chuckles, having spoken the sentence in English. Although we
usually conversed with the aid of an interpreter, Linh would sometimes break into
a jag of English, ending in a burst of laughter.*

*She is Khmer Krom, an ethnic Cambodian from the Mekong delta region
of Vietnam, which is referred to by Khmer as Kampuchea Krom, lower Cambodia. She is equally fluent in Vietnamese and Khmer, though she cannot read
or write either language.*

*At fifty, Linh's hair is grey turning white, though her face is unlined. She
has five grown Amerasian children by a succession of three black American
"husbands." Three of her children are here in the PRPC, along with three of
Linh's grandchildren. Thu, her twenty-three-year-old daughter, often was present when I talked to Linh and spoke briefly herself about her lot as a black Amerasian in Vietnam.*

*When we first met, Linh mentioned only four Amerasian children, and this
is the number she gave the interviewers of the Orderly Departure Program when
she applied to leave Vietnam. After we had spoken several times, she hesitantly
confided that she had one more Amerasian son in Vietnam, whom she had "loaned"
to her sister. This sister will apply to the Orderly Departure Program claiming to
be the mother of Linh's son. If ODP believes her story, her family will be allowed
to immigrate to the United States under the provisions of the Amerasian Homecoming Act. In this way, Amerasians become tickets to the States for those who
claim them as family. Linh explains, "If my son don't go with them, they cannot
go, because they have no Amerasian."*

Linh: I was born in Tien Giang province, in Kampuchea Krom. My
father died when I was still young, and I was raised by my mother and
sisters. I don't really remember too much about Tien Giang, but I can

remember a lot of fighting, battles. These were between the French and the Viet Minh. Because of this, the French forced us to move to Hau Giang province.

The French troops put us into small boats on the river, and they took us to Hau Giang. When I say French, I mean the officers were French. The soldiers were mostly Vietnamese or Khmer or *Ma roc [Black African French Colonial troops]*. I remember that we could not take our animals. All the farm animals were left behind. They moved us to a small hamlet inside the military camp, not only us, but people from many other villages were brought there. The villagers lived in the middle of the base, and the soldiers stayed towards the outer part of the base. The French gave each family land to work outside the base perimeter, so we lived inside and worked outside.

At that time Ba Cut, the leader of the Hoa Hao religious sect, was opposing the French, and the Hoa Hao army sometimes attacked the base. There were also attacks sometimes by the Viet Minh. Sometimes villagers would be killed or injured by stray shells.

The fields were just outside perimeter. When it was peaceful, we worked the fields. We had to give part of our harvest to the French for taxes, and the Viet Minh would also take rice when we were in the fields. So we had to pay two times, to the Viet Minh and the French, but we preferred the French. I remember that the Viet Minh would sometimes come and torch hamlets that they suspected of supporting the other side. They would give no notice, just set the place on flame immediately. That's why I didn't like the Viet Minh.

There was a Buddhist temple in the hamlet. I went there to pray, but I didn't study. Only my brothers studied there, so I never learned to read or write. It was the custom at the time that only the boys studied. Education was not considered necessary for girls. Girls were not permitted to go to school. Actually, there were a few girls in the village who did go, but it was not really proper. Most of the families were poor, so the girls would stay home and help in the house or outside. I always did farm work when I was young. I have no other skills.

I got married at seventeen. My husband was a Khmer Krom, like me. He was a soldier for the French army stationed in the compound, and that's how we met. We had two children, but both got sick and died, one at a month old. The other lived to three years old. We were married about five years when he was shot in a battle with the Viet Minh. You know, I had three brothers, and they are all dead too . . . soldiers. One was in the French army, and the Viet Minh killed him. The others were ARVN, killed by the VC. That was in the time of the Americans, not the French.

So the Viet Minh killed my husband, and I was alone. I stayed in Vinh Binh, my husband's town, and worked in the market selling vegetables. The French government, they gave me money, a pension, because my husband was killed in the French army. You know, I got that pension until the Communists came, then everything stopped. I had to destroy many documents because I was afraid of the VC. If they know you are connected with the French or the Americans, that's very bad. So I don't have the papers to prove that I was married to a French soldier anymore, to try to start collecting again.

A few years after my husband was killed, I went up to Saigon and worked as a maid for some Vietnamese people. I had a friend, Khmer like me, who worked in the bars by Tan Son Nhut airport. She come to see me, and she said, "You come with me, you don't work too hard. Maybe you get married with American and have an easy life." So I went with my friend to work the bars.

I didn't dance in the bar, I was . . . like a hostess. My friend taught me *titi [a little]* English, how to say "hello," "good evening," things like that. If some Americans want to talk to me, my friend translates for me.

Mostly black men were coming in that bar. There were some Vietnamese, and some white men, but not too many. I didn't get salary, but I got money when the man drank Saigon tea. One tea cost about sixty dong, and I got half. Each night it was different. Some nights I would drink five or ten Saigon tea, sometimes only one or two, but the money was good, better than working as a housemaid.

The bar gave me food, and if the police arrested me, the bar bailed me out. If someone wants to take me home or to go someplace, they pay the bar money, and the bar gives me half. The man would pay about twenty dollars for one night. The American customers, they are very nice. They don't talk bad like the Vietnamese. But I didn't go with many men, because after one month I met my "husband," and I stopped working at the bar.

His name was Bob. He was a black man from New York, a soldier in the army. When I lived with him, I didn't work bar no more. When I get pregnant with his first baby, he went back to the United States and he left me a lot of money, so I could stay home and take care of his son. He wrote me many letters and always sent his son money. After about two years, he come back again. Bob had a wife in America, and I was very sad when he went to America, but I didn't wait a long time. I got another husband, another black GI. He was also a very good man. His name was Terry. He was the friend of my girlfriend, and when he came to see my girlfriend, I met him.

You know, Bob came back when his baby son was about two years old. He wanted me to go back with him, but I was already with Terry. Bob was very good, he didn't get mad. He just told my second husband, "If you live with her, you must take care of her very kind." When Bob come back, he was stationed in Can Tho, but he came to Saigon every month to visit his son and gave him money.

I lived with Terry for four years, and we had two babies together. He didn't have other girlfriends, he just stayed with me. He loved my children. One time he went back to America. He stayed a month and came back to Vietnam again. He came back around Mau Than [*"the year of the monkey," used here to refer to Tet, the Vietnamese New Year, of 1968, the time of the Tet offensive*]. The Communists came to Saigon on that holiday and made plenty of trouble. My husband, he worked at Tan Son Nhut airport, and he had to stay there, he couldn't go out. There was too much shooting, many died.

In '69 Terry went back to America. He made a paper for me to leave with him, but I didn't go. I like Terry very much, he was very kind. I have had three American husbands, and he was the best one. But my mother was very old, and I had to take care of her. Terry, he was very sad. He wrote many letters, he said he missed me. He sent money, but I could not go with him.

When he went back to America, he left me some cash. I used it to buy a house in Saigon, and I opened a small coffee shop right in the house.

When Terry had gone, I met another black man, Clark. He was a civilian. I stayed with him more than two years, from '70 to '72. Then he went to the United States. Clark, he had many, many girlfriends. I had two babies with him. When he left, I was pregnant with the second. He didn't even tell he was leaving. He said he was going to work, and he never came back. He didn't leave me any money, he didn't even say good-bye.

You know, I lived with Americans for ten years. How come I can't speak English? When I was married to Americans, I could speak, but it's twenty years ago, and now I forgot, and I feel shy to try.

When the VC came in '75, I was in Saigon. The day before they came, my husband's friend was still in Saigon. He told me that if I wanted to go to America, he could get me out, but how could I go? I had three babies in the province, with my mother near the town of Co Do. I could not leave my children.

April 30, when the VC took Saigon, I was very afraid. People were saying that if you have Amerasian children, you must hide them, because the VC will cut off their heads. We were very scared, but they did not hurt my children.

When the Communists came, they said that we cannot stay in Saigon, that we must leave and go where we can work as farmers. So I went to Co Do and worked on my mother's farm. My mother had her own land, but the Communists took it and redistributed it. They gave us back a small plot to work. Anything we wanted to do, we had to ask permission. There was no freedom, no medicine, not enough rice. My kids went to school just a short time. Even before 1975, when my kids went to school in Saigon, the other kids bothered them because they were black. Vietnamese hate blacks, they hate American children . . . even before '75. Black and white, they hate both. The other children, they say my kids are dirty, that all blacks are dirty, so my kids don't want to go to study anymore. They just stay home and work in the fields, and they are like me, they cannot read and write.

Thu: Nobody liked me in Vietnam. That's why I want to go to America. Everywhere I went, in the town, at the market, people yelled at me, they insulted me. I never say anything, I don't listen to them. But I didn't like to go out and see other people. The Vietnamese hate Amerasians.

Linh: My mother never said nothing bad about my Amerasian kids. She helped me take care of them. There were no problems in my family; but the villagers, they don't like my babies. I don't have trouble with the VC in Co Do, but the neighbors looked down on me because I have *bu cu* American children and no husband. I always felt afraid of my neighbors, that they would tell the VC something bad about me.

In my town there were both Vietnamese and Khmer. Both hate American children. They hate it when one of them gets married to an American. They hate the husband, they hate the children, and they hate the women who marry the American husbands.

Now one of my daughters is in America. She is twenty-six. She escaped by foot into Cambodia, then to Thailand, and then resettled in California. She married a Khmer man there, but she gave all her five children American names. She lives in Sacramento and will sponsor my family. Recently she sent me money, $100. Before, she sent me $50 but I never got it. The Philippine post office stole it.

I have the name and address of my second husband. *[Astonishingly, Linh produces the military ID of her second husband, Terry, five feet, eight inches, 158 lbs., born June 17, 1951. It is not a copy, but a laminated original, dated 1971.]* You see, he is much younger than me *[Linh is laughing]*. I will not try to see him, he must be married again. I don't want to make trouble for him, so we will go live with my daughter.

There are many more things I can tell you about my life, many . . . but I don't want to remember the past.

I turn off my tape player and get ready to leave Linh's billet. A grandchild, a girl of about four, munches on fried bananas, mesmerized by the cassette recorder. Another granddaughter, a baby, is sleeping peacefully in a tiny hammock fashioned out of blue plastic cord and a Kroma, the multipurpose sheet of checked material used by almost all Khmer. Linh gently rocks the hammock with her foot, and hesitantly, again begins to speak.

SOMETHING I DIDN'T TELL you. . . When I was married to the Americans, I sold heroin and made a lot of money. Heroin, and opium for smoking.

My customers were all GIs. I lived in a neighborhood with many Americans, and many people were selling drugs. My neighbors showed me how to get set up, and they supplied me. My husband, Terry, knew about this and didn't like it. He wanted me to stop, but I didn't. I couldn't; the money was too good. I didn't really think about what the stuff did. For me it was just a way to support my kids. But one time, one of my customers, a GI, came to the house. He was sick, shaking, looking for a fix. I saw then what it did, that people were dying from it, and I got out of that business.

In 1978, I was arrested and put in jail for dealing drugs. I had not sold any drugs since before the Americans left, and I don't know for sure why I was arrested. I think a neighbor probably turned me in. I was accused of selling heroin, arrested without a trial, and sent to prison in Long Thanh, near Vung Tau.

They put me in a cell with about fifty people in a room about twice the size of this billet *[the billet is about ten feet by twenty feet]*. We each had two bricks of floor space to sleep in.

In the day we had to go out and do labor, farm work. For food we got corn, very bad corn, full of worms. Sometimes they gave us some kind of cereal. Hard work and bad food . . . many people got sick, some died. The prison, they gave us some training too. They taught us to sew and how to make hats *[the Vietnamese conical hats worn in the provinces by both men and women]*. We make the inside of bamboo and the outside of coconut leaves.

I spent five years in that jail. I got out in 1983. They never told me that they would let me go. They just came one day and told me to go home—and I did.

Mai Lien and Diem

"I no longer make offerings to the altar of my ancestors."

Diem is trouble-shooting his homemade fan. An ingenious contraption of scrap metal and bent spoons, it runs on five rechargeable D batteries. His mother, Mai Lien, only half jokingly calls it "An invention for the twenty-first century." The machine sputters to life, sending a tiny wisp of a breeze through the dense heat of the billet, and abruptly peters out. The only air movement now comes from the arc of the hammock in which Anh, Diem's wife, swings their ten-day-old son.

Mai Lien, slim and graceful at fifty-five, was born a farm girl, and before coming to the Philippine Refugee Processing Center, she spent most of her life in her small village. During the war, she moved to Quy Nhon to find work at the U.S. base there. While working at the base, she met her American boyfriend, Willie Smith. Diem, now twenty-four, was born of this relationship.

Mai Lien calls Diem over and asks him to put his foot up on the bench. She points to the long slim toe next to the big toe. The nail has grown in an unusual way. Rather than forming a single surface, there are two distinct nails, separated in the middle. "This is the same as Willie Smith," she says. "He can know that Diem is his son, he just has to look at his toe."

We speak through interpreters, but Mai Lien's command of English, though rusty, has not disappeared. When she is dissatisfied with a translation, she breaks into a brief torrent of English. Her point made, she lapses back into Vietnamese, deferring once again to the translators. Diem, American in appearance with his light complexion, brown hair, and wisp of a mustache, speaks only Vietnamese.

Mai Lien: I was born fifty-five years ago in the Tan Chau district of Long Xuyen province. Now they call it An Giang, the government changed the name in 1975. There were seven brothers and sisters in my family, but only three of us are still alive. I am the only one to leave Vietnam. My village, Phu Lam, was a farming village, and like all the other children, I grew

191

Diem's split toe nail, inherited from his American father, Willie Smith

up working in the fields and helping raise the chickens and pigs. My family
was very poor, they could not afford to send me to school. Most of the
villagers followed the Hoa Hao religion, but we practiced ancestor worship.
On an altar in the house, we burned joss sticks and offered fruit in honor
of our dead ancestors. Here in the PRPC, the Baptists showed us a movie
about Jesus. It was very convincing, and we decided to join their religion.
Now I no longer make offerings to the altar of my ancestors.

　　　When the rains came, we would bring out the buffalo to plow the
fields, and we would sow the rice. This is called *sa lua,* the scattering of the
rice seed. After the rains, when the rice was ripe, we harvested. Since the
Communists took over in 1975, we've changed our methods. Now we plant
the rice in a small field, and when the seedlings are big enough, in about
eighteen to twenty-five days, we transplant them to a bigger field. We just
make a hole with our finger or with a small stone and transplant by hand,
seedling by seedling. I like the old way, but some villagers prefer the new
method. Either way, if you care for your field, you can get a good harvest.

When I was a girl, my favorite holiday was "Via Ba," on April 25 of the lunar calendar. That's when we went to Sam mountain in Chau Duc province. Once there was a rock on Sam Mountain in the shape of a lady. The rock grew magically till it was so big that twenty men could not lift it, but the villagers sent nine virgins up to the mountain, and they picked up the rock and carried it to the fields below. The rock is known as *Ba [revered lady]*, and a temple was built around it. Many Vietnamese, and especially Chinese, believe that if you make a pilgrimage to her and light joss sticks, she will make you very lucky, so people come from all over the country to visit this magical rock. This was a wonderful time for me as a child. If you ever go to Vietnam, you can visit there and stay in my house. There is a boy living there now. I will tell him that you are coming.

When I was eighteen, I married a Vietnamese soldier. We had a small wedding in the army compound, and only my father came from my family. My other relatives stayed at home because there was a bandit group operating in the area called *Canh Buom Den [black sail]*, and people were afraid to leave their property unguarded. That husband was trouble. We had three baby sons, and then he got another wife. He actually brought his other wife home and wanted her to live together with us. I was *bu cu* mad. I said "no way," and I took my children and went home to my mother and father. I left my children with them, and I went to Quy Nhon and got a job for the American army. That's where I met Willie Smith.

His name was really Kenny Rays [*not a real name*], but I couldn't pronounce that name. Willie Smith is easy, so that's what I called him. He was from Georgia, and he worked as an MP. I changed my name too. In Quy Nhon everybody called me Mai Lien, and that's what I would like you to call me in your book.

I loved him very much; he was a very good man. I took him to my parent's house to see my children, and he treated them like they were his own. And you know, he loved to cook. He could cook very well, chicken, ham, pork, all very delicious. I had two babies with him. The first was Diem, his name is the same as the president of Vietnam. My second, Jacqueline, she died very young. She got sick at six months old. At first it wasn't serious, but Willie went back to America already, and I had no money to pay for a doctor. Two months later she was dead.

Willie, he used to tell me he wanted to take me back to America, but I said, "No, I cannot go." I had a sick mother and three Vietnamese babies. How could I leave them? But now, I feel very sorry. He is the father of my baby, and I miss him very much. I would like to see him again, but I don't want to make trouble for him. I don't want to make his wife jealous.

In 1968, during Tet, the Communists attacked. Willie Smith was driving to the base in a jeep, along with two friends. The Communists ambushed

Mai Lien in the 1960s (courtesy of Mai Lien)

the jeep, and one of his friends was shot dead. Willie was very shook up over that, and he didn't come home. When I didn't see him, I went to the base to find him, but he had already gone back to America. I felt so sad. He was a good man, he took care of me. *[Mai begins to weep, and cannot continue for several minutes.]*

Diem: I want to meet my father, just see him. If he wants to help me, okay. If not, that's okay too. I will tell him, "My mother told me all about you, and I'm very lucky now to meet you in person."

Mai Lien: On April 30, 1975, the VC came. We were in Long Xuyen. The rumor was that they would kill all the Amerasians, so naturally I was very scared. I was afraid to separate from Diem. I took him to the fields with

Mai Lien

me, I didn't let him out of my sight. When the Communists came, they called over a loud speaker for all the officials of the former government to assemble, and they took them away—first the higher officials and later the lower ones. But they never hurt the Amerasians.

We lived in a thatch hut. Because I had an American baby, I thought that the Communists would confiscate our house and land, so I dismantled part of the house and sold the materials. We stayed in the tiny remainder. Then I sold our land. Actually, I drew up a contract in which I leased the fields to another farmer for twenty years, because we couldn't sell our land outright, but really it was a sale. So where before I had a house and land, I wound up living in a tiny hut and working for other people. My own actions, the things I did out of fear of the Communists, hurt me more than anything the Communists actually did. But it was difficult for Diem. When he went to school, the other children were mean to him.

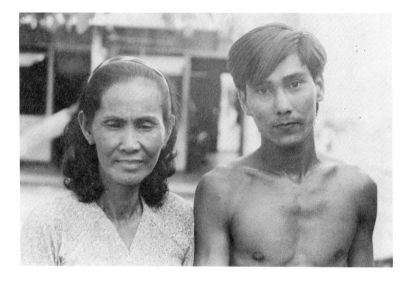

Mai Lien and Diem

Diem: I only went to school for two years. All the children teased me, called me *My lai [Amerasian]* so I had many fights and got beat up a lot. So I didn't want to go back, I just left and worked on the farm, taking care of the cows. I didn't understand why people called me that, my mother had never told me that I had an American father. When I was about fifteen, the police came around the village with a list of Amerasians and they called on us. That's when my mother said that, yes, I did have an American father.

We applied to leave Vietnam in May 1991. A few months later, I was working in the fields when the Vietnamese official came with a slip of paper calling us for an interview. I said to myself, "Okay, this is the time to go, because here we are very poor."

Mai Lien: After 1975 there were two markets, the government market and the private market. The prices at the government market were very cheap, but to shop there you had to have a food card, and to get a food card you had to work for the government. I didn't, so I had to buy at the public market. The vendors there are taxed heavily, so the prices are very high, and the food very expensive. So no matter how hard we worked, we were still poor.

I tasted American rice when I worked on the base. The long grain is very tasty, but the short grain is tough and takes a long time to cook. I know that in America you use machines for planting, it is a different way. Do you think that when I go to America I can get a hundred hectares from the government to grow rice? I would like to do that. I have always worked in the fields.

Dao Thi Mui and Thao (Patrick Henry Higgins)

"My mother may not live long enough to see America."

The door and window of Mui's billet are thrown open in a forlorn attempt to funnel any wisp of a breeze inside, but there is no movement of air. The March heat is almost hallucinogenic. Mui's billet is bare but for a table and a single stool. A hammock fashioned of plastic string is tied back against the staircase. Magazine cutouts and ads decorate the asbestos walls. Their messages are in ironic contrast to the severity of the setting: "Fortune Magazine, the hottest 50 companies; Find out what has been good this year." Below that, a duck-walking Chuck Berry declares, "Rock and Roll is back." Nearby is an ad saying, "Bring your IRA together with the nation's number one fund, Scudder," and there are also blurbs for Fidelity and Dreyfus mutual fund companies.

These plugs are lost on Mui and her son Thao, also known as Patrick Henry, the name bestowed upon him by his American father. They possess neither the English to comprehend the messages, nor the money to comply with them if they did. Although Mui and Thao inherited $40,000 between them in 1984 from the estate of Thao's deceased father, Henry G. Higgins, they have yet to see a penny of it.

We sit on the cement floor, trying futilely to get comfortable in the immense heat. Mui pulls a paper out of a sheaf of documents and hands it to my interpreter, who passes it over to me. The letterhead indicates it is from an attorney at law located in Miami Shores, Florida. The letter is dated August 16, 1984, and is addressed to Thao in Ho Chi Minh City. It is headed "Re: Estate of Henry G. Higgins, Deceased," and it states:

> *The court has directed and we have established a controlled savings account in your name with $30,000.00. This is your share of the inheritance. As you probably know, the United States Government does not allow the transfer of American funds to foreign countries and, therefore, it will be necessary for you to be in the United States to receive same.*

According to records that we have, your father carried you to the United States Embassy and recorded your birth as his son and, therefore, you are a United States citizen, which should make it very easy for you to leave Vietnam to come to the United States.

Leaving Vietnam, however, was not easy. Eight years passed, numerous escape attempts failed, and Vietnamese officials were bribed before Mui, Thao and his wife, and two of their three children would depart Vietnam for the Philippines through the Orderly Departure Program.

Despite the $30,000 inheritance and an additional $7,500 Veterans Administration government insurance benefit to Thao and $2,500 to Mui, the family remains without funds. Until they reach the United States, they have no access to the money. While his father's bequest gathers interest in a Stateside bank, Thao has been reduced to selling his clothes to obtain money for food.

Mui's appearance is extremely aged, well beyond her sixty-six years. She had three eye operations in Vietnam and wears glasses with a left lens so thick it is almost opaque. Her hair is snow white, and the single tooth in the bottom front of her mouth seems preternaturally long, due to the lack of others around it. Her hands are unlined, however, and the fingers delicate and youthful.

Mui has known loss. Her first husband and a daughter died in a car accident. Her American husband passed away from heart disease in 1983, fifteen years after he left Vietnam to return to the United States. Her oldest son, a bicycle rickshaw driver in Ho Chi Minh City, died of a liver ailment. And Minh, one of her two Amerasian sons, was evacuated from Vietnam just a few months before Saigon fell and placed with a foster family in the United States. Contact has been lost, and Mui doesn't know how to locate him.

As Mui tells her story, she often confers with Thao on details. There is a great rapport between mother and son. We speak for about an hour and a half, and Mui must then excuse herself. She is tired, her health is not good.

Thao is a very soft-spoken young man, and his English is minimal. At twenty-five, he has his father's light skin and brown hair. On his chin, a mole sprouts several long hairs, in a style favored by some Vietnamese. He worries that his mother may not live long enough to enjoy the inheritance they have waited so long to collect.

Mui: I was born in a small village in Kien An province in North Vietnam, but when I was still very young, there was fighting in our area, and we left home. I remember that we walked about a half day to another village, and that is where we stayed. It was a farming village not too far from Haiphong. Most of the villagers grew rice and fruit trees, but my family didn't farm, we were vendors. My sister sold soup in the market. My father died when I was young, and my mother entered the temple to become a Buddhist nun, so I was raised by my older sister.

When I was twenty-one, I married a Vietnamese policeman. I was the prettiest girl in the village, that is why my husband chose me. I first saw him at my engagement party. I remember being struck by how young he looked. He was two years younger than me. But everything had been arranged by our families, I had no say in the choice of my husband.

By custom, on the engagement date the husband's family provides the head of a pig, a bottle of red wine, a bag of tea, some biscuits, and sticky rice, and presents them to the Buddha at the altar. After the presentation, the family can eat them. For the wedding the husband gives a gift of jewelry to the bride and offers eight trays of betel nut and leaf, each covered by a red cloth, to the wife's family. That is the tradition, and that was how my wedding was. We got married in Haiphong, which was my husband's hometown.

My husband was a policeman, and his family worked in the office of the navy. A few months after my wedding came the great exodus to the south, including most Catholics, and also families who had worked for the old French regime. Since my husband's family worked for the Department of the Navy, they arranged for us transportation on a navy boat to Saigon.

In Saigon my husband joined the air force. He became a sergeant. We had three children, two girls and a boy. But my younger daughter and my husband were killed in a traffic accident, and I was forced to go out and work to support my family.

I got a cart, and I began selling fruit juice on the street. I worked in front of a bar, one of those bars that American servicemen like to go into. That's where I met Henry Higgins. Every day, he would buy out my juice, give me twenty dollars and pass the juice to the people all around. That's how we got to know each other. He was about forty-one, I guess, and I was about five years younger then him. I think that was 1964. He asked me, "You have husband?" I told him that my husband was dead. After about five months, he rented a house and we lived together. We stayed together for about three years, and we had two children, two boys. Henry, he worked in the communications section *[for the army]*, then he went back to America for a while. When he came back to Vietnam, he worked as a teacher at the military hospital. He had a wife in America, he told me that, but they were separated.

My two sons are Minh and Thao. Thao is here with me. His American name is Patrick Henry Higgins. Henry didn't believe that Minh was his son, because the eyes, the hair, the nose, the mouth were all different from his. Minh had blonde hair, it wasn't like Henry's. When Minh was born, Henry was still in Vietnam, living with me, and he stayed with me until Thao, our second, was seven or eight months. He didn't say anything about Minh, and he bought the same things for both babies, but he didn't include Minh in his will. Minh *is* Henry's baby, I told him that, but he didn't believe me.

In 1967 or 1968, Henry went back to America. He got sick there and

Dao Thi Mui and Thao (Patrick Henry Higgins) in Vietnam, circa 1968 (courtesy of Dao Thi Mui)

never came back to Vietnam, but he always sent me money for Thao. You know, when my husband was in America, the police would come around looking for handouts—money, camera, radios, things like that. They think I'm rich because I have an American husband. Even after the VC came, Henry sent money until 1978, then no more money came. *[Mui shows me a letter from Henry dated January 17, 1977: "I hope you receive the $50 I am sending you in this letter. . . . Maybe, in a few months, the mail will be faster. Your last letter took about 2 months to get here to me. The first letter took 97 days." A fragment of another undated letter states: "Hello Mui and Thao, I hope you received the $50 I sent you. Can you cash the money order? I hope the mail*

Thao and his brother in Vietnam, circa 1970 (courtesy of Dao Thi Mui)

gets better. "] Even when Henry sent money, it was not enough. I had to go out and sell soup to support my family. Then, in 1983, Henry died.

You know, when I was thirty-seven, I died and came back to life. This is what happened. I was six months pregnant, and I hemorrhaged. I was bleeding very badly. I was taken to the hospital. My husband was in America at this time. The last thing I remember is that the French doctor said in French that they would operate, "demain à huit heures et demi" *[tomorrow at eight thirty]*. The next thing I remember was waking up in a room full of people lying on stretchers. I thought they were sleeping. I walked past them to the door and tried to open it, but it was locked. I knocked on the door, and some doctors and nurses opened it. They were scared when they saw me, and they ran away. I made the *lay* sign *[palms together in Buddhist obeisance]*, I had no voice to speak. Finally a doctor came to me. That room was the morgue, where I had been put when I "died." I had been dead for eleven hours and had come back to life. That is why the doctors and nurses who opened the door were so scared. They thought I was a ghost. *[Mui and her son Henry are laughing at this.]*

My son Minh is in America. He went there in 1975, and I don't know where he is. My American children went to a school run by an American charity group, and they brought him to the United States before the Communists came.

Thao: We went to Catholic school for four years. Then we went to a school run by an American organization for Amerasians. We went there for two years. In February of 1975, a group of Americans came over from an agency *[probably Foster Parents Plan]* to bring Amerasians to America. My brother and I wanted to go. I asked if they could take my mother, but the organization refused, so I decided to stay with her while my brother went to America. We thought that he would sponsor us after he got there, but a few months later Saigon fell, and we could not leave.

Mui: We had an address for him, but it was lost, and I don't know how to find him. All we have are these. *[Mui shows me a few pictures of Minh in America; on the back of one is written "Johnny Vernon, Foster Parents Plan." Mui believes that he was given this name by his foster parents in America.]* I wrote to Foster Parents Plan, but they never answered us.

When the Communists came to Saigon in 1975, I moved to another part of the city, where I was unknown. I was afraid that if I stayed in my neighborhood, I might be denounced by a neighbor. I heard all the rumors of what the VC would do to the Amerasians, so I darkened my son's skin with coal dust from the stove and pots and kept him inside. We had heard that in Pleiku they had killed Amerasians and their families, and we were very scared. We stayed inside for a week.

Under the Communists, the new regime, we had to report to the work council. My son had to stay about ten days. He was very young at this time, maybe ten or eleven.

Thao: They made me clean the prison, clean their office, wash their clothes. I was very polite. I said, "Yes sir, yes sir," and I did what they asked. In a week they let me go home. There were other Amerasians there. The ones who did not speak politely they kept longer.

Mui: I brought rice to him twice a day. After I gave him the rice, I would cry and cry on the way home, right in the street. Why should they keep my son? He is only eleven, what is his crime?

Thao: After the Communists came, I couldn't go to school anymore. I didn't have the right ID. I didn't even like to go out anymore, people made fun of me. I mostly stayed inside.

Mui: The work council called me and told me that I would have to go to the New Economic Zone. I didn't want to go. I told them I was sick, and they sent me to a Communist doctor. Before I went to see him, I sold four bracelets, some of gold and some with blue stones. I took the money, stuck it in an envelope, and put it inside my clothes. When my turn came to see the doctor, I gave him the envelope and asked him to write me a note. He wrote that I had an enlarged heart, and this kept me and my family from going to the NEZ.

The note, however, did not exempt me from forced labor. The new government made us work for them for no wages. They called me and I had to go. They sent me to Hoc Mon, which was about thirty kilometers from Saigon. I had to dig canals for the Communists. The women are the ones who do the digging. I was chest deep in water all day, scooping up earth and piling it on the banks. I had to get up at four in the morning, and they drove me in a bus to the site. We worked until seven P.M., then they drove me back to Saigon. For lunch we had rice and rotten meat. It was worse than prison. From Hoc Mon they sent us to Cu Chi and then to Le Minh Xuan, the place named after the Communist hero. We got no pay, it's all forced labor. To get money for my family, I sold gasoline on the street on the weekend.

I worked for several months. Then finally I bribed someone at the work council and they let me go. I had gotten malaria on the job. I went to the Communist clinic, and they gave me some orange medicine. It didn't do anything, so I had to go to the market and spend money on malaria pills, and these cured me.

In 1982 we applied to leave Vietnam through the Orderly Departure Program and waited and waited. We did not know the way to bribe the Communists. Finally, in 1989 my daughter got to know someone who was a friend of a member of the application committee. He arranged the bribe, and we paid two bars of gold. Even with the bribe, we waited three years because we had to change our documents. We wanted to take my daughter, but she was denied. Then Thao got married, and we had to make documents for his wife. He and his wife have three children. The last one, a girl, was born about a month before we left Vietnam. We had to leave her behind. We couldn't get her included on the documents. We will try to bring her over once we get to America.

Thao: Before we were accepted by ODP, I tried to escape Vietnam four times, but I failed each time. The first time I tried to escape with my wife and one child and my brother-in-law. I only had one child then.

We had made arrangements in Saigon, and our connection took us to Ha Tien in the south *[on the Cambodian border]* and put us on a small boat. We were supposed to meet a big boat which would take us to Thailand. The big boat didn't show, so the captain took us to an island and asked us to wait there while he located the big boat then he would come back. So he dropped us off on a small island, completely uninhabited.

Well, the whole thing was a setup, they never came back. The island was inside Cambodia, and some Cambodian fishermen came by to fish off the island. They could speak Vietnamese. I told them what had happened to us. They were very kind. They took us to their home on another island, and we stayed with them for about twenty days. When they went to the Cambodian mainland, they took us with them. Their island was a long way off the coast. It took many hours for us to get to the mainland.

The fishermen took us to the bus station and loaned us some money, and we got on a bus for Pnom Penh. In Pnom Penh there were many Vietnamese vendors in the market. I didn't want any one to know why I was in Cambodia, so I approached one and said, "I have been visiting my relatives here and I am trying to get back to Vietnam, but I am lost." They directed me to a boat on the Mekong River, which took us to the Cao Lanh district in Dong Thap province. *[I asked Thao why, once he was in Cambodia, he didn't continue on to Thailand. He said that he had no guide and was afraid to continue without one. My interpreter concurred, saying that police in Cambodia are very aware that many Vietnamese use that country as a conduit of escape into Thailand, and it is very risky to try it without a guide.]*

When I got back to Ho Chi Minh City, my family told me that the boat owner had come by to collect the money for the trip, saying that we had reached Thailand safely. But before we had left, we devised a coded message which I would telegraph once we reached Thailand, to let my mother know that we had gotten there. The message was simply, "We reached the island safely." Since the boatman didn't know the message, he didn't get the money.

When I got back to Vietnam, I went to ODP to check on the progress of my application. They told me that my application was lost. At that time people weren't moving. Everything seemed stalled. I made the ODP papers again, but I had to think of escape.

I arranged to try and flee Vietnam again through a Saigon contact. We took a bus to Vinh Chau, a few hundred kilometers south of Saigon. My wife had had another child since the last escape try, and she was with me along with my two kids. We had paid four gold rings as a down payment. If we escaped, the plan again was to send a coded telegram to my mother and she would turn over four bars of gold.

We waited two days in a hotel there. My contact used his documents to get us a room. After two days they took us to a small thatch hut by the

Mui, Thao, and his sons

sea, where we were supposed to board the boat. The police noticed that there were people in that small town whom they had not seen before. Since it is a seaside town and people have escaped from Vietnam from there, they are always on the lookout. They came into the hut, demanded our documents and arrested us. Then they took us to jail in Vinh Chau.

That same night my wife, who was having her period, began to bleed very heavily, and passed out. They sent her to the hospital, and after three days she was released and her and the kids were sent home.

I was not that lucky. They kept me two months in Vinh Chau jail, and then I was transferred to Long Tuyen prison in Can Tho province. There was no trial, or anything like that, and I was never told when I might be released. The police didn't even inform my family that I was sent to Long Tuyen. My family came down from Saigon to Vinh Chau to visit me, and only then did the guard tell them that I had been transferred.

They stuck me in a cell with about sixteen other men. It's unbearably hot there, like a furnace. There was a hole in the floor for a toilet, and the place stunk. We were never let out. We just stayed there all day and night.

The cells are tiny and crowded. There's really no room to lie down and sleep. People would roll over in their sleep, knock into another person, and a fight would start. This happened all the time. Or if one person had food and another didn't, there might be a fight over that. Sixteen people were in a small space; every day there were fights. If they got too bloody, the guards would come in and take the prisoners involved to other cells. But

a few days later, they'd bring them back, and the fights would start all over
again. The guards don't care at all what happens in the cell. They just let
the *dai bang,* the chief prisoner, and the other inmates handle the problems.

When I got into the prison, the dai bang saw that I was Amerasian, and
he asked why I had been arrested. I told him that I was visiting relatives in
Bac Lieu and I had no documents, so the police arrested me. If I had told
the dai bang that I was trying to escape Vietnam, he would have figured that
I had money and would have strip searched me to look for it. He was a big
fat guy with tattoos and had been in prison a long time. He didn't bother
me much, I stayed out of trouble. The worst he did was force me to lie near
the stinking toilet.

There were many Thais in Long Tuyen, mostly fishermen caught in
Vietnamese waters and pulled in by the police. They more or less roamed
around the grounds, not caged up like us. They weren't given rations, and
so they begged for food from the Vietnamese. They are very aggressive, and
there were a lot of them. I was afraid of them, even the guards were wary
of them.

The police questioned me: "What was I doing in that hut by the sea?"
I told them that I was just visiting relatives, that the man in the hut was my
uncle. I was caught in the hut and not on the sea, so I stuck to my story.
After a month or so, they let me go. If I had been caught on the boat, I
would have been in jail much longer.

My third escape attempt I was set up again, I believe, though my
neighbor's son made it to Indonesia on the boat that was also supposed to
take my family. I paid five gold rings in advance to get on that boat. We
waited in Vung Tau, and the boatman was supposed to contact me. I
waited for a day and finally got suspicious, so I went to talk to the landlord
of the house. He said that the boat had already left. As I said, my neighbor's
son made it to Indonesia on that boat, and his family received a letter from
him. He said that the boatman took him to the boat to help make arrangements for food and water, but when he got there, they sailed off unex-
pectedly, and the boatman wouldn't let him go back to get me. Why the
boat left without me, I don't know. Anyway, we lost five gold rings on that
deal. *[Stories of passengers being left behind during boat escapes are far from rare.
Many times the boat pulls out just ahead of capture by the police. People and
cargo are often left behind in the scramble.]*

We tried one more time. This time we got on a boat in Ba Ria, near
Vung Tau. The police saw us, and the captain beached the boat. We ran
away, and the police didn't get us.

My father left us a lot of money when he died in 1983; but it is in
America, and we have not been able to get any of it. We received a letter
from my father's lawyer, telling us that we had inherited the money, but

that it couldn't be sent out of the United States. So all these years we have had that money in the bank in Florida, but we were very poor. Here we have no money.

My mother has a problem with low blood pressure. Every week she has to go to the doctor. Last week she fainted and was brought to the hospital and they had to give her oxygen. The doctors here do not treat refugees kindly. They are often nasty to us, so it is unpleasant to use the hospital. *[When Thao says this, my interpreters nod in agreement.]* One of the doctors said that my mother may not live long enough to see America. I worry about this, and I wish we could go to America right now.

My mother is very weak. She needs good food, but we have no money. I wrote to my father's lawyer, asking if there is any way that we could get some money here from my father's inheritance, but I have not gotten a reply. I have been selling our clothes, piece by piece, to buy food. I have almost nothing left.

When I get to America, I hope to find work as a tailor. That's what I did in Vietnam. Eventually, I'd like to study and become an army doctor, like my father was. I will put my father's inheritance in the bank and use part of it to help orphans in Vietnam. And maybe I will have to use some to put my mother in a home. I don't want to do this, but I learned in Cultural Orientation class about old age homes, and my cousin from California wrote me that that's what Americans do with old people.

My cousin in California, she is sponsoring us now, but I hope that my father's lawyer can sponsor us instead. He is in Florida, and that's where I want to go. That's where my father's grave is.

Postscript: *I remained in contact with Mui and Thao through August of 1992, when I left the PRPC. Mui's health had stabilized, though she was easily prone to fatigue. At Mui's request, I wrote a letter to Foster Parents Plan, the organization which she says brought her son Minh to the United States in 1975. We hoped to get some information which could aid her in locating him. In May, I received a reply from a representative of Childreach Sponsorship, a program of Plan International USA (formerly Foster Parents Plan). It stated: "I asked some employees who worked here during the year 1975, if it were possible that our organization brought some of the Amerasian children to the United States. I was told that it was possible but that we would not have any records in which to verify that information. I'm very sorry that I was unable to help you."*

A letter also came in from the Pearl S. Buck Foundation, Inc. They have a data base on Vietnamese Amerasians who are searching for family members. Childreach had forwarded our inquiry to them. Unfortunately, Minh's name did not appear on their database. Their representative suggested Mui contact the American Red Cross and the Citizen's Consular Service of the Department of State. Mui says she will follow these leads when she gets to the United States.

Nguyen Thi Mai and Thuy

"The VC, they killed my mother."

Despite political and military developments indicating the contrary, many South Vietnamese never believed their country would fall to the north. Mai is one of the many Vietnamese women married to Americans who waited too long to try to leave Vietnam. Mai's husband had sent her and their daughter Thuy one-way tickets to the United States in the spring of 1975. By that time, however, the government in South Vietnam was crumbling. Chaos ruled at the airports, and Mai and Thuy were stuck.

I first met Mai when she was a student in an ESL class in which I was assisting. Weeks later I ran into her near her billet in neighborhood two of the PRPC. It was about 6 P.M., and the camp water, which operates only a few hours a day had been turned on. Refugees were waiting in line with buckets to gather the evening's ration. Women sudsed up little children by the side of the water tanks that supplied the neighborhood, and teenage girls squatted beside plastic buckets of laundry. The early evening break in the intense March heat and the turning on of the water, which had been erratic of late, had buoyed everyone's spirits.

Mai was returning from her last day of ESL class. There had been a party, and Mai and her companions, all women in their mid-forties, were resplendent in their ao dai, *the flowing pantsuits which are the traditional dress of Vietnamese women. She invited me into her billet and said a few words to a neighbor's boy in rapid fire Vietnamese. The boy disappeared and returned moments later with an armful of Cokes.*

Thuy, Mai's twenty-one-year-old Amerasian daughter, sat along with her husband and small daughter on the raised platform of wooden slats which serves as a bed in the PRPC billets. Freckle-faced and willowy with long flowing brown hair, Thuy more resembles a midwestern farm girl than a Vietnamese refugee. Extremely shy, with very little knowledge of English, she deferred to her mother whenever a question was directed to her.

Mai lit a cigarette and began to talk about her life. As she spoke, the window filled up with children's faces. Occasionally squeals of "My, My" [American] could be heard. The word was out that an American was around, and the neighborhood kids came to see what was up.

Mai was to continue her story over four meetings. Her English was fine, though a bit rusty after years of disuse. After our second meeting, she asked that I bring an interpreter along the next time we met. I did so, but whenever there was a difficulty in understanding, it was Mai, and not the interpreter, who came up with the correct translation.

Mai spoke with composure and wit. Even when describing subjects as disturbing as her imprisonment by the North Vietnamese government or her daughter's misery at the taunts of her classmates, she retained her aplomb. Only when speaking of her mother's death of a heart condition which Mai believes was exacerbated by government harassment, did she lapse into tears and bitterness.

Mai: I am from Bao Vinh village, two kilometers from Hue. My father was a soldier; and I am the oldest of my five brothers and sisters, so I can only go to school two years. I have to stay home to help take care of my young brothers and sisters, and I help my family plant rice and bananas.

When I was nineteen, I went to work at Phu Bai base in Hue. It's an American and Vietnamese base together. I was a waitress at the NCO club. My boss at the club, his name Hal, we fall in love. He be about forty, I am only nineteen. He went back to America, stay six months. Then he come back Vietnam again, as a civilian. He work aero-sci, fixing airplanes, and we go all over—Hue, Nha Trang, Saigon, Bien Hoa—but our base is Da Nang. That's where he was stationed.

One time we go to Da Nang from Hue. That be Mau Thanh *[the year of the monkey, often used synonymously with the 1968 Communist Tet offensive]*. There was bad fighting in Hue. We went back four months later. It was all rubble. Many died, the VC bury many alive. There were many famous buildings in Hue, the Khai Dinh temple, King Minh Mang temple, King Thu Duc temple, Linh Mu pagoda. So many were destroyed in the fighting. Bao Vinh was destroyed, my parents' house in pieces, several of my friends were killed. My husband gave my family some money, and they built a new house there.

Me and my husband had a good life, a nice house, two maids. My parents didn't want me to marry an American, but I got pregnant, so what could they do? They must accept it, but they think it's not good for a VN woman to marry an American man. People think that such marriages are made for money and not for love, and they look down on the woman.

Hal left May 30, 1974, for a long stay to work in the United States. He was supposed to return July 1975. He wrote me every week. In '75 he realized that the VC would win the war, and he sent tickets for me and my daughter to go to the United States. We had tickets to leave from Da Nang on March 27, but it was too late. We went to the airport and it was closed, nobody was working. *[Da Nang fell to the North Vietnamese three days later on March 30]*. So we took a boat to Saigon.

In Saigon, I stayed with a friend on Nguyen Minh Trieu Street. I tried to go to the airport a few times, but it was crazy, packed. Everybody want to get out Vietnam. I call the Vietnamese army. I tell them that I am married to an American, and I have to get out; but they don't care about that. They have their own problems. I call my husband's Saigon office, in the airport. Nobody answers the phones. We were trapped. All women with Amerasian kids were scared, they thought the VC would kill us and our babies.

So I destroy my marriage paper, I be afraid the VC kill me if they see I am married to an American. The VC come, I stay in a friend's house, hiding, worrying. After about a month, I took a bus back to Da Nang with my daughter. I cut her hair, so no one would know that she was American.

My idea was I go to Da Nang, not so many people know me. They don't know that I have an Amerasian, it be easier for me and my daughter. Hue is a small town. If I go back there, everybody know that I have an American baby. The VC, maybe they kill us.

In Da Nang I start to sell medicine in the market, but I have many problems. The police, they call me in, and I be afraid to lie. I think they know already about me, and maybe they kill me if I don't say the truth. So I tell them that I had an American husband, even that I had the tickets to go to America. They hate me for that and because I have an American daughter. Many times they come to my house in the middle of the night. There would be that banging on the door, and they take me down to the office and question me, harass me. "You're no good. If you were any good you wouldn't have an American baby. We're going to send you to the mountain" *[New Economic Zone]*, things like that. I cried, what could I do? Sometime they keep me for a few days. Then one time they tell me, "Next time we will send you to the mountain." So when I go back to the market, I was crying. I don't know what I will do. Since I be a little girl, I never lived in the country or work as a farmer. How can I go live on the mountain? So one man he work in the market with me, he say he will help me. He paid the bribes to the police to keep me out of the NEZ. He had to pay many times but still the police never gave me papers *[to live legally in Da Nang]*.

Soon after that, we get married, but we don't make paper ... you know. We just live like husband and wife. I am his second wife, he has one more wife besides me. She live a few kilometers from my house. We were very friendly, we don't be jealous. We often ate together, our children play together. I have two children with him, and his other wife have three. My husband, he still in Vietnam. He stay with his first wife.

So I have a husband, and I still work buying and selling medicines. I go up to Hanoi by train four times a month and buy medicines to bring down and sell in Da Nang. The trip from Da Nang to Hanoi takes about twenty-five hours. It is illegal to buy and sell medicine, but many people do it. I had some contacts in Hanoi, they had a son studying in the Soviet Union. He sent them medicine from there, and they would sell the medicines for profit. These were North Vietnamese Communists, but they were capitalist Communists. They were VC, but still they hate the VC, and several of them have left Vietnam by boat.

Now Hanoi is rich, at least the upper and middle classes, but before 1975 it was a poor town, they had nothing. When they took Saigon, they took all the goods, refrigerators, televisions, everything, and sent it north to Hanoi. So now, everybody has a TV, a radio, a refrigerator, but it all was stolen from Saigon. The people up there, they are liars. They cheat when you do business with them, when you buy and sell. There are some good people, like the people I get the medicine from, but many are deceitful. They are very different from southerners, from the people from Saigon.

One night I was on the *Thong Nhat [Unification Train]* in Hanoi, on my way to back to Da Nang with a bag full of medicine to sell, when the Economic Police boarded the train and came right for me. They didn't even look at anyone else, so to this day I believe that they must have been tipped off, maybe by the Da Nang police. They took all my medicine, and they took me to Hoa Lo prison in Hanoi. It's where they kept the captured American pilots during the war. *[It was known to Americans as the "Hanoi Hilton."]* It's a huge building, it was built by the French.

When I was in Hoa Lo, the police went to my house in Da Nang and cleaned it out. They took everything I had, my TV, my cassette player, all my medicine, and all my money. They found two hundred dollars that my husband had hidden in a cabinet. We had changed some gold for these dollars in the market, but the VC accused me of getting that money from the father of my Amerasian daughter. This was not true, but that's what they said. My husband was also arrested. A woman in jail heard that he was being brought to Hoa Lo prison and she told me, but I was not able to see him or speak to him. He was released after three or four months.

In Hoa Lo we had to wake up at five, and at about seven we would have to go outside for attendance. They would call our numbers. Then they would send us back inside, and we just stay in the cell. At about eleven they fed us … rice and sauce for six months, *troi oi [my God]*, terrible! Then we sleep, and they give us some food at four o'clock, then nothing to eat until eleven next day. We didn't work, just stay in the cell.

The first month I was there, another prisoner take my food every day. She don't let me eat, so for one month I don't eat anything. I don't fight with her, I give my food.

In the cell there were a hundred and thirty-six prisoners. After a while, they made me the prison leader. The other prisoners voted me that. I think it's because they thought I would be there for a long time. I had to check the number of prisoners, line them up for food and bath, things like that. Prisoners were in for different reasons. Some were taxi girls *[prostitutes]*, some bought and sold on the black market like me, some were even government workers who got caught taking bribes.

Every night they wake me up and take me to interrogation. I never sleep, I never eat, I become very thin. They ask, "Where you buy medicine?" I say, "I buy at the market" because I don't want to get my friends in trouble. The VC don't believe me, they beat me. A young woman guard, about the same age as my daughter now, she beat me, hit me many times. They ask, "Where did you get the dollars?" I tell them that I buy in the market, and that's true. But they think my American husband send them to me, and they hit me for that.

On December 26 they sent me to trial, and I was convicted of being a capitalist, of hoarding goods. I had already spent five months in jail, so they let me go with two years probation and a big fine. I was broke. They kept all my medicine, all my money. They took everything in my house.

So what did I do? I went back to Da Nang and started buying and selling medicine again. This was how I made my money, so that's what I did. I still went to Hanoi and bought medicine and sold it in Da Nang, just like before.

Thuy: I went to school for five years. That's where I found out that I wasn't Vietnamese, that I was Amerasian. The other students let me know. I was the only Amerasian in that school, and they always put me down, make fun of me. They tell me that the Amerasian has twelve assholes . . . *[part of a derogatory rhyme used to taunt Amerasians]*. Students who made friends with me were threatened by other kids. They said they would beat them up if they made friends with "the American." People didn't like me, and finally I didn't want to go to school anymore.

Even when I quit school and went to help my mother at the market, people would insult me. Vietnamese just don't like Amerasians. So many times I wished that I was Vietnamese, so people would like me.

Mai: My daughter married in 1988. Her husband was our neighbor in Da Nang. His mother and father worked with Americans before, so there was no problem, they didn't care that my daughter was Amerasian. That same year we applied to go to the United States. We had to pay a bribe to the officials, but not too much. The American from ODP who interviewed us, his name was Bob. He could speak Vietnamese very well. He asked us why we wanted to go to America. Thuy said she wanted to go to America to find her father. We have no sponsor in America, we go free case.

Thuy: I would like to find my father in America, but I don't know how. We have no sponsor in America. I don't know where we will go, who we will meet.

Mai: After the fall of Saigon in '75, I got a letter from Hal. My father didn't accept it, he was afraid the VC would do something to us because we got a letter from America, so he said that it wasn't for us and had it returned. That was the last I ever heard from Hal.

I can say my husband's name, but I can't write it, how will I be able to find him. His name is Hal Dellin. I will try to talk to people who worked for the embassy or the bank in Da Nang, who might remember me or my husband. Maybe they can help me.

Thuy: My biggest worry is learning English and finding a job. I would like to do nails. That's what I did in Vietnam before I came here. My husband Minh was a welder. He hopes he can find a job doing that in the United States.

Mai: I will do any job in America, wash dishes, anything. There was no future in VN. The VC didn't give me papers, no ID card, so it's very hard to stay there.

I tried to escape from Vietnam twice. The first time me and my daughter got on a boat in Quy Nhon, but the police caught us and took us to jail, fifteen people in all. I think someone probably informed on us.... You know many people will inform to the police for money. I lost one bar of gold that time, and we had to stay in a tiny crowded cell with many people. We took off our clothes it was so hot. We only had enough water to take a bath twice a week. After two months they sent us to Da Nang, and my husband paid off the police and they let us go.

I tried to escape again in 1990. We had already applied to go to America through ODP, but under the old rule the wife can only take either the husband or the mother, not both. *[That rule has since been changed, and both spouse and mother are eligible to go.]* My daughter cannot take me and her husband, so I try to escape. This time I went to Hanoi, to the north, to try to escape through China to Hong Kong. I did business with Chinese, and they told me that they could get me to Hong Kong. I went to Lang Son, all the way in the north. I was supposed to be there at nine P.M., but there were many checkpoints, and I got there late. No one was there, they had left without me. I was supposed to pay the guard at the meeting place, so at least this time I didn't lose any gold.

The VC, they killed my mother, you know. In April 1975, they took Hue. They found out that I had an American baby, an American husband. I was not even in Hue, but they went to my mother's house. They started to bother her, "Where is your daughter? Why she has an American husband?" My mother got very scared and nervous, she had a bad heart and couldn't take it. Finally she had a heart attack and died... *[Bitterly, in tears]* I very hate the VC.

Nguyen Thi Nguyen Tuyen and Nguyen Ngoc Minh

"I hope you, sir, can help rescue my beloved orphans."

Outgoing and exuberant, Nguyen Ngoc Minh does not want to use an interpreter to tell her story. "I can speak for myself," the nineteen-year-old Amerasian says, and she does. Minh, an orphan, was raised by Buddhist nuns, and five of the eight people who accompanied her to the Philippine Refugee Processing Center are women of the cloth.

As we enter her billet, one of the nuns, a young lady in grey habit, a sock hat pulled over her shaved head, looks up from her English text and greets us warmly in Vietnamese. In about a half hour, the head nun, Minh's "auntie," arrives.

Nguyen Thi Nguyen Tuyen, sixty-five years old, is in orange habit, her hair close cropped, her smile perpetual. We begin to speak through an interpreter, and she talks predominately of the orphans she left behind in Vietnam, those who were not approved for resettlement in the United States. There is a strange dynamic between Minh and her "auntie." Although Minh exhibits deference and respect to her auntie Tuyen, who adopted and raised her, Minh makes funny faces in the background when Tuyen speaks. Tuyen decides that it will be easier for her to write her story in Vietnamese than to tell it. It will be ready the next day, she assures me. Before I leave, she shows me a packet of photos taken in her orphanage in Vietnam. I ask if I can borrow them to have them duplicated. She is hesitant to let me do so, and the matter is dropped.

After I've walked a hundred meters or so from the billet, I feel a tap on my shoulder and turn around. Minh is there, an impish smile across her face as she hands me the packet of photos.

Nguyen Thi Nguyen Tuyen: I was born in the countryside of Long An province, near Saigon, in 1928. My father was a woodcutter, my mother a housewife. When I was still a girl, I was touched by the suffering of my

Orphans at the temple in Vietnam in the mid-seventies; Nguyen Ngoc Minh is in the front center, next to the statue (courtesy Nguyen Thi Nguyen Tuyen).

country, the fires and death of war, and I decided to lead the religious life. I had no desire for the loving that goes on between a man and a woman, the marriage, the beautiful clothes. I have never coveted gold. At sixteen I became a vegetarian, and at twenty-five I shaved my head and entered the pagoda.

A few years later, I went Pleiku in Central Vietnam and worked in the Co Nhi Vien Nhut Chi Mai orphanage. We had forty-six orphans, eight of them Amerasian. We took care of many children of South Vietnamese soldiers who had been killed. I often went to the 71st hospital in Pleiku to look for orphans, and that's where I found Minh, on New Year's Day in 1975. She was very sick and small. Her mother gave money to some people to take Minh to the hospital. She was afraid to keep her, afraid of the VC.

I also founded the Bao De school for children, hoping to earn a little money with which to support the orphans. I tried to help children whose parents were dead or who had been abandoned or separated from their parents in the turmoil of war. I love these children very much.

The war affected me so much. I will tell you a story: A colonel in the South Vietnamese Army, he was eating dinner with his family when a rocket hit his house, killing him and his six children, scattering pieces of their bodies everywhere. Only his wife, who had been in another room when the rocket hit, survived. She was pregnant and had been badly wounded. The doctor told her that he could save the baby, but in doing so she would not live. She agreed, and the baby was born. The doctor brought him to me, and showed me how to care for him, and I raised him. This child's name is Quoc Thoi. He is a beautiful curly haired boy, but he was taken away by the Communists and now lives abandoned in Vietnam.

In early 1975 the VC were moving south, and I left Pleiku for Saigon, bringing the orphans with me. Minh was only a few days old. The climate in Saigon was too hot. The children were itching, and the town was dangerous. I did not want to stay. I sent the boys to an orphanage at Cau Hang in Bien Hoa province and brought the girls to Bao Loc near Dalat. The climate is fresh and cool there.

When Saigon fell, we were in Bao Loc, and the Communists came and took four or five of the kids in my care. They wanted to give them to others to raise. Many of these children didn't like their new families and eventually ran away. I suffered because there was nothing I could do to stop the government from harassing us. I divided the rest of the orphans into two groups; one went with another nun and one went with me. My group had three Amerasians and five or six Vietnamese orphans. I cut off all their hair, so no one would know who was Amerasian, and we fled to Bau Cat in Cuu Long Province, very far away. We settled on a farm and supported ourselves by selling soy bean curd and soy milk.

In 1982 I heard that Amerasians would be allowed to go to America, but I felt mine were still too young. In 1984, I sent them to Saigon with another nun, so they could attend English classes at night and learn to read and write the language of their father's country.

The children who were taken from me by the Communists, they couldn't live with their new parents. Some came back to me, and some went to the other nun. In 1987 we all applied to come to America, but these

Minh as a baby in Vietnam (courtesy Nguyen Ngoc Minh)

kids have no household registration, so they were not accepted. And three of the Amerasians were not accepted because of a mix-up with their documents. They are real Amerasians, even though they look Vietnamese. So these children are in Vietnam, neglected, homeless, and miserable, and I am sure that they are falling into bad situations, these orphans I have helped bring up since they were babies.

I cannot sleep at night, worrying about my orphans. I expect the U.S. government to look into their cases and allow them to come to America, and I hope you, sir, can help rescue my beloved orphans.

Nguyen Ngoc Minh: I lived in Tinh Xa Ngoc Temple in Saigon. I don't know anything about how I got there. I think my mother left me outside, and my auntie take me. I got no mother, no father, only auntie, but she loves me very much, just like a mother.

There were many orphans, maybe a hundred, living in the temple. About half were Amerasians. When I was young, my auntie sent me to school. After school I work in temple, cleaning and sweeping. In the evening I go to my friend's house outside the temple to study about English, or I go to the temple and pray.

Many of the orphans became nuns, but for me, I don't want to, because I want to marry. I see many people become nuns, and after a few years, they go out to marry, and no more nun. I don't like that. I am

"Auntie" Nguyen Thi Ngoc Tuyen and Minh in the PRPC; Tuyen is holding a picture of orphans she raised in Vietnam.

Buddhist, but I have a boyfriend in Vietnam, so forget nun for me. My auntie was very angry about that boy, she says that I am too young, I must wait till I am twenty-five, then I can do what I want. Now I am very sad because two months after I left Vietnam my boyfriend got married to another girl.

When I was about nine years old, I go to school and the teacher asks, "You Amerasian?" I do not know, that's the first time I heard that. So I ask one Vietnamese if I am American, and he tells me yes. But I have no problem in Vietnam, I studied the same as a Vietnamese. I live in Vietnam since I was baby, and I am good. Many people half–Vietnamese and half–American are no good, but me, I'm not like that.

I liked Vietnam, but I want to help all my sisters go to America. We are all orphans, no mom or dad, and I am the only one who speaks English. We will stay together, just like in Vietnam. Our sponsor is a Buddhist nun in California.

I also go to America to look for my father. I don't know his name, but I want to find him. And I want to continue high school. I'd like to be a doctor because there are many people in Vietnam who are very poor, they can't have a doctor. I'd like to go back to Vietnam to visit my friends, to visit

Nguyen by mural of the Buddha in the PRPC

many poor people, and to visit the temple and the nuns. Maybe I can give money to people in the temple. I don't want to live there again, I just go back to visit one or two months, then I go back to America.

Here in the refugee camp I am sad, because I miss people in Vietnam. When I go to school I be shy. All my friends in the classroom, they say,

Inside Tuyen and Minh's billet in the PRPC; left to right: Le Thi Thu (interpreter), a young nun, Minh, and "Auntie" Tuyen.

"You have no father, you have no mother," and I feel very embarrassed. I'd like to have a mother and father, then I would be very happy.

   Postscript: *Tuyen, Minh, and the other seven women who accompanied them from Vietnam were resettled in California in July of 1992.*

Nguyen Thi Van and Phat

"The first time the VC call me it was a crisis . . .
but later I was just bored."

As we settle down to conversation, Van pulls out a sheaf of photos and papers, documentation of a life lost. "When I show ODP my photos, they be suspicious," she laughs, recalling her interview in Ho Chi Minh City with the American Orderly Departure Program. "They ask how did I keep all these photos when the VC come? I just do this . . ." Van laughs again and makes a digging motion with her hands. Most women with photos or documents linking them to Americans burned the evidence as North Vietnam marched south. Some, like Van, buried their pasts in gardens or fields and dug them up years later.

There are plenty of shots of her American husband, Air Force Captain Ken F. Eckman, Jr. In several he is holding their baby son, Phat. There are a few photos of Eckman on a field telephone on maneuvers in Thailand and some of Van, a stunning twenty-year-old in a traditional flowing white ao dai, having dinner with her husband. A few photos are snapshots of their wedding. In a large white file folder is a series of 8×10 black and white glossies of Ken's father, Air Force Colonel Ken F. Eckman, Sr., and his family at a banquet in his honor. Ken Jr. appears in some of the pictures with his two sisters, both married to air force captains. The occasion is Ken Sr.'s retirement from his post at the Technical School at Keesler Air Force Base in Mississippi. Although the date is not listed, from the clothes and hairstyles, I would place it in the early seventies.

I spoke with Van on numerous occasions in the summer of 1992, generally in her tidy billet. She spoke in competent English, without the aid of an interpreter. Van is a petite woman with short black hair who appears to be in her early forties. Her English, learned from her husband and from the Hoc Chuc My [American school] in Saigon, where her husband sent her, was clear and often colloquial. She occasionally broke into GI jargon, referring to the Viet Cong as Charlie.

As the overwhelming heat of June lapsed into the monsoon rains of July, Van's moods turned melancholy. She worried and wondered what her life would

221

*be like in America. Van had married Ken Eckman in 1972, and he left Vietnam
that same year as part of the pullout of U.S. forces. Van completed the paperwork
which would enable her to accompany her husband to America, but when the time
came, her mother asked her not to go, and she compliantly remained in Vietnam.
In 1973, Eckman returned to Vietnam for the birth of their baby son Phat. It was
the last time Van would see him, and the only time Eckman would see his son.
With the fall of Saigon in 1975, all communication between Van and her husband was cut. Now, twenty years later, Van and Phat are on their way to the
United States. Van says that all she hopes for is that her son can see his father
at least one time. She has written to her husband's 1973 Mississippi address but
received no reply. One day she showed me an envelope addressed to Eckman.
Why had she not mailed it? "I think about him, maybe he's married already,
so I feel very jealous, I get very angry. I take the letter and I throw it away. I
don't need him, I can take care of my son."*

Van: I was born in Cholon, but when I was seven, we moved to Long
An. My father was a cyclo driver in Cholon, and my mother sold fruit in
the market, but in Long An my family became farmers. I went to school
for five years, but my father, he got sick and died when I was still young,
and my family moved to Ap Truong in Lai Thieu district, Binh Duong
province. We lived right in the market, where my mother sold food. There
was no school there then, so I couldn't study. Anyway, we were very poor,
I had no time for school. I helped my mother make money at the market.

When she saved a little cash, my mother built a small house. Later,
when I got married, my husband gave me the money to build a big house
for my family in Lai Thieu. My husband liked my town. I took him around.
We went to the market, they have many foods he loves. Lai Thieu is famous
for its porcelain bowls. My son knows how to make those. He went to
school four months before he came here and learned.

When I be about eighteen, I see my mother is still very poor, she
doesn't have money to live, so I go to Long Hai, you know Long Hai, near
Vung Tau. There is a big base there, B-36, and I went to work there. I was
a laundress, I worked for Major Lang.

I worked at B-36 maybe two weeks, and one lunchtime my friend takes
me to a restaurant. Eckman, he comes, he sees me, and he tries to talk Vietnamese with me. I have many friends, but he doesn't like them, he wants
to talk to me. He says he wants to go dancing with me in the nighttime,
and I say okay. So, many times he takes me out. We go around, walk, talk,
look. One night he says, "I love you, I want to marry you." I say, "Okay,
I love you, too." He loves me, but that time, I don't really think I love him.
I say okay, because I need money; my mother is very poor. He wants to find
a house to let me stay with him, and I say all right. Only later, after me and

Nguyen Thi Van, circa 1971 (courtesy of Nguyen Thi Van)

him stay together a long time, four or five months, I fall in love with him for sure.

I meet him in '71, and we get married in '72. I get married, and I think it will be easy to make paper to go to United States, you know . . . but later I change my mind, because I see my mother is very sad. She don't want me to go.

We stay in Long Hai one year, then he go to Saigon to work at Tan Son Nhut airport, and I go with him. We stay together until he goes to the United States in '72. He wanted me to come with him, but I cannot go. I cannot leave my mother. Before he goes, I tell him I'm pregnant, three or four months already. So he knows when I will have the baby, and he comes back to Vietnam to see me in 1973 when the baby is born. He stayed with me one month. My mother was old, very sad, nobody to take care of her. My sister was still too young, so I could not go with him to America. Every month he sends me money, writes me a letter. Before *Charlie [the Viet Cong]* came, my husband writes me, he tells me that the VC are coming . . . but I don't think so. I think never the VC come. He tells me, sure. He says, "Please honey, take my baby, come to America. Charlie will come kill you." I don't believe him but in 1975 Charlie comes. My husband cannot write me anymore, and I feel very stupid. I feel crazy that I didn't listen to him.

April 1975, one morning, very early, the VC come. I was living in Lai Thieu. Everybody, especially mothers of GI babies, were very scared, don't go outside. If you had an American baby, you wouldn't be scared? If you go outside, maybe Charlie will kill you. So, I stay inside three hours, four hours, then I go out. The [South Vietnamese] army, they took off their clothes, they only wear shorts. 'Cause if the VC see [them in their uniforms], maybe they kill them. So in the street there are many guns, many clothes, many grenades. Many, many, I cannot count. I be very scared, too scared to count. I have an American baby, and I am afraid Charlie will kill my baby.

Where I live have many VC, but before Charlie come, they don't let us know they be VC. In 1975, when Charlie come, many stand up and say, "Oh, I am VC, I am VC." So I feel very scared. I think, "Before they don't say nothing, but now they say they are VC." I don't know what to do, who I can trust. When Charlie comes, the VC that live in Lai Thieu, they say, "Oh, Miss Van, before she married an American." So, Charlie calls me to go to the monkey house [jail].

Charlie gave me many troubles. He says, "Why you marry with an American?" He makes me go to [reeducation] school, many things I cannot say now because I cannot speak very well English. He don't like my family because I married an American. He brought me to monkey house for one month. Every month I go to police and study politics. They say, "VC very good, only you don't know what they do [for you]." You know, the first time the VC call me it was a crisis . . . but later I was just bored. They say, "VC very good, Americans very bad," every day, every week, every month. "VC very good, Ho Chi Minh very good, Americans not good." If I say that the Americans are good, he Chac ca dao me [cut off my head] and throw it away. After one month, school is finished, but he say if he don't like me, he will come back and make me go to school again. And he do that. Sometimes he calls me again, makes me go once a week, sometimes twice a week, sometimes every day.

Before '75 it was very easy to go to market and sell something. After '75 we cannot. I try to sell food, mangoes, coffee, but VC don't let me. He takes my things and throws them away and makes me go to the monkey house. He says I have no paper [for residing in Lai Thieu]; he makes it very difficult for me.

In 1977, 1978, it's very hard for people to work. If you have money, they let you go to the market and sell, but you must give them something. I have no money. How can I give them beer, cigarettes, money? They don't let me sell at the market, but I do it anyway. I have to take care of my son. I'm not scared of them. If they kill me, I die, okay.

I feel so sad in Vietnam. I can't talk to anybody, there are too many VC. Some people they escape by boat, but I never try that. I have no money, so how can I pay? And I'm scared my son might die, so I don't want to try the boat.

My son he went to school, but the teacher don't like Amerasians, only Vietnamese. He stayed in school five years, but many times the children say, "American, American," and talk bad to him. Finally, he didn't go anymore.

We applied in 1990 to ODP to come to America. I paid some money *[a bribe]*. My friend said she knows how to make the paper, so I gave her money. I don't know who she paid, but she made the paper, and I left Vietnam. It's very easy, if you pay them money.

I wanted to stay in Vietnam and let my son go to America to look for his father, but he didn't want to go without me, so I had to come too. Better he goes to America than stays in Vietnam, 'cause what can he do in Vietnam? We were very poor. He had a job, but the money was very little. I want my son to go to school in America, to learn English. Later when he speaks English, he can find a job, a very good job, make good money, and later get married. When he gets married, okay, I will feel very good inside.

My son wants to find his father. He looks at the pictures, the photos, and he says, "Let's find father quick." I wrote my husband a letter in '76, but I don't know what happened. I didn't get an answer. I wrote him again from here, but still I haven't heard from him. *[Van shows me a letter addressed to her husband in America. I ask why she didn't send that one.]* Why I don't send this letter? I think about my husband. I think maybe he's married already, so I feel jealous, I get very angry. I take the letter and I throw it away. I don't need him, I can take care of my son myself.

Phat: I have my father's picture, and I will find him. I will just knock on the door and when he opens it, I will ask, "Father, do you recognize me?"

Van: What will I say to my husband if I see him? I will say, "Hello, long time no see. I am very surprised to meet you again. I come because my son wants to see you. I don't want to make trouble for you if you're married. That's the main thing. I don't want to make trouble for you ... but you see my son, for a long time he misses you. I just want my baby to see you and call you father."

Postscript: Van and Phat were resettled in Newark, New Jersey, in the late fall of 1992. After being temporarily housed in a refugee shelter, they found their own apartment. Within a week of her resettlement, Van got a job in a box factory. Phat is working as well. Van has written me several times. The following is an excerpt from a letter dated February 1, 1993:

Nguyen Thi Van and friends in Vietnam, 1971 (courtesy of Nguyen Thi Van)

I haven't located my husband yet because no one has been able to help me. My case worker said he was going to help me but he hasn't done anything to locate him. . . . The United States is a very sad place for me right now. I only know the streets to go to work and to come home. I haven't learned my way around.

In December of 1993, I received a short note from Van. The Red Cross had succeeded in locating her husband, but he has declined to contact Van and Phat or to let the Red Cross supply them with his address or phone number.

Lam Thu Cam Lien
and Sophie

"The Americans, when they want something,
they just speak straight to you.
They don't go from this side to that side.
... But Vietnamese speak far and then come close."

Carefully dressed and impeccably coiffed, Lien appears much younger than her fifty-four years. She is the mother of five children, including a twenty-four-year-old Amerasian daughter named Sophie and two children by a Korean husband. The latter three children, along with Sophie's daughter Linda, are in the PRPC together with Lien.

Lien acted as my interpreter in a tutorial class for Amerasians. When she learned that I was collecting the stories of women who had Amerasian children, she volunteered to tell her own. Much of what Lien speaks about centers on the difficult relationship between herself and her American "husband," Floyd Derault. Most of their problems, she believes, had their roots in differences between their respective cultures. Lien puts it succinctly, "I don't understand him too much, and he don't understand me either."

Lam Thu Cam Lien: I was born in Saigon and lived with my parents, three brothers, and three sisters. We lived in a middle-class house, not so big, not so small. My father was a clerk for Air Vietnam. My mother stayed at home, she was a housewife. She is still in Vietnam, but my father, he died already. I went to school nine years, I studied Vietnamese and French.

When I was young, my house burned down. My family lost everything, and we became poor. My birth certificate burned, too. I have to make new birth certificate, and we make my date of birth 1935 instead of 1939, so it is easier for me to get a job. After I finished school, I went to work for the Vietnamese army. At this time Ngo Dinh Diem was the president. There were no Americans, the French stay in Vietnam.

I am so young when I start working for the army, only fifteen years old, but my birth certificate says I am eighteen, so I can work. I did social work. I worked as a nurse, clerk, psychologist. I did everything, I helped the wives, too. Often when someone from out of the country comes to Vietnam, I am the first one in Vietnam to meet them. I go to the airport, greet them, and give them a flower.

Many Vietnamese officers, they like me very much. I have one boyfriend. He says he loves me so much, but when I ask him about getting married, he says no. His family don't want him to get married with a poor girl, with no house, not "high class." I feel very sad about that.

After a few years I meet a captain, and I live with him four years. We don't make the marriage document, we just stay like boyfriend and girlfriend in the same house. I have two sons from him, they still live in Saigon. After I born my two sons, I find out he's already married. You know, the first time we meet he likes me, so he says he's single, and he never told me he had a wife.

I went back with my mother, and I look for a place to make money to take care of my two sons. I start to work as a cashier in my brother's nightclub. It's called "Twenty-Five" because it's at 25 Tu Do street. Many Americans come there to have a drink, listen to music, and talk to the girls. After I worked there about a year, I met one American, this was maybe 1965 or 1966. The first time he meets me he asks me some things about my family, and then, about two or three months later he says, "You want to be my girlfriend?" I think, "I have two Vietnamese sons, but I am very unlucky, because my Vietnamese husband he is already married. I think maybe, if I stay to work in the bar, maybe people look at me no good. Maybe I stay with him better than work in bar." So I stop work with my brother, this man rents a house, and I go live with him. He was a civilian, he worked for Air America. I was about twenty-six or twenty-seven, he was about forty-five. His name was Floyd Derault [not a real name].

He treats me sometime very good, but sometime not so good. What I mean is that sometime I don't understand him too much, and he don't understand me either. Like, you know, he has friends come to the house, and he says to them, "This is my girlfriend." I already have one daughter with him, and he calls me "girlfriend." I don't like that, it hurts me. I say, "Why you don't call me your wife, why you call me girlfriend?" He says, "You not my wife, you my girlfriend." I ask him why, he says because we don't have certificate of marriage, the American way is like that. He says if we stay together, but don't have certificate of marriage, we cannot call ourselves husband and wife. Many Vietnamese women living with American men have trouble like this.

I stay with him four or five years, but we have many problems. I have some trouble because of the birth certificate I changed when I was younger. When I meet him, he asks me where I was born. I say, "I was born in Saigon." After we stay together one or two years, he sees my birth certificate. It says that I'm born An Hoi, Binh Trung. He gets very mad, he says, "Lien, why you not be honest with me?" I say, "Why you say that? I don't understand." He says, "Even your birthday, your birthplace, you don't tell the truth. If you be honest with me, I can give you a house, a car, anything you want. But now I don't do anything for you because you a liar woman."

But you know, I'm not liar woman, but I don't understand American people. When he first come to my brother's nightclub, I tell him I was born in Saigon, but that time I don't speak English so well, so I don't explain him everything. I don't tell him that when I be young my house burned down and when I make new birth certificate I change date from 1939 to 1935, so I seem older, so I can get a job. When I do this, the lawyer also tells me to change my place of birth, so we write An Hoi, Binh Trung.

Because of the problem with my birth certificate, my American husband don't trust me. When I born my daughter, he don't believe it's his. When I go to hospital, he don't come to see me, and I'm hurt. I ask him when I come back home, "Why you don't come to the hospital to see me?" And he say, "I'm afraid you born one Vietnamese boy or Vietnamese girl, and when people look at me, what will they think? They will think I am stupid or something, that's what." He don't trust me. He thinks he is not the father, that I have another boyfriend. But when he sees my daughter, and he looks in her eyes, her face, he sees that she looks like him too much. At that time he cries, and he says, "Oh Lien, I'm sorry because I didn't trust you. I thought that you stay with me because of money, and after that you get another boyfriend. I don't go to hospital to see you, now I feel sorry. Because now, I know this girl is my daughter."

When my daughter was born, I don't call her Sophie.... Tran Dai, that's the name I give her. And I don't write the father's name on the birth certificate, I put down the last name "Lam," same as my last name. When he looks at that certificate, he says, "No, I don't want this, you must find out how much it costs, I don't care. You must change her last name, she must have my last name." And I did. I have two birth certificates here. On one her last name is mine, and one it's her father's. And Floyd, he likes the name Sophie, so that's what we call her.

After I born my daughter, he gave me one new car, and he said "I am sorry, maybe I make you feel bad." And I say, "Thank you," and I forget all.

Floyd, he drink one month about ten bottles of vodka, but he only could get six bottles from the PX. One day I just joking with him, I say,

"Honey, this afternoon I go buy for you more four bottles of vodka." And he say, "Sure, thank you, that's very good," and he go to work. I stay home, I feel tired, I don't buy the vodka for him. When he come home, he say, "Where's my vodka?" I say, "Oh honey, I'm sorry, I don't feel so good. I will buy some other day." He get angry and he say, "No, I don't like that, when you say something to me you must do." Because when he say something he mean it. He don't want me to do after a few days, he don't like that.

I see he loves my daughter very much. Every time he finishes work, he comes home, he see my daughter, and he's very happy. But between him and me, it's not good. I know we don't love each other.

After Sophie was born, I stay with Floyd about two more years. Every year he has one month vacation, and he go back to the United States. When he go, I go back to work at the nightclub with my brother. One time he come back, he get angry. He say, "Why you go back to work? I tell you to stay home." He's furious. I say I feel very sad, very lonely. I want to go work at the club, no problem. He say, "No, I don't want you to." I say sorry, but he tells me, "No, I don't want that. I don't want to stay with a woman who don't listen to me, who don't do what I want."

After a few months he starts again, "Why you go work? I told you not to go there." I say, "We talk already, why you make trouble?" He say, "I think maybe you have another boyfriend." I say, "No, why you don't believe me?" So I tell him, "If all the time we fight like this, maybe I have to go back with my mother." He say, "Okay, you can go back with your mother, but you let Sophie stay here, and I take care of her." But I tell him, "No, I born her and I have to take care of her." He says, "You not a rich woman, you cannot take care of her." I say, "I don't care. I can work, take care of her. I don't need you." Finally he agreed that I take care of Sophie, and he say that he give Sophie a hundred dollars a month, for her, not for me. So I go back to my mother, and every month my maid goes over there, and he puts a hundred dollars on the table, and she brings it home to me.

I send Sophie to see him once or twice a week. I see him sometime, but when I see him we just talk about Sophie. He went back to America in 1969 or 1970, I don't remember. After he left, I opened an account in the Man Nhat Tan [Manhattan] Bank. He say, "One month, one hundred dollars," but now that he go back to the States, he give one year, maybe two, three times, not like before. We got that money for about two or three years. In 1975 the VC came, and then it stopped, and I don't have any more news from him.

American and Vietnamese husband very different. The American, when they want something, they just speak straight to you. They don't go from this side to that side, they don't beat around the bush. But Vietnamese speak far and then come close.

Lien and Sophie in Vietnam, late sixties or early seventies (courtesy Lam Thu Cam Lien)

My American husband, sometime he hurt me like this. Sometime he say, "Lien, I want you to look for me one girl have long hair and be young, younger than you." First time I think he's joking. I just smile, don't say anything. But after he speaks again, I get mad, I say, "Why? If you want to look for girlfriend, go look yourself. You can tell me, 'Oh Lien, I'm busy, I want to meet some friends at home.' You go back to your mother's house and stay there.' I don't want you to say I look for you for a girl, I don't want you to say that."

After Floyd go back to the States, I get married again, with one Korean. He work for RMK company as an engineer. This time I make the paper, I have a marriage certificate. I have two children with him, one boy and one daughter.

I stayed with him four years. In 1972 or 1973, all Americans must go back to America. At that time he's out of a job, and he don't want to go back to Korea, but he says he must find a place to work, to make money.

In March of 1973, he went to Australia alone. At the time he left, he didn't have a job for almost one year, so we didn't have the money for me and my family to go with him. We owed money, we had debts, and we had to pay them off. After two or three months, he starts to send me money, two hundred dollars every week. After about six months, he started to make the papers for all my family to go to Australia, except for my two Vietnamese sons, my two oldest children. They always stayed with my mother, she always took care of them. So, I think we will go to Australia in March 1975, but when VC come, everything stopped.

In 1974 my husband wrote me one letter from Australia. He says, "Oh, Lien, you must hurry to get out of VN because the VC come." You don't have to take anything with you, only take care of your three babies, go with them. Just you hurry to go."

And that time I ask my brother, "Will the VC come?" My brother, he works in the army, he says, "The VC can't come here, never, because we take care of Saigon very good." So I wait for my passport to come, and I think I will go to Australia by airplane. I never thought the VC would come, so I didn't hurry. But, you know, my brother was wrong, and when VC come they put him in jail because he work for the ARVN. I can't get out of Vietnam, and I never heard from my Korean husband again.

Years later, when my brother got out of jail, he asked my daughter Sophie, "You know your father's address?" And she says she knows, and she gives it to him. And my brother wrote a letter in Vietnamese for Sophie and sent to Sophie's father in America. But Floyd, Sophie's father, cannot speak Vietnamese, he cannot understand anything. After about two or three months, he send me a letter. He say, "I read, but I don't understand nothing. I have to go around and around to Vietnamese people, they read for me." You know, that time there are not too many Vietnamese people in the States, so it took some time for him to get a translation. He sent a money order, four hundred dollars, for Sophie, but we could not exchange it. We went many places, but they would not accept it. Finally we find a way to change it, but at a very cheap rate.

He and his sister wrote me a letter. His sister wrote, "The VC came, but you are still okay, and I'm very happy about that." And he asks in the letter, "Sophie, you want to go to the United States?" And my daughter, she don't know how to write English, I teach her, and I ask my friend to help me find the English words to write. My daughter write her father that she wants to go to America, but she will not leave without her mother and her family. This was about 1983, and we don't hear from Floyd again.

You know, all my life I stay in Saigon City. I never really knew much about the war, I only read in the newspaper. Only in the country, have many trouble about VC. In Saigon, we don't know nothing, but we have trouble in 1968, the VC came into the city. At this time it was Tet, and I hear many bombs. I stay with my mother one day, and maybe seven o'clock next day, I go back home. Floyd, he was home, and he was very glad when I came in. He tell me, "One day I stay home wait for you. I think you have trouble, I worry much, but I'm very happy to see you come back."

I never thought the VC could take Saigon. In 1975, when finally I knew that the VC were coming, I was very afraid. At that time I had many nice clothes, I threw them out. The first time they came, they don't know nothing about me, that I have foreign husbands. But then, they come around the neighborhood, and somebody tells them, "Oh, this girl, she get married to American, or, she get married to Korean." Then they don't like me. But Koreans, they have black hair, black eyes, just like the Vietnamese, so they can't tell my babies are Korean. But Sophie they can tell. She has brown hair, she looks like an American. They know that she is American, not Vietnamese. Then they say, "Oh, this woman, she got married with the rich foreigners. Now she must do something very dirty, like go out and clean the garbage. She must do that because before she's rich, she have everything, and we didn't have nothing." So they made me go around and collect garbage in Saigon, one week maybe two or three times.

One week before the VC come, the Man Nhat Than Bank, where I put my money . . . it closed. So I cannot get my money, and I have nothing. I have to sell everything in my house. That time was very bad, I cannot tell you. I sell everything to buy some food. I don't work. They don't let me, they don't need me. I sell my clothes, I go outside and buy something and then I sell that. I buy maybe two cans, I sell two hundred and fifty dong, something like that. I sell sometimes clothes, sometimes rice, sometimes oil, anything.

The VC said whoever got married with American people must go out of the city, far from Saigon. The VC wanted me to go to the New Economic Zone. I didn't want to go. I never planted rice or did farm work in my life. I don't know how, and I have to take care of my babies, so my mother says she will go in my place. My mother tells the VC, "My daughter don't want to go, I go for her." She took my older son and my youngest brother with her. She was too old to work, so she just stayed home and cooked, but my son and my brother had to work very hard.

My daughter Sophie went to school five or six years. She looks like an American. When she go out, many people look at her and laugh, they say something bad, *My Lai muoi hai lo dit, dit lo nay xi lo kia.* That means Amerasian have twelve asses, when you shit you shit twelve times, and then twelve times come more." *[More literally, Amerasians have 12 assholes, if they fart from one, gas comes out the others.]* I don't know why they say that. It's just a rhyme they say to tease the Amerasian. My daughter come home, she cry. She say, "Why you born me American? Why you no born me Vietnamese, because they always laugh at me. I don't like that." So she didn't want to stay in Vietnam.

Sophie, sometime she listen to me, but sometimes, I say, "Sophie do this," and she don't listen. She must do what she do. My Korean babies don't make me any trouble. They look like Vietnamese and they act like Vietnamese. When I say something, they do. But Sophie, she say, "I want

Left to right: Lam Thu Cam Lien, Linda and Sophie in the PRPC.

to do something, let me do. ... You don't have to tell me to do this or do that." If she want to do something, she just go ahead.

Sophie has a baby girl from her Vietnamese boyfriend. They lived together in Vietnam. Now he went to America already, but they are finished. She don't want to see him no more. Her daughter Linda she is here with us.

We are going to Long Beach, California. My sponsor is my young sister. She went there nine years ago, and now she works as a manicurist. I will take any job in America, but I think I cannot speak very well English, so I don't know what job I can find. Maybe when I study in W.O. *[Work Orientation course in the PRPC]* I know better about the job.

You know I made the paper to go to America in 1983. I wait seven years till they call me. I never pay no bribe. I don't know how, I don't know who to pay. When we make the paper, there is a sign on the wall, "No bribes," so I am afraid. But many people did pay bribe, and they leave Vietnam fast.

My Vietnamese son, he also want to go to America, but he is thirty years old. That's too old *[the non–Amerasian children of applicants must be under twenty-one to accompany them]*. I don't let him lie about his age because of all the problems I had with my birth certificate. I was afraid to do that. But many people, they buy Amerasians in Vietnam, so they can leave to go to America with them. They not the real mother or husband.

They just buy them and make the paper to leave. I think here in the PRPC, eight out of ten families bought their Amerasians. They not really the same family.

I hope in the future my children will have a better life in America than in Vietnam. I don't want to live in a Vietnamese neighborhood in America. The Vietnamese people, I hear, they see the new Vietnamese people come, they look down on them. I don't like to stay together with Vietnamese people.

The first person you meet walking into Sophie's billet is her two-year-old daughter Linda. She grabs you by the knees and keeps you in limbo until her mother or grandmother lets out with a cease and desist order in Vietnamese. One afternoon in May, I noticed that Linda's belly was terribly distended. Worms and other intestinal parasites are among the most common ailments of the refugees, as well as the local Filipinos, but neither the PRPC hospital nor the tiny farmacias in the nearby village of Morong carried any remedies.

I called to a friend in Manila to send up a bottle of Quantrel, the standard treatment. After receiving a dose, Linda passed a quantity of worms, but her stomach never really seemed to lose its bloat.

The walls of Sophie's billet are hung with professionally shot photos of her in a variety of poses and costumes, remnants of the days she modeled for Tribeco cola, a popular Vietnamese soft drink. In a classic instance of typecasting, she received an offer to play an Amerasian in a Vietnamese movie production. Sophie was set to leave Vietnam at the time and could not accept.

Sophie's modeling career ended with her short term live-in relationship with a young Vietnamese man. He objected to Sophie posing before the camera. Sophie and her boyfriend soon separated, and shortly after he went to the United States, Linda was born of this relationship.

In the PRPC, Sophie helps out at Community Family Services International, a counseling and mental health service for the refugees. She talks to new arrivals about stress management and gives them orientation to CFSI's services. "Here I can introduce the program and do everything," she says. "In Vietnam an Amerasian could not do that."

We speak without the aid of an interpreter. Frequently, Sophie and her mother confer in Vietnamese over meanings of difficult words before Sophie answers in English.

Sophie: When I was about five or six years old, I had brown hair and brown eyes. When I went outside, many people called me *My lai, My lai.* That means Amerasian, but it's very impolite.

I asked my mother about that, and my mother told me that I had an American father, not Vietnamese. Then I realize that I have many differences between me and Vietnamese. When I go to school, I feel very different because all of the people have black hair, only me brown hair.

Some of my classmates, sometimes they don't like me because in the lesson the teacher teaches about the bad way of the Americans. After that, the people look at me and say, "Oh, she's the daughter of an American. She's not good because she has the same blood."

The lesson always says that Americans come to Vietnam and make many families fall down and cause many problems for the Vietnamese. Sometimes I disagree with my teacher and my friends because my mother tell me about my father, and I think my father is very good. I don't think he is the same as what the teacher teaches about America.

When I am growing up, I think the people around me are not good because they are always saying my father is bad. They always want to put me down. Sometimes I feel afraid to make friends with Vietnamese people.

When I go to school, I always study very well, but my teacher discriminates against me. My Vietnamese classmates sometimes study not as well as me, but the teacher prefers them to me. Sometimes my school has a program, and my friends want me to introduce the program, but the teacher doesn't agree. She works for the Communists, and if she puts an Amerasian up before many people, it's not good for her. I always have many troubles in my class. I only have Vietnamese classmates, only I am Amerasian. I have some friends, but not good friends, because when I am growing up I feel only I can understand myself. People don't care about me, don't understand me, so I don't have a best friend.

If I have a friend and I think she is my good friend, and I go to her house, sometimes her parents don't want her to stay with me. They say, "Oh, if you are friends with Amerasians, you have many problems because Communists don't like Amerasians." I always hear that. And if I go to a friend's house and I see her father, I am very sad because I don't have father. So many times I just don't like to go out.

As a girl, I am always very busy. My mother teaches me English, and also I study in school. But the food is not enough for my family, so at night I must sell many things. Sometimes I sell cigarettes, and sometimes I sell cakes. Always, I feel very sad. My happiest time is only when I get a letter from my father.

I went to school for nine years. In 1983 my father write me a letter, and he say he want me to go to America, so I stopped school and I start to study English. But I don't go, because my father says he wants only me. He don't want my younger sister, my younger brother, or my mother to go with me. I think that is wrong, because when I am growing up I have mother, younger sister, and younger brother. If I go to America, all my family must go too. I think it's no good for me to go alone, so I don't agree with my father. He don't understand me when I say I want to take my brother or sister. He says, "Why? That's no good for you." He want me to go right away. I think he is very angry, and I wait from 1983 until now.

When I get to America, I will contact him. I have his address, but he has many houses. When my father was living in Vietnam, he was very rich. He tells my mother that he wants me to be like Ngo Dinh Nhu, the first lady of Vietnam. He says, "If Ngo Dinh Nhu can do many things, than my daughter can do the same as her."

I know that my mother and my father have a problem. But I don't worry, I think I can understand him. When I am growing up, I do many things. I can take care of myself, but I want to know him. I want to see him, I think I love him so much. Because when I am growing up, I never have a father. I think he is very kind, and I think he can love me too. I believe that.

In Vietnam, I always have many problems and I am very sad, but I always believe that my future would be good. Vietnamese people were not kind with me, I don't trust them. They always want to make me fall down. That's why I want to go to America.

In America, the first thing, I want to see my father. Then I want to study more. This is very important to me. After that, I want to have a good job. I would like to sell clothes because in Vietnam I have experience with that. I only hope my family will have a good future, that my younger sister and brother can go to school and have a good job, and my mother can have a good job too. And I hope we can help my two elder brothers, who are still in Vietnam.

I was born in Vietnam, but Vietnam could not give me a good future, so I must go to the United States. I think I will have many problems because my English and my customs are different, but I try. I believe America will be very good for me. I have American blood, and I want to live there. But what's good in Vietnamese culture, I keep, and what's good in American culture I keep. I never ask myself if I am Vietnamese or American, I don't worry about that.

Postscript: *On July 12, 1992, Lien and her family left the PRPC for Long Beach, California. For several months they stayed in the home of Lien's sister, and in December they rented a house of their own in Garden Grove. Sophie quickly found work as a waitress in a Vietnamese nightclub. Lien is presently looking for a job. I asked Lien if she knew any of her neighbors. She replied, "No, I never see anyone. In California, every door is closed." Her feeling, though, was one of optimism, "but anyway, the life in the U.S. is more better than Vietnam, because if we have job we can take care of the life."*

Sophie's search for her father ended in disappointment. She was able to make contact with her father's sister, only to find out that Floyd Derault died several years ago, of an alcohol-related illness.

MOTHERS

I, like a river
have been turned aside by this harsh age.

Anna Akhmatova, "The Fifth"

Nguyen Thi Lang

"Then one day we heard that Amerasians
can go to America ... My son, he says,
'You say one day you write father.
Mother, now you write.'"

"You say you come, then you must. I wait for you, but you don't come."
Lang spoke in a firm, gentle voice, and I was chastened. We had met in her
English-as-a-Second-Language classroom a week before, and I had arranged to
speak with her in her billet the following evening. Accustomed as I was to the Viet-
namese's relaxed sense of time, I thought it would cause no problem that I was
unable to keep our appointment. I was mistaken. She had written a short
paragraph indicating her disappointment over our missed meeting and showed
it to me for correction. Lang, I was to discover, took every possible opportunity
to improve her English.

Despite her meager three years of schooling, Lang has a love of the written
word. She told me that she had kept a diary in Vietnam and often handed me
short pieces written for class, for my comment and correction. Her attitude
towards learning the language was earnest. When we spoke, there invariably was
an English-Vietnamese dictionary within reach, ready for consultation.

At forty-seven years old, her eyes framed by wire-rimmed glasses, her speech
measured and thoughtful, Lang exudes a scholarly demeanor that belies a lifetime
spent working in the fields. We were to meet regularly over a period of three
months as she told her story. Our initial meetings were without benefit of an inter-
preter, and when the descriptions of her life went beyond her knowledge of the
English language, Lang would patiently pause and refer to her dictionary. Our
later discussions took place with the aid of a translator.

Our first conversation took place on a very windy February day. Months
had passed since the monsoon rains, and the gusts clawed on dry earth, depositing
layers of grit in the refugee quarters. Outside Lang's billet, children flew minu-
scule kites of used notebook paper and plastic bags. Several had wrapped around
the power line and fluttered erratically in the wind. Just inside the billet hung a

240

small wall altar on which rested a tin can laden with joss sticks. Hanging nearby was a likeness of Jesus. Lang is a follower of Cao Dai, a religious sect native to Vietnam. In its days of power in the 1940s, it counted over a million disciples and maintained an army which opposed both the Viet Minh and the French. The religion reverences both Jesus and Buddha and numerous secular figures as diverse as Sun Yat Sen and Victor Hugo.

As we spoke, the room filled up with neighborhood children. Occasionally one would be unable to resist the urge to explore my camera or push buttons on the cassette player, but would desist as soon as Lang issued a gentle reprimand. Several Amerasians dropped in just to meet "the American." One young man, mistaking me for someone of authority, earnestly requested me to aid him in bringing his wife over from Vietnam.

Lang has six children. Her oldest two, both sons, remain in Vietnam with their families, including all three of Lang's grandchildren. In the PRPC with Lang are Minh Hanh, her twenty-three-year-old Amerasian son, and her two young daughters and youngest son, all under ten years old. The three younger children are from Lang's marriage to a former ARVN soldier who had escaped from reeducation camp and settled in her town of Xuan Loc in Dong Nai province. Seven years after his escape, he was rearrested and held incommunicado. Two years later, Lang was to read of his execution in the newspaper. She was never informed.

Standing about five feet ten inches, his hair and eyes brown, Minh Hanh, according to Lang, bears a strong resemblance to his father, Lloyd E. Grow. Lang and Lloyd had met and fallen in love when Lang worked as a housekeeper at the Bien Hoa army base, where Lloyd was stationed. He left Vietnam when Lang was five months pregnant, and Minh Hanh never met his father.

Aware that Amerasians were being resettled in the United States through the Orderly Departure Program, Minh Hanh wanted to go. He asked his mother to try to contact his father, but Lang was hesitant. She worried that the Vietnamese government would persecute them for writing to America. She says, "I wait until 1990 to write him. I wait because I am scared of the VC. In 1990, I see many people write letters to America, so I write too."

Lang wrote to the address Grow had given her seventeen years before. Remarkably, he still lived there. Grow immediately agreed to sponsor Lang and her family, and they will be going to his home in Minnesota.

Grow was able to enlist the aid of his congressman in expediting Lang's departure from Vietnam. In a recent letter to Lang he writes of plans being made for her arrival: "There will be a party for you on May 23 to meet the family. Among the invited will be Congressman Vin Weber, without whose help you may have never made it out of Vietnam."

I WAS BORN on Jan 24, 1945, in Lai Nguyen village, Ben Cat district in Song Be province, about fifty kilometers from Saigon. I am the last of five children by my father. He was killed shortly after I was born. My mother remarried three years after his death and had five more children.

Lai Nguyen was a farming village of between three and four hundred families. There was no electricity in the village, and a few lambrettas provided the village transportation. We had a small battery radio we would listen to, and sometimes some people from the city would come and show a movie at the village, an action movie.

Our family, like most in the village, followed the Cao Dai religion. We lived in a wooden house with a thatch roof and got our water from a well outside. We had our own fields and grew coffee, rice, corn, and mung bean. When I was a girl, my day was like this: I would wake up, feed the animals, prepare the breakfast for the family, take care of my younger brothers and sisters, prepare lunch, feed the animals again, take care of the children, and then make dinner. Sometimes I would help out in the fields, planting while my parents turned the soil. This was my routine. I only went to school for three years.

This is the story I was told of my father's death. When I was only twelve days old, the French army took control of our village and we moved to another one. My father, who bought and sold tobacco, was not there when the French came, he was away buying tobacco. The Viet Minh were suspicious of him. They believed that he was out of the village because he knew that the French were going to come, and they accused him of being a spy for the French. One day, almost a year later, they waited for my father to return from the market. They took him to the forest and shot him.

My uncle had secretly followed them and saw what happened. He then took my family through the forest and across the river to the Cao Dai army post. The Cao Dai had an army made up of followers of the religion, and they opposed the Viet Minh. We went to their village stronghold and settled there.

My uncle attempted to avenge my father's death. A year after my father was killed, my uncle saw my father's executioner going into the forest to defecate and followed him. My uncle attacked my father's killer with a machete, but he only succeeded in slicing off the man's ear.

I was married when I was eighteen. The marriage was arranged by my family and that of my future husband. His family consulted with my uncle, who acted as a go-between and contacted my parents. I had known my future husband for years, we had worked in the fields together. My mother asked me my opinion of him, so I had a little say in the matter, but very little. I told my mother that since I knew him already and liked him, he seemed suitable but that the final decision should be the parents'. In Vietnam, children don't marry for love. It's the parents' responsibility to chose a suitable partner.

The members of my future husband's family came to meet my family.

Nguyen Thi Lang

They brought two bottles of wine, two bags of tea, and four pieces of betel and four leaves. On the engagement date they repeated these gifts, but added earrings and a ring and some money to help my family prepare for the engagement. My uncle, who was skilled in astrology and palm reading, asked our birthdates, read my palm, and chose an appropriate wedding date.

On the wedding day the groom's family came to my house, brought jewelry, gold chains, and bracelets, and took us to their house for the wedding. Once we married we stayed with my husband's family, as is the Vietnamese custom.

In 1968 my husband got sick and died. One day he lay down, and he could not get up. He never got up again, and in six months he was dead. We went to the doctor three times, but then we could not go again. We had no more money, we were poor farmers. We had one son, and I was six months pregnant with another when he died.

After my husband's death, I went back to my village to live with my parents. At this time there were problems in the village with the Viet Cong. The Thieu government controlled the village in the day, but by night it belonged to the VC. Anyone the VC suspected of collaborating with the government would be taken away. These people were never seen again. *[The Vietnamese had a slang term for these areas controlled by both the VC and the government—"vung xoi dau," sticky rice with bean—the idea being that you can't separate the sticky rice from the bean, i.e. the government from the VC.]*

The VC didn't show itself as a large unit. They worked in small groups, hid in the daytime, and entered villages at night to get food. Often at night they would force the villagers to construct barricades made of earth and stones on the road two kilometers from the village. In the daytime, government troops would come and force us to tear down the barricades we built the night before. It went on like this, several nights a week, for about a year.

Finally, in 1969, the Thieu government forced us to relocate. One day American soldiers came to our village in GMC trucks. We were used to seeing Americans. They often went out on patrol near our village. This time though, they came to relocate us. They were polite, but they told us we had one hour to move. Some of the villagers protested, especially the wealthier ones, who didn't want to leave their homes and fields; but there was no choice, everyone had to go. I was not sorry to leave, the village had become too dangerous. The soldiers helped us get our belongings on the trucks and moved us to an ARVN base about twenty kilometers away.

Our village was one of many in the area that was being relocated. We were sent to the ARVN camp and then told to clear land about a kilometer away. We were paid sixty dong a day for our work. A camp for the evacuees was to be built here. Dwellings were built, one for each family, about twenty in a row, each house six meters away from the last. They just built a cement frame, like columns, and a corrugated iron roof. We had to make the walls. The richer people made wooden walls, and the poor people used thatch. We made ours of thatch, and it took me ten days to finish. As dwellings were completed, families were moved in one by one. My family was the last on the list, and the last to be called. It was six months before we were able to move off the ARVN base and into our new house, and while I waited to be called, I worked clearing land for dwellings for other villages that had been relocated.

The American military offered jobs on the base to all those from my village who wanted to work. Those that didn't went back to farming or worked at the market. I took a job as a housekeeper at the U.S. army base at Bien Hoa, near Lai Khe, working with the Second Batallion, Eighth Cavalry, First Cavalry Division. For me, it was easier than working out in the hot sun like I had always done. A bus came and took me to work and took me back home again.

After six months, the army moved to Dong Nai, and I went with them. I rented a house there in the town of Tam Hiep near Long Binh in Dong Nai. I left my children with my family in Song Be, and each week on my days off I would travel the fifty kilometers back there to see them.

While I was working on base as a housekeeper for the communications section of the first cavalry division at Bien Hoa Army base, I met one American. His name was Lloyd. I knew that he had a wife and children in the States, but he was very good to me, and we became like boyfriend and girlfriend. Sometime we stay together in his room, but in the day, not in the night. One day his officer saw me and him in the room. He told me to come into the office. I say that Lloyd is my boyfriend. He said that he didn't like GIs to have Vietnamese girlfriends. I didn't speak English very well. Some things he said I couldn't understand. I told him that we weren't doing anything, just sitting and talking, but after one week, he took my boyfriend and sent him to the fire zone. My boyfriend, he told me, but I didn't understand. I thought he went home to America. I was five months pregnant with his baby.

Excerpt from letter to Lang from Lloyd dated March 14, 1990:

> *I knew you were expecting a baby before I departed Vietnam, but I was not sure it was mine. Captain Vitachi, The officer who caught us in the hootch, asked me when I had to report to his office. Since I was put on a plane and sent to the fire base, I did not get a chance to ask you about it. When I departed, I was not sure. . . .*

My mother was angry that I'm going to have an American baby. She sees I am pregnant with American baby, she's very sad. She says that a Vietnamese woman to be pregnant with no husband, that's very bad. My mother loved me, but she was ashamed of me. When I gave birth to my baby son, I was scared of my mother, so I went to Dong Nai city and rented a house. I lived there alone. After my baby was born, three months, I went back to see my mother. I say, "I'm sorry, I very love my boyfriend. I didn't take care of myself. Mother, you understand me." She sees my baby, she loves him, and she's not angry no more.

In 1972, after I have Lloyd's baby son, I moved to live with my sister in Vung Tau. I sent Lloyd a letter to America. I could not write English very well, I look in the dictionary to help me. I had his address, he gave it to me before he left. *[Lang carefully unwraps a piece of waxed paper and takes out a yellowing slip of paper. On one side is Lloyd's military address in Fort Sill, Oklahoma. On the other is his address in Minnesota. Lang kept this piece of paper well hidden in the years after '75, for fear of reprisals from the government.]* Lloyd, he sent me a letter back too. In 1974 I wrote him again. He wrote me back and said he would send me money, but we moved to live in Xuan Loc, Dong Nai province. After we moved, I didn't get any more letters. In 1975 the VC came, and I scared if I write a letter to America, the VC say, "You have a husband in America," and he take me to jail. I'm scared of that, so I cannot write.

I stay in Xuan Loc and work in the fields. In 1978 a former soldier of the Thieu regime escaped from reeducation camp, where the Communists had sent him in 1975, and came to Xuan Loc. He worked for many people as a farmer. In the morning he goes to work, in the afternoon the landlord pays him, and he goes to buy rice to eat. I see him, he works for everybody. I tell him, come work for me too. So he works for me in the morning, and in the afternoon I pay him the money. He goes home, he stay together with my brother. He sees that I no have husband, that I am a widow. He comes to talk to me, he says he loves me. He wants to marry me, so we get married and we be together for seven years. We had three children, two girls and a boy.

In 1985 the army come to Xuan Loc to find him. They know he escaped from reeducation camp, and they take him go to jail again, to P4 prison in Tay Ninh. I traveled there many times, but they never let me see him. I ask, "Why I can't see my husband?" but they don't answer me. I bring him food, but I don't know if they give it to him or not. I never get letter from him. I never saw him again.

One morning in 1990, I go to the market and buy a newspaper. I see in the newspaper that the court of Tay Ninh sentenced my husband to death. They killed him on June 27, 1990. They never tell me about it. I only found out in the newspaper, they say he die. They never even let me know, I don't know why.

You know, my brother was killed fighting the VC. Another brother also a soldier, was wounded, and cannot use one leg.

Before the Communists came, one person could work and take care of a family. Under the Communists, even with a whole family working we could hardly survive. We had to sell a part of our crops to the Communists and a part we could keep or sell outside. The Communists paid a very low price for our rice, but the price of food was very high, the price of fertilizer too. So we could barely afford to buy food after growing and selling our rice.

Before the VC, I used to go to the Cao Dai temple, but after '75 I didn't go because I was afraid that the Communists would see me. The Cao

Nguyen Thi Lang and her family outside their billet in the PRPC

Dai opposed the Communists before 1975, and I was worried. So I just prayed at home and kept an altar.

Hanh, my American son, went to school six years. Some people are very cruel. They say to him, "Hey, you, American ... you don't have father. I am Vietnamese, I have a father." Hanh says to me, "I don't remember my father." I tell him, "I had many pictures, but the VC come, I burned all."

My son has many problems because he is Amerasian. I tell him, "I am your mother, I will take care of you. I have your father's address. Maybe one day we can see him." But I never really believed this.

Then one day we heard that Amerasians can go to America. My son, he say, "Mother, you have my father's address. Let me see." So I show him. He says, "Mother, now we make paper to go to America. You say one day you write father. Mother, now you write."

So I write a letter to Lloyd. I tell him that now Amerasians can go to America. I say to him that the Communists are no good. If you can help us go to America, you write me a letter back. I write many letters. Finally, I get a letter from him.

Letter from Lloyd to Lang dated February 19, 1990:

> *My Darling Lang,*
>
> *I received your letters and the pictures of Minh. I tried to answer your last letter, but it was returned, you must have moved to a new address. Since I'm unable to read and write in Vietnamese, I have found a family who can interpret for me. We are pressed for time now. I must receive a copy of Minh's birth certificate, as soon as possible. I must register him as a child of a U.S. [citizen] born abroad before his 18 birthday. Once registered, both of you will be able to come to the U.S. on the Orderly Departure Program of the U.S. This program is handled by the U.S. embassy in Bangkok, Thailand. You need to contact them immediately. They have all the info on me and have been trying to contact you. Please hurry, I hope to be able to bring you to America before the end of this year. I hope you can find someone to interpret this letter for you. I'm rushed so will close this and get it in the mail. Thinking of you both, and hope to have you here with me soon.*
>
> *Love,*
> *Lloyd*

Letter to Minh Hanh:

> *Dear Minh,*
>
> *I'm writing you from far away. I only wish we could have been together when you were growing up. There are many things I could teach you. Thank you for being a loving son and taking care of your mother. I'm trying to get you out of Vietnam and to the U.S. I need a copy of a birth certificate before your 18 birthday. I need it immediately, your date of birth and place of birth. As soon as I can find a way to send money, I will do so. I owe you a lot. Your brothers and sisters say hello, and hope to see you soon.*
>
> *Love,*
> *Dad*

[Although it seems clear that Lloyd is welcoming Lang and her family into his life, she still is preoccupied.]

Lloyd is sponsoring me . . . but I worry. I worry that he is married. I know that he got divorced in 1976, but I don't know if he married again. I hope not, I hope we can be together.

My two sons from my first husband are still in Vietnam. I could not take them with me. They are over twenty, and my oldest son has no name in the family book, so I could not bring them. When I get to America I will send money to them. I hope I can sponsor them to come to the United States too.

Excerpt of Lloyd's letter to Lang of March 31, 1992:

> *It's a 90 mile trip from the airport to the house. Home is 4 bedrooms. It's warm. I have 30 lbs. of rice and 25 lbs of deer meat and about 20 lbs. of fish stored. My daughter Susan will be there to help you and the children learn to use appliances. The children will have to learn to use the bathroom facilities, the hot and cold water so they won't be scalded. We hope to make the transition a smooth one, but life is very different than in Vietnam.*

In Vietnam, I always worked as a farmer. I like farm work very much. I can plant rice and coffee. You think I can work farmer in your country?

Postscript: *Lang and her four children left for the United States in the spring of 1992. The day of her departure she was understandably uneasy about the transition she was about to face. A few months after her arrival in the United States, she wrote Cora Alcalde, her English teacher in the Philippine Refugee Processing Center. The following is a translation of that letter:*

Dear Cora,

Today I write this letter to you, I hope you receive it. First, may you have luck and beauty forever. Now I would like to tell you what has happened to my family since leaving the PRPC.

It took three flights to get to Michigan. When we arrived at the last airport, my son carried the suitcase and walked ahead. When he met his older half-sister, she was so happy that she ran quickly to her father and shouted, "My young brother looks just like you."

I recognized my husband immediately. . . . His appearance had not changed very much. We looked at each other, but could not speak. Finally, he took my hands and said, "Lang . . . how do you feel, seeing me again?"

I felt so shy and embarrassed I could not answer his question.

He held me closer and said, "I am so happy, why don't you say something to me." Finally I got my voice, and I answered, "I am happy too." We were taken with emotion and wept.

I met his older sister and his daughter. We went to his sister's house, where they had a lot of food prepared for us, but we could not eat, we were so tired from the trip. . . .

Lloyd then drove us to his house. It was a three-hour drive. On the way he told me that when he divorced his wife fifteen years ago, he decided that he would wait for me on the chance that we could be together again. Now, he said, it had come true.

I asked if he still loved me as before, since I had three kids with another man. He told me that he loved me, he loved my children too, and he accepted them as his own children.

Now we are living happily. On my son's birthday we had a party with Lloyd's brothers and sisters. My husband's sister took me aside and told me, "When my brother divorced fifteen years ago, I advised him to remarry, but he refused. He thought of you, he wanted to wait for you. Now his dream has come true, and I share your happiness, because my brother will never be lonely." Her words touched me deeply.

Lang and Lloyd were married on December 26, 1992.

Dung

"I'm not scared of nothing."

Dung brings out a dish of roast pumpkin seeds from the makeshift kitchen at the back of her billet. "I cut pumpkin all morning at work in Food Distribution," she tells me, "and they let me keep the seeds." Her survival skills are well honed. From the GI bars to the streets, from the New Economic Zone to Vietnamese jails, Dung has learned how to make do for herself and her two black Amerasian children in any situation. Her English, learned in the bars of Pleiku and Saigon, is direct and utilitarian, particularly when she describes her ongoing conflicts with the post–1975 Vietnamese government: "When they [the government] talk bad to me, I tell them, "VC, you know, I been four times in jail, five times in jail, and now I'm not scared of nothing."

Unschooled and illiterate in her own language, at thirty-seven Dung is learning to read and write for the first time. In a tiny student notebook, she shows me her early attempts at writing. "My name is Dung, I am from Vietnam," is put down in tentative, skewed letters. "I practice many times," she tells me, "and now I remember."

I COME TO SAIGON with my mother when I be a little girl. I never went to school, we be too poor, so I never learned to read or write. I had a friend who was up in Pleiku, working bar, making good money. I wanted to help my mother, to take care of her, so, in 1968, when I was fifteen, I go up there to work bar, too.

The first time I go to work, I don't know nothing. My friends at the bar, they teach me—how to drink Saigon tea, how to talk to the Americans, everything. So I work bar, and I get pregnant with my son. I'm not sure who the father was, maybe this guy Winger. You know, when I work bar, I have many boyfriends.

In 1970 I go back to Saigon and work the GI bars down there. The next year I meet Johnson. He's army, from Texas. I live with him one year, and I get pregnant with my daughter. When he goes back to America, I go back

251

to the bar. Johnson, he sent me letters from the States, he sent me money, he sent me anything I want.

Back at the bar, I meet Dinkins, a civilian from New York. He worked aero-science, he taught about planes. So Johnson, he's still sending me letters and money, but I'm living with another guy, Dinkins.

Early '75, Dinkins, he had to go up to Da Nang. When he comes back, he says to me, "Dung, you better come with me to America. If you want, I'll take care of you." I say, "No." You know, I never liked him too much. He had many girlfriends, and he always was telling me lies. Anyway, he tells me, "Soon, the VC will come to Saigon, and they will kill you." I say, " The VC won't come yet." I never believe that the VC could come to Saigon.

So he went to the airport, and that night he did not come home. But the next afternoon he came back, I say, "Mother fucker, you say you go to America, why you here?" He say, "They got no plane." The next day he goes back to the airport, and this time I never see him no more. Before he leaves, he say, "Dung, in one week the VC come." I don't believe him, but he be right.

Before '75, I had everything; my own house, papers *[for residing in Saigon]*, ID card, my babies' papers and ID cards. When the VC came to Saigon, they took it all. The VC tell me, "Get out, you have no job, leave Saigon. You have two American babies, you have two American boyfriends. Get out, you have to go away." They sent me to Tay Ninh *[to the New Economic Zone]* to break stones. I didn't have money, I didn't have food to eat either. I work all day, you know what they pay me? Three cups of rice. I didn't eat, I gave to my son and daughter to eat.

So they send me out of Saigon, and I escape and come back. But I have no ID for Saigon anymore, the VC take that already, so they catch me and send me back to Tay Ninh. I escape back to Saigon again. I try to sell something to make money, the VC they catch me and send me to jail. Why? Because the VC don't want you to make money, they don't let you sell. If you don't make money, how can you eat? So I go out to sell—shoes, clothes, anything. They catch me and send me to jail again. Sometimes I play cards, and they catch me and send me to jail then, too. I been in jail many times.

When I go to jail, my children, they stay with my sister or my brother. When I come back, we all stay together. They didn't go to school. You have to have money, you have to pay to go to school. My son, one time he tried to go. There were all Vietnamese children there. My son's an American baby, he be very shy. All the children would be laughing. They say "American baby, American baby." After that he don't go no more.

My children are very good, they listen to me. My daughter, she worked in Vietnam, she helped some people *[as a maid]* in their house. My boy, he's number one son. He work building houses, made good money. When I go to jail, they go to work and make money.

The VC always talk bad to me, they tell me, "You have two American boyfriends." They talk about me everywhere. One night in 1975, I was sleeping, and they come knocking on my door at 2 A.M. They yell, "Open the door." I don't open the door, I hide. I be afraid for my children, they are very young then. Years later, when they *[the VC]* talk bad to me, tell me, "You are the wife of an American," I don't listen to them. So many people call me that, you know, that I don't even pay attention. I tell the VC, "VC, you know, I been four times in jail, five times in jail, and now I'm not scared of nothing." And that's when I made the paper to leave Vietnam with my children.

Here in the PRPC, me and my children, we get along very good. They listen to me. Now they be in school, I cook, and they come back and eat. Then I go to school, and when I come back, they cleaned the house, washed the clothes, and got water. Yesterday, my son, he had a headache, he wanted to stay home from school. I say, "No, you must go. Be careful, if you are absent too much, you won't go to America."

My family is going to North Carolina, but we don't know our sponsor. I want to work when I get to America, I'll do anything. You know, in Vietnam I raised piglets and sold them. I can do many things. I'm not scared of going to America, I'm not scared of nothing."

Thanh

"The UPI tells me my husband
was taken by Cambodian soldiers."

I am struck by Linda's appearance. With her thick wavy hair and liquid brown eyes, she seems almost Brazilian. In explanation of her daughter's Latin features, Thanh, Linda's mother, tells me, "Her father was American, but his family came from Portugal."

We are sitting in Thanh's billet, as her family wanders in and out. She has five grown children, three of them Amerasian. Thanh's former husband, Terry Reynolds, had come to Vietnam as a soldier, and became a freelance journalist after his tour of duty. Thanh shows me a letter of recommendation written by Colonel Altman for Reynolds. It extols his excellence in the battlefield and as a writer and mentions that Reynolds could be found, especially after the Tet offensive, in orphanages and hospitals, donating soap and other items that he had purchased with his own money. Thanh also produces a document from United Press International describing the incident in which her husband was abducted by Communist forces in Cambodia while on assignment, never to be heard from again.

Thanh, fifty-three, was born in North Vietnam, fifteen kilometers from the China border. She moved to Hanoi with her aunt when she was three and to Saigon in 1954. Although she speaks to me in English, Thanh occasionally enters into a Vietnamese discussion with my interpreter, who then gives a translation.

MY AUNT HAD three or four houses for rent on Truong Minh Giang Street in Saigon. An American came and rented one. I saw him many times; he came into my store. Soon we fell in love, we were both about twenty-three. We live together and I have a son. My aunt gets very angry and fights with me, so we go away to a different house. After two or three years she finds me, and I go back there with my husband.

Terry was in the army, but after that he became a reporter. I worry about him, that he will get killed. Saigon has many troubles, and he goes

Thanh, family and friends inside her billet in the PRPC; Thanh is second from left, Linda is second from the right in the second row, her brother next to her.

out every day. Many times he goes on the aircraft carriers. He goes for four or five days and comes back, then two weeks later he goes again. And sometimes he goes to Cambodia.

Vietnamese people look at me very bad when I stay with an American. My husband knows about that, but he don't care. He comes home and reads a book, eats, sleeps. He don't talk to nobody. My husband don't like Vietnamese food, so I learn to cook American food.

He says to me to get married and go to America with him. I say I don't go, and we stay together in Saigon. Finally, he tells me that if we don't get married, and something happens to him, my baby won't get nothing. So, after seven years, we get married, and then he gets lost.

It happened in Cambodia, in 1972. He was abducted by Cambodian Communist soldiers. One Australian woman, one American, and two Vietnamese men come to my house and tell me. One girl, she's Korean, she works at UPI too, she tells me to stay home, and she goes to Cambodia *[to look for him]*. In three days she comes back. One Cambodian man saw him, and told her he's still alive. One or two weeks I hear about him, then I don't hear no more.

I ask Hanoi *[for help]*, but they don't answer to me. I want to go to Cambodia, but I am afraid because the Cambodian people, they kill the Vietnamese. I don't know what to do. What can I do? I just stay home and wait for my husband.

Linda and Thanh in the PRPC market

When I go to America, I want to find my husband's mother. She is angry at me because he got killed. She blames me. She told her son he would have problems if he married a Vietnamese girl. I wrote her a letter, but she never answered. I want to see her, to make amends.

The UPI tells me my husband was taken by Cambodian soldiers. They say that after six months, if there is no word, they pay me six months' salary. UPI says he works as a freelancer, so they don't want to pay more. So I wait, and then they pay me two hundred dollars every month for six months. I had to sign a paper to guarantee that when my son get old, he don't make no trouble *[file further claims]*. I have babies, I don't have money, so I have to do that, but then I hire a lawyer to try to get my husband's insurance. He tells me that if I didn't accept the six months' salary, maybe we could do something, but since I got that already . . . *[He couldn't help her].*

I thought maybe the army would give me some money. My husband was in the army seven years, but they don't give me anything. One or two months after my husband got killed, the Americans left Vietnam and went home.

In 1975, I ask UPI for a loan of two hundred dollars, to help me take care of my children. They gave me one hundred dollars, and they say the next day they give me more. That night there was a lot of trouble. The next day, the VC came to Saigon.

Anh

"Linh's father was not my husband. I was raped."

Anh and I first met in neighborhood four of the PRPC on a scorching day in February. I had come from teaching a class; she was attempting to find an agency that would provide her with some clothes. Anh was eight months pregnant, and her own worn clothes were woefully small. Clothing is for sale at the camp market, but shopping requires funds, something that Anh, with seven children at home, was perpetually short of. She approached me, asking in near fluent English for ADRA [the Adventist Development and Relief Agency], where she had heard that used clothing was available. With the help of some neighborhood children, we located ADRA, but they had already closed their doors for the day. Anh and I walked back to her billet. In front of the entrance, several of her children were playing the Vietnamese equivalent of jacks, using chopsticks and a rubber ball. Her husband was poring over an English textbook. Shortly after we arrived, Linh, Anh's black Amerasian daughter, walked in. Anh stiffened immediately, the tension between them was palpable.

A month later, Anh came to see me in my office. She had given birth to a daughter and invited me to come by and see the newborn girl. As we walked to my car, she began to talk about her daughter Linh. "You know, she said, "Linh's father was not my husband. I was raped, that's how I got her, and that's why I never loved her as much as my other children."

MY FATHER DIED when I was still a young girl, and my mother sent me away to a Catholic school outside of Saigon. That place was my home for about eight years. When I was about twelve, I went back to my village near Phuoc Vinh and continued my schooling there.

When the U.S. army came to Vietnam, I studied English, and I got a job at the U.S. army base in Quy Nhon. I brought my mother up there to live with me. I started as a waitress at the open mess, but after two months they saw that I could speak English well, I could read and write, so they sent me to be a secretary. I was about eighteen at this time.

A black GI used to give me a ride to work and drop me off near my house at the end of the day. One day there was a very heavy rain. I could not get out of the car to walk home. He said that he would take me back to the office and I could watch TV until the rain stopped, then he would take me home. I told him that I didn't want to go because it was already late and my mother would be worried, but he insisted. He didn't go back in the direction of the office. He turned into an isolated area, and he raped me in the car. Then he drove me home. I was crying and miserable, a young girl, a virgin.

The next morning he came to pick me up to take me to go to work. I wouldn't get into the car. He apologized for what he did, but I would not go with him. After that I didn't see him anymore. His time in Vietnam was up, and he went back to the United States. I didn't know then that I was pregnant.

Rape is a terrible shame for a girl in Vietnam. I couldn't tell anyone what happened, not even my mother. Finally, when she saw that I was pregnant, I told her what happened. She was furious, she blamed me. She beat me and sent me away to a church in Saigon, where they took care of me.

After my baby was born, I moved back to my village in Phuoc Vinh, but people there looked at me bad because I had been with a foreign man. That's why I had to go away. I went to Long An and got a job on the army base there, again as a secretary. But a few months later, the U.S. army was leaving Vietnam, and I had no more job.

I went back to my village, and I got a job as an elementary school teacher. In 1974, I married a Vietnamese soldier and moved back to Quy Nhon, where we stayed with his family. My mother took care of Linh, my Amerasian daughter. I didn't tell my husband that she was my child. A Vietnamese man doesn't want a woman who has an American baby.

The next year the VC came. They made it very difficult to find a job. You could only be a farmer or a housewife, something like that. So we were farmers. My husband worked in the fields, and I took care of our children. We lived with his family. We had no money for food or for anything. We were broke. That same year the VC took my husband away, but they would not tell me where. Later, I found out they killed him.

In 1978 I married again. This husband is here with me now. He is also from Quy Nhon, and we lived with his family there. I told him that my Amerasian daughter was really my mother's godchild, and not my daughter. In Vietnam it is common for a child to live with her godmother, so he believed me. If you tell a Vietnamese man that you have an Amerasian child, he will think you are bad and will not marry you.

By 1983 we had two babies. Money was a problem, my husband's family could no longer afford to feed us. I went back to my mother's house in Phuoc Vinh with my babies, and my husband stayed in Quynhon. You know, my husband is younger than me, and my mother never liked him. She kept on telling me, "Your husband is much younger and more beautiful than you. He will not take care of you forever. You must leave him."

A few months later my husband's grandmother died and left him a little gold. He came down to Phuoc Vinh to stay with me, but he could not stand my mother, so he used his inheritance to buy a small house there in Phuoc Vinh. My mother was still trying to break us up. Finally, she told him that Linh was really my daughter, not her godchild. She figured that if he knew I had an Amerasian daughter, he wouldn't want me anymore.

So now my husband tried to find out the truth. He asked me so many times, "Is Linh your daughter or not?" I tried to hide it. I didn't want him to find out because in Vietnam when somebody knows about that, it's very bad. One night he was asking me again, over and over. "How will you feel if I tell you that she is my daughter?" I asked him. He said, "Go ahead, let me know." So, I told him. He almost cried when he found out. He wanted to know, but when he knew he almost cried.

Anh's husband speaks: When I knew Linh was her daughter, I was very sad because if you have a good family you can't have an Amerasian. In Vietnam, many people think it's bad when a woman has an Amerasian child, that she hasn't a good heart.

Anh: You know, my husband treats Linh well, better than me. I was raped by her father, so I never loved her as much as I loved my other children. Sometimes I would get angry at her, but my husband would say, "You cannot act like that. You must be good to your daughter."

Linh always stayed with my mother, and my mother loves her very much. She stopped school after two years. You know, the Vietnamese children do not like that color skin, black. They teased her so much, and she wouldn't go back.

In 1983, I heard about the Amerasian program, that Amerasians and their families could go to America. The government didn't tell us anything about it. A friend mentioned it to me, and then I heard about it on the radio, on the BBC. When I went to make the papers, the officials asked, "Who told you about this?" and things like that. They didn't want people to leave Vietnam. They would make us stay there forever.

I made the application and left it with them. I waited four years until they called me, and then they made me come five or six times. Each time it was the same, I had to give them bribes, some money or cigarettes. I had just given birth, and I had to take my baby daughter on the bus with me each time I went there. It was very tiring. And they made us wait three more years to get out of Vietnam. They didn't let us leave until 1990.

I never tried to escape by boat because it was so expensive. You have to pay thirty gold rings to the captain. If you have a hundred dollars, you can buy two gold rings, and for one person you have to pay thirty rings. I had so many people in my house, how could I go by boat?

Since I came here to the PRPC, I have had problems with my Amerasian daughter. She is always going around, she don't like to stay home. She says that she should have come here with another family and gotten money. You know, in Vietnam if you want to go to the United States you can pay money to an Amerasian child *[to say that she is your child]*. She is very angry at me because I don't have any money.

Before the Amerasian program, it was difficult for the Amerasians in Vietnam, especially the black Amerasians like my daughter. The Vietnamese don't like that color skin. But since the Amerasian program, now that people know that if they have an Amerasian child they can go to America, the attitude towards Amerasians is different. Now everybody wants them.

Here in camp the Amerasian children have become like mothers and fathers instead of children. They tell the family what to do, and anything they want you must give them because they say if not for them you could not go to America. If you have a hundred Amerasians, ninety-five think like that.

When I was in Vietnam, I wanted to go to America very much. But now that I'm here, and my daughter is giving me so much trouble, I'm sorry that I came. I think it would have been better for me to stay in Vietnam and my daughter to go to America by herself. I'm afraid she will give me more trouble when I get to the United States. You know, she tells everybody that when we are called to go to America, if she doesn't want to go with me, she will cut my name *[by claiming that I am not her real mother]*, and I will have to stay here forever. I hope that's true, because I don't want to go with her anymore, she gives me trouble. *[Anh's voice is breaking.]* You know one time, she got angry, and she took a knife to my little daughter, and she said she would cut off her head. Now Linh lives in another billet, she doesn't stay here anymore.

She is very lazy. Three of my other children are in school here, and they are learning fast, faster than me. But Linh, she always goes to school late and leaves early. In one week she might be absent two times. She doesn't want to do anything, but she likes to spend a lot of money. I know that in America, she will come and ask for money, and if I don't have, she will give me trouble.

Ironically, Linh enters the billet just as Anh is speaking about her. The two converse briefly in Vietnamese, and Linh leaves almost immediately. Anh obviously upset, continues speaking, her voice tinged with resentment:

She went to play cards. She asked me for money, "Give me some money, give me some money," and she went to play cards. You know my country is very poor. I didn't have enough for my family . . . but she always spends money on coffee shop and cards, and I don't know what. I don't love her anymore. I don't want to stay in the house with her anymore.

Postscript: *Anh and her family resettled in San Jose, California, in April of 1991. They were sponsored by a boyhood friend of Anh's husband, who had himself resettled in America several years earlier.*

In June, I received a letter. Anh and her daughter Linh continued to quarrel. Relations soured between Anh's family and their sponsor, and the family left his home and rented a small house. Linh remained in the sponsor's home.

De

"I had put away lots of gold
from my more successful days."

*Even in the crowded, bedraggled atmosphere of the refugee camp billets, De
exudes an aura of sophistication. Poised and self-confident, she has been able to
ride out the difficulties with relative aplomb. Unlike the majority of women who
mothered Amerasian babies, De was able to put away a healthy stash of gold to
tide her through the rough times after the fall of South Vietnam.*

*De's English, despite years of disuse, comes easily and smoothly, though she
is frustrated by the occasional word that slips her memory. She is in the Philippine
Refugee Processing Center along with her twenty-year-old daughter.*

MY PARENTS LIVED in the north of Vietnam, where they had a tailor
shop. My father died before I was born. He was murdered by the French.
The Viet Minh had attacked a French ship, and many Frenchmen were
killed. My father spoke French and tried to explain to the French soldiers
that no one in the town was responsible for the attack, that there were no
Viet Minh sympathizers in the town. While he was talking, one of the
French soldiers knifed him. My mother, at thirty-eight, was left a widow
with four children and me in her stomach.

In 1954 my mother went to the South with her five children. She was
able to support us by doing embroidery. She was very skillful and was
known for her work. We lived in a bamboo house. It was not fancy; there
was no running water or indoor plumbing.

I went to high school in Bien Hoa. I studied English there and at the
Vietnamese-American Association. Because of my skill in English, I was
able to get a job at Long Binh base after my graduation. At first I worked
as a secretary. There was an American man there, he kept telling me he
could get me a better position, one where I'd make more money. My
mother always warned me that American men would trick girls into prostitution, so at first, I did not trust him, but he was honest and got me a job

262

managing a tailor shop on base, supervising ten workers. I worked there from 1968 to 1971. Then I transferred to Tan Son Nhut air base in Saigon, doing the same job. It was there that I met Rick.

He was an air force man, about twenty-five years old. He always came around when I was working and stared at me. Finally one day I asked him what he was staring at. "Oh, nothing," he said, "I'm just looking for a friend." Later, when he became my boyfriend, he admitted that he really came there to look at me. He was from Alabama. His parents were divorced, and he was brought up by his grandmother. He was very poor. I was a virgin when I met him, and he couldn't believe that. We were supposed to get married, but he was sent back to the States early. We didn't know when he left Vietnam that I was pregnant.

I got three or four letters a week from Rick. Before he left he bought me a cassette player, and we sent tapes back and forth to each other. He used to send me Elvis Presley tapes, Elvis was his favorite. When he found out that I was pregnant, he wanted me to make the papers to come to America. He said he would send money for my plane ticket. Then he wrote and said he didn't have the money yet, so I knew something had changed. After all, six hundred dollars was not so much to get, even in 1972.

That's when I stopped writing to him. I did contact him when our daughter was born, and he wrote me a few times after that, but I never answered. I just forgot about him and concentrated on being a good mother. Being a mother made me feel strong. I never doubted that I could take care of myself and my daughter.

In 1975 my mother buried all of his pictures, fearing the Communists, so my daughter never saw a picture of her father. I told her, "Just like me, I never saw my father." I really never wanted to know anything about him, and my daughter doesn't seem interested in knowing anything about her father. She once told me that her family is complete, her grandmother, her mother, and herself is enough. She is a good girl, she never caused me any problems. But since we came to this camp, she is getting very fat. I told her that in America it is not good for a young girl to be fat, but this doesn't seem to bother her.

In 1974, I opened up a bookstore in Bien Hoa. It did very well. I traveled to Saigon a lot to buy things for the store. It was there I met my other boyfriend. He was a civilian working for the 3M company, I met him at the country club pool. I was young, beautiful, and very stuck-up, the way young rich Vietnamese girls act. He wanted to take me traveling, but I never went. I had my daughter and my own business to take care of. Also, my mother told me that I had made a mistake once, I shouldn't do it again. I had a good business and could take care of myself, and I liked that.

On April 1, 1975, he had to go to Hong Kong on business. He knew that Vietnam would soon fall. He called one of his Filipino employers and told him to make papers for me and for everyone in the company. I and many others from his company went to the airport on April 27. We were supposed to go to Guam, but the plane never showed up and we were stranded. By April 30, Saigon had fallen.

On May 5 he sent a telegram to his own house, I saw it there. He was asking about me, asking if I could get out of the country and how. One of the employees in the company told me not to answer, that he might be involved with the CIA. I was afraid of what the Communists might do if I answered, so I didn't reply.

A year later the woman who was his secretary got a letter asking where I was. He still wanted to find me. She got in trouble with the VC for receiving that letter, a letter from an American. Later on that woman went to America, and she saw my boyfriend. He asked about me, but she had her own reasons for not telling him how to contact me. She was in America having an affair with my brother-in-law and didn't want his wife, my sister to know. She figured if my boyfriend got in touch with me, somehow my sister would find out, so she didn't tell my boyfriend anything about me. I found all this out many years later, but it didn't matter, I felt I didn't have to depend on anyone, I would get out of Vietnam myself and arrange my own reunion with my boyfriend.

In 1975 I had to sell my bookstore, and I became a vendor, selling things right in front of my house. I had put away lots of gold from my more successful days, though I lost a chunk of it on an attempted escape from Vietnam. It was a set-up. They took my money, but the boat never came.

In 1980 I opened up an illegal billiard hall. The VC tried to make me go to the New Economic Zone with my mother and daughter, but each time they bothered me I paid them off. If you can bribe them, they leave you alone.

My daughter went to school for seven years, but finally quit because she couldn't take the teasing that most Amerasian children get. She studied English at home and helped me at the billiard hall.

So now we are going to the United States, but I am afraid to contact my boyfriend. Maybe he is married. That would make me sad, and I don't want to hurt his wife. After a few years when I am well established, then I'll contact him. I don't want to be dependent on him. In the United States I want to open up my own business, see my daughter get married, and then return to Vietnam to visit my mother. I have a nest-egg, I still have five thousand dollars. Just before I left Vietnam, I sold my house to someone who had relatives in America, and the money is waiting for me there in the United States.

Postscript: *De and her daughter were resettled in Westminster, California, in August of 1992.*

Mai

"I was a country girl, not the same
as many girls in Saigon."

*Mai, thirty-eight, is a self-described "country girl" from Thu Duc, formerly
on the outskirts of Saigon, now a part of Ho Chi Minh City. She is in the Philippine Refugee Processing Center with her Vietnamese husband and her six
children, including her Amerasian son. She speaks good-naturedly about her
former relationship with an American navy man, which ended in a long distance
divorce; she chalks it up to youthful naïveté. Mai told her story in competent
English, without the aid of a translator.*

MY FAMILY WERE farmers in Thu Duc, and I lived there all my life. In
1965, I went to work in a restaurant, that's where I met my husband. He
came to eat in the restaurant; many Americans ate there. We served French
food, but the owner was Indian. I washed dishes from '65 to '68, and in
'69 and '70, I carried food for the people to eat, what do you call this, ...
waitress.

He was in the navy, Seabee *[naval construction worker]* 10-6004. I lived
with him for three or four months in 1970, and then he went back to
America. He came back to Vietnam in '71 and worked as a mechanic in
Saigon. A month after he came back, our son was born. He saw my baby,
and he made a marriage paper with me. On April 2, 1972, my husband went
back to America, and because he was in the military, I couldn't go with him.
He said that when he finished the navy, maybe I could be with him. I was
so young, maybe only twenty. I was a country girl, not the same as many
girls in Saigon, who work in a bar, understand everything. I was country,
I didn't understand nothing.

My husband was very nice, but he didn't give me ... I didn't have
clothes, nothing. I just liked him. I loved him. I wasn't the same as the girls
in Saigon. If they have an American, if he has money, they stay, if not, they
go. No, I loved him. My husband said he only had little money, *titi* money.

I lived with my family. My father had rice, I could eat, I could feed my family. He didn't have to take care of me and baby.

Every week he called me and took me to where he lived. I'd stay with him Saturday night, Sunday, and then Monday morning I'd go back home. We didn't have a house, we didn't live together. He said he didn't have money to rent a house, because of the navy, but I know he had many, many girlfriends. I was very sad about that, but I didn't know how to talk with him. I was too young. He was thirty-eight, I was only twenty. When he got married with me, I was his fourth wife. He got one wife, divorced, another one, divorced, another one, divorced, then me. In 1972 he went home, and he divorced me too, and he got another one. By now, I don't know how many wives he's had.

After my husband left Vietnam in 1972, he wrote only one letter, no, maybe two or three letters, that's all. The last one, he wrote me and said, "I have another wife, I can't come to Vietnam."

He gave money to a lawyer, and the lawyer sent me a paper from Guam. I don't have it here. If I had it, I'd show it to you. I lost it in Vietnam. I couldn't understand the letter when I got it, so I gave it to another man to read to me. It said "divorce." I was very sad. I was waiting for him . . . and I had his baby.

You know, when I worked as a waitress, many people liked me, loved me, many, but I said, "No, I have a husband." When he went to America, I had his baby, but many people liked me. They say, "I want to sleep with you," but I said, "No, I have a husband, I wait for him." When I got the letter that said "divorce," I was very sad, but I didn't know how to write a letter and ask him, "What did I do wrong to you?" I didn't know, I didn't understand.

In 1975 the VC came. That year, everybody, all Vietnam, had American children, and some people threw their babies away. Some people told their [Amerasian] children, "Go out." I was scared, you know, because I had an American baby, so I thought I'd get one more husband, and he'd take care of me and my baby. I got a husband, but when his family heard that I had an American baby, they said, "No, no, that's no good," and they took my husband away from me. In 1980 I got married again. This husband doesn't care that I have an American baby; he says, "I love you, I love baby too."

Lien

"I call my bar 'Simone,' that's my French name."

It's easy to imagine Lien as an entrepreneur; she has that kind of energy. Indeed, she was the owner and "mama-san" of her own bar in Saigon. For several years, her boyfriend and helper in the bar was Johnny Price, a black American from California. They have remained in almost continuous contact since he left Vietnam in 1972. Despite a recent automobile accident that left him walking with the aid of a cane, Price is sponsoring Lien and her family; they will shortly be joining him in the United States. Lien is one of the very few women I've spoken to who will be reuniting with an American boyfriend or husband. Her family includes children from various liaisons; her eldest son, fathered by a French paratrooper, was resettled in France in 1978. Her daughter from a soldier from Ohio, and her son and daughter from a Hawaiian merchant marine are all with her in the PRPC and are bound for California, as is Tuyet, who is also called by the English translation of her name, "Snow." She is Johnny Price's daughter.

Lien laughs as she recites her litany of boyfriends. As is common, all are referred to as husbands, irrespective of qualifying documents. Price, she says, was her last and most lasting husband, and Lien claims that she hasn't thought of another man since he left. As the topic changes, and she recounts the indignities she suffered after the fall of Saigon, her mood changes from levity to bitterness.

As we speak, several members of her family drop into her billet, sit for a while, and wander on. On the tiny concrete strip in front of her billet, several Filipinos, probably part-time workers at the camp, engage in a card game. Little kids come by to check out the oddity of an American with a tape recorder in the billet.

Lien, at fifty-five, has never learned to read or write in any language, though she has no trouble expressing herself in English or French, in addition to her native Vietnamese. She speaks easily and confidently without the aid of a translator.

267

YOU KNOW JAPAN? Japan killed my father in the war. He was half-French, half–Vietnamese. He was in the army before, working as an interpreter for the French in Hanoi. After he finished the army, he opened a fruit and vegetable store. When the Japanese came to Hanoi, father told me and my mother, "Get out of Hanoi, go to the jungle, go to Quang Tri." When we went back to Hanoi after the war, my father was dead. Japan told my father, "Hands up." He no hands up, so they shot him, his brother and his two sisters. They threw them in a big grave with many people.

After the war, my mother owned a restaurant. She sold meat, she sold potatoes, all kinds of food. I went to school only two or three years. My mother said, "Lien, you go study," but I was very lazy, so I stayed home. That's why I can read and write Vietnamese only a little, not too much.

After 1954, after Dienbienphu, many Vietnamese people went south to Saigon. I go too, with my boyfriend. He was a Frenchman, a paratrooper. My mother had a new husband and two children, and she stayed in Hanoi. I never saw her again. She got sick one night, there was no medicine, and she died.

My boyfriend went back to France, he had a wife there, and I stayed in Saigon. I have one son from him, he went to France in 1978. *[Lien pulls out a sheaf of photos of her son and his wife, sent in letters from France.]* The French government took him, the same as the American government takes Amerasians.

In Saigon, I opened a bar, a cafe, near Tan Son Nhut airport. We had food, and music, coffee, whiskey, scotch, beer . . . and girls. I open it as an American bar, you understand, not a Vietnamese bar. Many GIs come there. I have two policemen stand outside. They take care of my bar, make sure there is no trouble and no bombs. One come to work with me in the morning and we check everybody, all the girls that come to work there. If I like her, I let her work. If I don't like her, she doesn't work. I call my bar "Simone," that's my French name.

A very attractive black Amerasian walks into Lien's billet, and takes a seat near us. Lien introduces her as her daughter "Snow." Snow's entry turns Lien to talking about her children.

So, I have one French son, he is in France now, and I have three girls and one boy, from three different American husbands. One white man, his name was Georgie, he was army, from Ohio I think. I had a baby girl from him, three months old, when he went back to the States. He go back, and he never wrote me.

Then I have one Hawaiian husband. He worked on a ship, you know, like merchant marine. He only comes to Saigon two times in one year, but he always bring many things when he comes. I have two babies with him, one boy and one girl. You know, I just get a letter from him. He tell me

Lien in her billet in the PRPC

he wants to come here *[to the PRPC]* and see me, but I don't care about him anymore.

After he left, I met Johnny Price, a very nice boy. I miss him now. For eighteen years now, since he left, I never get married, didn't have no boyfriends, nothing. I stayed with Johnny from '69 to '72. He helped me run my bar. In '72 he go Arab *[Saudi Arabia]* to work, and he send me money every month. I was two months pregnant with his daughter Snow when he left, so he never saw her, but he always wrote me, until 1975, when the VC came. Even now, I still get letters from him, he never forgot me. He will sponsor my family. We are going to his house in California, he is waiting for us. Look, he is very kilo *[fat]* now.

Lien goes back into her sheaf of papers and photos and takes out a recently received letter and pictures from John Price of Long Beach, California. Price is the father of Snow, who is also called "Diamond." He is a very large black man, walking with a cane in one picture and drinking with a friend in another.

>*My wife Simone and daughters, Diamond, Mai, and Phuong,*
>
> *From my accident I walk with a walking cane. I'm still not well. I hope to be well soon so I can take care of my beautiful family. Now I weigh 250 lbs., more of me to love. I love you to the bone. Get well soon.*
>
>   *Big Daddy Price*
>
>*P.S. I'm an old man now.*

When VC come in '75, I burn my letters, around midnight, but I hid two. I don't know what will happen. Maybe they kill me, maybe kill all my daughters. I don't want them to see any letters from Americans.

When they come, all letters from Johnny stop. Then, about two years later, in 1977, the VC say that we can write and receive letters from America. That's when I start to get letters from Johnny again. After 1977 Johnny sent money to the bank. The American bank sends money to the VC bank *[Lien laughs at the irony]*. He wrote me a letter, he said, "Honey, I sent you money." I say okay, and I go to the bank, and I see the check. I get many letters from him. He says that he wants me and my daughter, his wife and children from Saigon, that's all. He say he don't have no American wife, no American girlfriend. I don't know, I don't see, I only read his letters. I want just him, that's all. I don't have nobody, don't have no boyfriend, just me and my children, that's all.

After 1975, the VC don't let me work. They steal my house, my car, my store, everything, money, too. I had three houses, they steal two. Everything in my house, my diamonds, all my gold, they steal all. They sent me to jail too *[Lien is sobbing]*, because I married an American and had American babies ... I'm sorry, I can't talk anymore. *[We pause for a few minutes. When Lien regains her composure, she continues her story. Her anger is apparent.]*

They took me to jail, and every morning they take me out to ask me questions. "What you do, why you stay with Americans?" I say I didn't do nothing. I work, I took care of my babies, I opened store, I opened bar ... that's all.

They say I love Americans, I don't love the VC. They say I work for the Americans, I work for CID *[Criminal Investigation Division of the U.S. Army]*. That's not true. I never work CID, but that's what they say.

I tell them that I didn't do anything bad. I loved an American, lived with him, and took care of my children. They say, "Well, then you American too," and they sent me to the mountain *[the New Economic Zone]*.

Lien's daughter Snow

My children were very young, they cry every day. There was no school there, very bad food. You know what we had to eat? . . . Wet rice, rotten wet rice. VC steal all my money, my house. I don't have nothing, and he gives me rotten rice. He wants to shoot me. I say, "Okay, shoot me, shoot my family too." He put us on the mountain, it's the same thing. He don't care if we live or die.

I could not stay in that place. After six months, I took my children back to Saigon. I want to put them in school, but the VC teacher told me that American babies can't go to school. Before the VC, all can go. But now, if the parents worked with Americans, the children cannot go.

*Lien goes back to her sheaf of letters and pulls out a few from Johnny Price
for me to look at. One letter states, "Tell that asshole that beat you not to come
[to my house in California], he's not welcome here." I ask Lien who this
"asshole" is.*

It's my son, he's no good. I was very sick, and he gives me rice to eat,
but I couldn't eat it. It was no good, it smelled. I tell him, "Okay, take these
two kilos of rice and change for another rice. He don't want to do that, he
tells me, *Du ma.* In Vietnamese that's the same as, "Fuck your mother, . . .
mother fucker." I'm very angry, I tell him, "Okay, you cannot live here with
me, you talk number ten mouth. I take care of you since you were a baby,
you never had a job, and now you talk very bad to me." I say to him, "All
right, now you get out of here." He gets angry, and he wants to beat me.
Now he moved. He left here about twenty days ago. I wrote my husband
Johnny. I told him, "My son told me 'Fuck your mother.' Don't sponsor
him, don't let him come to your house."

I never had any problem with my son in Vietnam, but now he is very
bad. He has a wife here, and one baby in Vietnam. The baby was born after
we made the paper to leave Vietnam, so he couldn't come. He had to stay
behind in Vietnam.

When we were in Vietnam, they told us we were going to America, but
they sent us here to the Philippines . . . *Troi oi [My God]*, bad food here.
In Saigon I ate very good food. Here the food is so bad, I can't eat it. The
rice they give us stinks. The meat, fish, the eggs . . . they are very old, no
good. Johnny sends money every month, and I go to the market and buy
good food.

When I go to America, I'll ask Johnny what he has been doing, how
many wives, how many girlfriends he has. He says he don't have any, but
I don't know. But he's a very good man, and I want him, nobody else. You
know, his baby, my Snow, she's eighteen years old. Since she was born, I
didn't have no boyfriends, no husband. I just wait to see Johnny again.

Postscript: *Several members of Lien's family tested positive for tuberculosis in the PRPC and had to undergo a mandatory six-month treatment. In the
spring of 1991, Lien's married daughter Phuong gave birth to a baby girl. These
events delayed the family's departure for the United States by several months. In
this period, Lien continued to receive letters from Johnny Price. As the date for
her departure grew closer, the letters took on a more romantic nature, recalling
their days in Vietnam and looking towards their future together. Lien, though
eager to reunite with Price, was understandably nervous. "Eighteen years for me
already," she liked to joke. "Maybe I forget how."*

Price also expressed concern for his daughter, Snow, especially since Snow's older sister Mai had become pregnant from her Filipino boyfriend. Every letter admonished Lien not to "let any boys hang around Snow."

Lien and her family finally left for Long Beach, California, on July 8, 1991. After several months without any word from her, I attempted to call John Price. A recording indicated that his phone was no longer in service. Letters to him were returned with stamped post office messages indicating that he no longer resided at this address. In September, I met a girl who had received a letter from Lien's daughter Mai. The information was scant but unhappy. Lien's reunion with John Price had not gone smoothly. After a brief period together, they had separated and Lien and her family had moved to another location in California. Snow, Price's daughter, remained with him.

Hanh

"People say to my daughter,
'Your mother went with GI, she was a whore.'"

*Hanh comes from southern Vietnam, from the region that once belonged to
Cambodia and is still heavily populated by ethnic Khmers like herself. Khmer is
her native language; she didn't learn to speak Vietnamese until her teenage years.
At forty-nine, she is extremely slender for having given birth to eight children.
Three of the five Amerasian children she has borne have died. One, a daughter
in her early twenties, is with Hanh in the refugee camp. Her other surviving
Amerasian child, a son, is still in Vietnam, caring for his grandmother. Hanh
speaks in clear English, learned from the American GI with whom she lived for
four years when she was a mess hall worker on the U.S. army base at Quy Nhon
in central Vietnam.*

MY FATHER WAS a soldier for twenty-five years. When France is Vietnam, he serves in the French army. When the Americans come, he fights
on their side. He was stationed in Vung Tau, near Bien Hoa.

My father stays with the army in Vung Tau. I stay with my mother and
brother and two sisters, in my place in Kien Giang. We have twenty *cong
[20,000 square meters]* of rice fields there.

I never go to school. When I am very young, the Viet Minh and French
fight, and I run all the time, no have place to go to school. The French come
to my village. They don't know who is Viet Minh and who is not. They
don't care, they shoot anybody. The village was very small. We have to go
hide in the fields or in the U Minh forest.

When I am about twelve years old, my family moves up to Vung Tau,
where my father stays. At this time, I cannot speak Vietnamese very well,
only Khmer. One day, working in the rice field there, I met a man. He was
a farmer like me, but he also was a soldier. He tells my friend to tell me
that he loves me, and soon we get married. I was sixteen.

We are married for four years, and I have two daughters with him. One

274

morning he's walking on the street in Bien Hoa, and there is some disturbance. He goes to see, and the VC shoot him dead.

I go back to my father and mother, I feel very sad then. I have two children. I don't know what I do, how I work and get money to care for them. My friend is going to Quy Nhon to work for the American army, and I go too.

I work in the mess hall on the base there, that's An Khe base, and there I meet Kerry. He was a cook. He tell me that he's from California, and he has a big tattoo here *[on the upper arm]*. He's first sergeant, a black man, and he speak sweet, so I like him.

We live together outside the base about four years. I meet him in '66, and he goes back to America in 1970. We have four children, three boys and a girl, but the three boys die. One die very young, he's just a baby, one die just after the VC come, and the other, he die in the New Economic Zone. The VC sent me there. It's very hot, and he got sick. We don't have any doctor, any medicine, and he die.

In 1970, Kerry goes back to America. He tells me that he will come back to Vietnam, but I don't know. He stay in the army a long time already. He was a first sergeant, and I don't think he will come back. I think maybe he's telling me a lie. If GI, American, tell me lie, how can I know? Now I am old, so I can know, but before, I cannot tell. I think he lies, just the same as Vietnamese.

So when Kerry goes back to America, I get another boyfriend, Gleason. He don't live with me, he stays in the barracks. When he goes back to America, he don't even tell me nothing. His friends say, "Oh, Gleason, he went back already."

But Kerry comes back to Vietnam, and he wants to take me to America. He comes to see me, and he says that his friend is making a party, and he will pick me up early, about ten o'clock. I just cry, I can't say nothing. Before he comes to pick me up, I go hide, I'm very scared, because I'm pregnant with a baby from Gleason. I know that Kerry will kill me if he knows.

I'm very sad because I wronged him. He is a very good man. He loved our daughter very much, and she looks just like him. His mother be very old. Every year she talked to me on the telephone, telling me to learn more English, to get ready to go to America. Kerry, he taught me to speak, he send me to school. He was a very good, very sweet man, but when he come back to take me to America, I hide. I don't go, I don't see him no more. I do wrong for him.

After 1972, I move up to Dalat, in the mountains, and I work as a vendor. I marry with one Vietnamese man there; he drives a truck. He was married before and had six children. When the VC come, he can't work anymore. The VC round up vendors, everybody, and they send us to the New Economic Zone at Bong Bo. My husband get sick, he can't work, so I work for him. Eventually, I went back to Kien Giang. I tell my husband to wait for me, that I must make some money, and then I will come back for him. But he couldn't wait for me. He got another girlfriend, so we are through.

In Kien Giang, the VC didn't bother me, but the people looked bad at me and my American children. When my children go to school, when they go around, people say *"con lai [half-breed]*, you have twelve assholes" *[from a popular derogatory rhyme about Amerasians]*. My daughter didn't want to go to school. She be shy because she is black. People say to her, "Your mother went with GI. She was a whore, she go for money, that is why you born black." They look at me the same as a dog. My son wouldn't stay in school, he got angry when they insulted him. So my children can't read and write.

Before 1975, nobody talk nothin' to me . . . just behind my back, so I can't hear. They don't talk loud, but I know, they say that I have a GI friend. But after 1975 when I go back to my place, some people look at me the same as a dog. I be very angry, but I can't say nothin'. I just go to work and come back and take care of my children. In 1979, I hear people say you can make a paper to go to America, but I don't know, I think maybe somebody is lying. Anyway, I got no money. Then in 1983, my friend, she has money *[to bribe Vietnamese officials]* and she goes to America. Me, I got son and daughter, I got no money. I got to work, work hard. I do anything, help people, work in the field, anything. I keep my money, and I pay many money to VC to make my paper *[application for exit visa from Vietnam]*. I don't eat. I keep that money to give VC. My son looks after water buffalo. When he gets paid he gives his salary to me. I pay to make paper in 1987, but I still wait five years to leave Vietnam.

Postscript: Hanh and her daughter left the Philippine Refugee Processing Center for Dallas, Texas, in August of 1992.

Chau

"Why you had to marry with black people?"

One afternoon in early February, as I was walking past the small clinic in neighborhood six of the PRPC, a black teenage Amerasian girl motioned to me from inside. Ngoc clearly had something to tell me, but she was unable to convey her message in English. With the aid of the nurse's Vietnamese interpreter, I grasped that Ngoc had heard that I was gathering the stories of Amerasians and their mothers. She wanted me to meet her own mom, whom, she claimed, was "number 1" in English.

Ngoc was certainly right about her mother. Chau rarely groped for words when we met a week later in Zar's restaurant, a tiny Filipino eatery fronting the parking lot of the neighborhood five market in the PRPC. Although she claims that her English was learned in Vietnamese high school, the ease and fluidity with which she handles the language certainly came through her contact with Americans.

Chau, forty-one, is herself of mixed blood, the dark-skinned offspring of a Vietnamese mother and a North African soldier who died fighting for France at Dienbienphu. She is the biological mother of two of her five children. Her first child, Ha, now a young man of twenty-four, was conceived through Chau's liaison with a white American soldier when she was barely seventeen. Her youngest, Hong Van, a five-year-old boy, is the result of her marriage to a Vietnamese man which ended in divorce in 1986.

In between, Chau adopted three children. Son, whom she believes is half-Korean, and Ngoc came from an orphanage. The parents of Thu, Chau's fourteen-year-old adopted daughter, were, like Chau and her family, sent by the government to work the New Economic Zone in Tay Ninh province. When Thu's parents died, Chau became her caretaker. Apart from her own children, Chau's billet in neighborhood two is often filled with unaccompanied Amerasian kids, who drop by for food, advice, or just to hang out. Many of them view her as a surrogate mother.

I HAVE FIVE KIDS, three are Amerasian. Ha, my first son, he's Amerasian, and my last child, Hong Van, he's only five years old. They are my
only real children. All my other children I adopt.

I never knew my father. I was four years old when he died, I only saw
his picture. He was a soldier. He fought and he died in Dienbienphu, that's
all I know. I have one young brother with the same father. He is in New
York now, he went there in 1990.

I had many problems because I am black. In '75 the Communists
threw me out. They told me that all my family have to go up the mountain
[the New Economic Zone] to be farmers. My children were very young, Ha
only five years old. I stay for two years, then I go back to Saigon. My mother
paid a bribe, and they don't send me back to the mountain, but they don't
let me have paper, no ID card, no nothing. That's why I couldn't make
paper to go to America, 'cause I don't have ID card. My children the same
. . . I can't send them to school. They say for school is only for Vietnamese
children. My children, black, white, they don't let them study.

When I was young, other children always call me "black, black," they
make me feel bad. I be very embarrassed, and I don't want to study no
more. My mother, she cry, and she say, "What can I do? I can't do nothing." I get angry with her. I say, "How come you don't marry with white
people?" She say, "What you say? What you talkin' about?" I say, "Why
you didn't marry with white people? Even you marry Vietnamese, okay?
Why you had to marry with black people?" I was very angry and very sad
because all the children they don't like me. All the time they call me "black,
black." I don't like that. Now I understand my mother, but before I have
my own children I can't understand. She can't change nothing.

It was the same for my brother, he fight with other children every day.
He stayed in school eight years only, but me, I finished high school. I learn
English there. I knew I had to keep myself cool, I had to forget what they
say to me.

My mother got married again when I was four years old. My father
died only two months before, and she got married again. My stepfather, he
don't want to take care of me and my brother, so they send us to my grandfather.

My grandfather lived in Phan Thiet, about two hundred kilometers
from Saigon. That's where I went to school. I didn't have any friends, the
Vietnamese don't like me. I feel this, so I stay by myself. I read books,
sometimes go to the movies. When I went back to Saigon, after high school,
then I had many friends. Some were Vietnamese, some were black like me,
others white, you know. Their fathers were French. I had some Cambodian
friends too. But when I be a young girl in Phan Thiet, I am alone. There
were no other mixed race children, just me and my brother.

Every six or seven months my mother would write my grandfather and tell him to send us to Saigon, and we'd go to stay with her for a week or two, or maybe a month, but I felt very angry at my mother for sending me away.

My mother had five children with her Vietnamese husband. One died, and the others live in Saigon. My mother is still there, but my stepfather, he killed himself two years ago. I don't know what happened to him, he just took too much medicine *[poison]* and died. We never liked each other anyway.

After I finish high school, I go back to my mother's house and take care of my mother's children. But my stepfather, he fight with me many times. One day he beat me, he tells me I have a hard head. He tells me that if I don't talk easy *[be polite]*, I have to go out and never come back to his house no more. I feel very bad. I know he don't want to put me out, you know, he just talkin', but I feel very bad because when he say that, my mother was sittin' right there, and she didn't say anything. He say to me, "I tell you what, you got a hard head. You do anything you want to do, you don't care about other people." I say, "How come I have to care about what other people like? If I like, I do. If it's no good, I don't do. I never do nothing bad, I'm a good person." So he say: "Don't say anything else, or you have to get out. If you be here you have to talk easy with me, or else . . ." I wait, I don't say anything. Then he ask me, "What you say now, what you do now?" I say, "I go out." He say, "All right, but you better remember, if you go out, you never come back my house no more." I say, "Okay," but when I say that, I don't know what I'm gonna do. I just feel so angry, he hurt me very much. And I hate my mother, I think she is very, very weak. She didn't say anything, she just sit quiet like that.

So I left that house in ten minutes, but I didn't know where I would go. I just walked and walked, and I was crying. I don't have no money, nothing. So I think I wait till late, when everybody go home, and I kill myself, on the street. I think, but I don't do; I be scared. I'm chicken, you know, I'm only seventeen years old. I don't want to die.

So I go to my friend's house. I told her what happened to me. She tell me that her sister married an American, and she ask me, "You want to go with an American?" I say, "Yeah." She ask why, and I say, "Because I can't go back my home anymore. I don't want to die. I need someone to help take care of me." She say, "Remember, you not even seventeen years old yet." I say, "Yeah, next month I be seventeen. Please help me."

So she told her sister, and her sister tell her husband; and he bring his friend home to see me, and I get pregnant, the first man who come with me. You realize what I say? I'm seventeen years old, the first man in my life, and I get pregnant. So I have Ha, my first son.

I lived in Saigon with that man, my first boyfriend. He was an MP. He got a house for me. Then he went to An Khe, and I went with him. After nine months he left for the States. He wrote me, he sent me money, but he have a wife in the States I didn't know about that. Three months after he left, Ha was born, that was 1969, and then I went to work in a club, you know a dancing club. I be a cashier. I don't have that guy's address now because after '75, when the VC come, all my addresses and pictures, everything, I burn all. People told me if the Communists come in your house and see American pictures, they kill you. So I'm scared, I burn all.

In 1971, I got my children Ngoc and Son from an orphanage. I think maybe Son is Korean, I don't know about him. Ngoc is black like me.

In 1975 the VC come, and they throw me out of Saigon. They tell me I have to go to the mountain. If I don't go there and be a farmer, they gonna put me in jail. They put my mother in jail, yeah. They say she work for the CIA. I don't know why they say that. They put many people in jail. Oh, you know, they say you work for the CIA and then they arrest you.

They sent me and my kids to Tay Ninh. I stayed there two years and worked as a farmer. There was no school, no hospital, nothing. I go to work, and the kids just stay in the house all day. One day I think my kids will die, because they tell everybody to go to work, but they don't give us no rice, no nothing. So we go to work, and after two hours we come home. Our children don't have food. My kids are all laying down, sick, hardly moving. I realize then that if I stay there we die, so I have to get out of that place. I don't want to think about that anymore. *[Chau is in tears and must pause.]*

So we left Tay Ninh. I walked, me and many people, we walked, from seven at night to four in the morning. We had no ride, no bus. We walked for two days. We walked to Saigon, all the way, many people. We hide from the Communists. We don't walk in the daytime. We walk in the nighttime so they don't see us.

When we get to Saigon, we go back to my mother's house and stay there. My stepfather was gone, he went off to live with another woman. My mother paid off the Communists, so they didn't make me go back to Tay Ninh, but they never give us no papers to stay in Saigon and no ID.

In 1982 I married a Vietnamese man, but we get divorced in 1986. He was a very bad person, he smoke cocaine. One month after I divorce him, I have my baby son Hong Van.

In Vietnam, so many people they bother my Amerasian kids, Ngoc and Ha. They say, "Go home, American," . . . so my kids come home and cry. I say, "Forget about that, just don't go out." My children, they are good, but Ha sometime in Vietnam he drink, somebody call him "American," and he fight. Then it's a problem. But that's only sometimes. Ha is smart, he study good; but he always going after the girls, too many ladies. . . . That's why he doesn't remember his English. In Vietnam he had a Vietnamese girlfriend. He wanted to marry her and bring her here, but she don't have an ID card, so they did not let her come here.

Son is smart, Thu also. My children, they didn't go to school in Vietnam, but I taught them at home. They can read and write. Because in Saigon you have to have the ID card. If you don't have it, you can't go to school.

We left Vietnam because there was nothing to do there. What would happen to my son and daughter there? They can't do nothing. We can't have job, we can't make money, we don't have no freedom. What we do there? I apply to go to America in 1982, but I have no paper, no ID, and the Communists say, "If you have no ID, you cannot make paper to go." So we wait, almost ten years. Always they tell me, "It's not time for you to go yet."

I could have gone to America in '71 or '72. In 1970 I have American boyfriend, you know. He went back to America, and he tells me that he will come to Vietnam again, but I don't believe him, you know. I think that he will forget me. But three months later I got a note from the American Embassy to go there. So I go and they tell me to make a paper, and I can go to America in only two months and marry my boyfriend. But I change my mind. I don't know what would happen to me if I go myself. If he be in Vietnam and we make paper together, okay, maybe I go. But only myself, I be scared . . . and the paper was only for me. It didn't have my children's names. Now I'm sorry that I didn't go. I won't look for him now when I go to America. It's a long time already. He has his life, I have mine. He maybe forgot me already, I don't want to bother him. I never bother no people. I think nobody like me when I'm young, so I never bother anybody.

Ha, he talks about seeing his father. He wants to see what he looks like, to stay with him, to know him. I say, "Yeah, your father very handsome, but don't you talk about finding your father and being with him, because he has his own life. He may have many children, he may have a wife. If you see him, okay, that's good for you, but if not, forget about it." He very sad when I say that, but what can I do?

Here in the PRPC I have some problems. Ha, he went down to the stream, he fell down and break his arm. So he have to go to the Balanga *[the provincial capital]* hospital for two weeks. One month later, my five year old fell down and break his arm, I have to go to Balanga again.

One time Ha get drunk, he drink after a class party. He talk not good with his teacher, so he go to jail. He only say, "Teacher, you loco, you no good," and they send him to jail for twenty days. No big thing, but I feel bad, because I tell him not to do that.

My kids learned some English here, but Ngoc, she very shy. When she comes home, I ask her, "What you study in school today? Tell me, I want to listen." She say, "I know, I know," but she don't want to talk. I say, "You can speak English, come on, me and you will speak English." But she very shy. I tell her, "You too shy. When you go to America, what you gonna do? Nobody can speak Vietnamese with you."

Postscript: After about two hours of talking, Chau felt that she had pulled up enough emotions for one day. "I got more I want to tell you," she said, "but let's save it for another time." Several days later Chau worked with me as an interpreter for an interview with an Amerasian boy incarcerated in the PRPC rehab center, but had no chance to continue her own story.

About a week later, I spoke to Son and Ngoc, the two children that Chau said she had adopted from an orphanage. When I mentioned this adoption, the kids looked puzzled. They spoke rapidly among themselves, then Son spoke directly to my interpreter. "We're not adopted," he told her. "Chau is our real mother."

I immediately backed off the topic, but resolved to ask Chau about it. Four days later I went up to her billet in neighborhood two. A neighbor was out watering his small garden, dipping a perforated Dole pineapple juice can into a plastic bucket and sending an arc of droplets up and down the rows of vegetables. He paused when he saw me, his expression told me that I was too late. "Chau not here," he said in halting English. "She go America yesterday."

APPENDIX

Changes of Province and City Names in Vietnam After 1975

Provinces in the North (above the seventeenth parallel)

Before July 2, 1976	After 1976 (As decided by the 4th session of the National Assembly)
1. Lao Cai, Yen Bai (before 1975)	Hoang Lien Son (since 1975)
2. Ha Giang, Tuyen Quang (before 1975)	Ha Tuyen (since 1975)
3. Phu Tho, Vinh Yen	Vinh Phu
4. Thai Nguyen, Bac Can	Bac Thai
5. Bac Ninh, Bac Giang	Ha Bac
6. Quang Yen, Hai Ninh	Quang Ninh
7. Hai Duong, Hung Yen	Hai Hung
8. Hoa Binh, Ha Dong	Ha Son Binh
9. Nam Dinh, Ninh Bin, Ha Nam	Ha Nam Ninh
10. Nghe An, Ha Tinh	Nghe Tinh
11. Quang Binh, Quang Tri, Thua Thien	Binh Tri Thien

Provinces in the South (below the seventeenth parallel)

12. Quang Nam, Da Nang	Quang Nam Da Nang
13. Pleiku, Kontum	Gia Lai Kontum
14. Ban Me Thuot, Quang Duc, Phu Bon	Dac Lac
15. Tuyen Duc, Bao Luc	Lam Dong
16. Quang Ngai, Binh Dinh	Nghia Binh
17. Phu Yen, Khanh Hoa	Phu Khanh
18. Ninh Thuan, Binh Tuan, Binh Tuy	Thuan Hai
19. Binh Duong, Binh Long, Phuoc Long, and parts of Bien Hoa and Gia Dinh	Song Be

283

20. Bien Hoa, Long Khanh, Phuoc Tuy, one district of Binh Tuy	Dong Nai
21. Long An, Hau Nghia	Long An
22. Dinh Tuong, Go Cong	Tien Giang
23. Kien Hoa	Ben Tre
24. Sa Dec, Kien Tuong, Kien Phong	Dong Thap
25. Vinh Long, Vinh Binh	Cuu Long
26. Can Tho, Ba Xuyen, Chuong Thien	Hau Giang
27. An Giang, Chau Duc	An Giang
28. An Xuyen	Minh Hai

Cities and Special Zones

29. Saigon, Gia Dinh (province), Cu Chi (of Binh Duong province)	Ho Chi Minh City
30. Hai Phong, Kien An (province), and part of Quang Yen	Hai Phong
31. Vung Tau, Con Son (district of Ha Giang province)	Vung Tau-Con Dao (special zone)

Recent Changes

1989: Binh Tri Thien (#11) has been divided into Quang Binh, Quang Tri, and Thua Thien-Hue provinces.

Nghia Binh (#16) has reverted back to its pre-1976 division of Quang Ngai and Binh Dinh provinces.

Phu Khanh (#17) has reverted back to its pre-1976 division of Phu Yen and Khanh Hoa provinces.

Thuan Hai (#18) has been divided into Thuan Hai and Ninh Thuan provinces.

1991: Dong Nai (#20) has been divided into Dong Nai and Ba Ria provinces.

1992: Cuu Long (#25) has been divided into Vinh Long and Tra Vinh provinces.

GLOSSARY

Amerasian Park: The nickname of a small park in Ho Chi Minh City near the Independence Palace, Ministry of Foreign Affairs, and the offices of the American Orderly Departure Program. Its proximity to the latter two locations, where, respectively, exit visas for Vietnam are granted and interviews for acceptance to the United States via the Orderly Departure Program are held, made it a convenient gathering spot for Amerasians, as well as any other Vietnamese trying to leave Vietnam for the United States. It was known to be the place where Vietnamese proficient in English filled out Orderly Departure Program applications for potential immigrants—for a price. Most Amerasians who are not Ho Chi Minh City residents now wait for departure from Vietnam in the Dam Sen Amerasian Center in another part of the city.

ancestor worship (Dao Tho Ong Ba): A Vietnamese religion of Chinese origin. Practitioners venerate and pray to their forebears.

ao dai: The traditional dress of Vietnamese women and girls, consisting of a long flowing blouse slit on both sides, worn over loose trousers.

ARVN: Army of the Republic of Vietnam

billet: Refugee quarters in the Philippine Refugee Processing Center. Constructed of wood and asbestos, each two-story billet is about eight feet by twenty feet and is part of a row of ten such connected enclosures. As many as twelve people may share a single billet.

blue guard: The blue uniformed Filipino security guards at the Philippine Refugee Processing Center.

bu cu: A lot, plenty. From the French "beaucoup."

Cao Dai: Vietnamese religion which reverences figures as diverse as Buddha, Jesus, and Victor Hugo. From 1938 to 1955 the Cao Dai maintained a private army and wielded considerable influence in the Mekong Delta region, as well as in areas northwest of Saigon. The center of the Cao Dai religion is in Tay Ninh province.

Charlie: Viet Cong.

CID: Criminal Investigation Division of the U.S. Army.

cluster sites: American cities which, by virtue of their reputedly adequate resettlement and social services, receive large numbers of Amerasian free cases. In 1992 there were fifty-five such sites.

CO: Commanding Officer

Community and Family Services International (CFSI): Implements a program for mental health for refugees in the Philippine Refugee Processing Center. Included in their services are guidance and counseling, mental health education, paraprofessional training, and treatment of psychiatric cases.

con lai: Person of mixed blood. Often used derogatorily, carrying the connotation of "half-breed."

cong: A measurement of land in Vietnam equal to about one thousand square meters.

dai bang: Eagle. It is used to denote the chief or the top man. In prison, it refers to the chief prisoner, the boss of the other inmates.

Dam Sen Amerasian Center: Holding center for Amerasians and their families awaiting departure for the Philippine Refugee Processing Center. The center is located in the Dam Sen area of Ho Chi Minh City.

dan gao: Vietnamese string instrument.

Dienbienphu: Village in northwestern Vietnam which was the site of France's final defeat by the Viet Minh in 1954.

dong: Piaster. Vietnamese currency. In 1992 the dong exchange rate in Vietnam was 10,800 to the U.S. dollar.

Economic Police: The post-1975 branch of law enforcement in Vietnam that cracked down on capitalist activities such as vending and trading, often confiscating merchants' goods.

family book (Ho Khau): Also called household register. The document in which the names of all the people residing in a given household appear. Without a name in a proper household register, one cannot legally live in a place, work, or study. Authorities often revoked the household register of families or individuals they wished to force out of their current residences and to the New Economic Zones, leaving them little choice but to comply.

free case: A refugee or refugee family in the PRPC that has no sponsoring relatives in the United States.

gold case: A term used in the Philippine Refugee Processing Center to denote a Vietnamese family or individual that has "bought" an Amerasian. Many Vietnamese will pay the bribes necessary for an Amerasian and themselves to secure exit visas from Vietnam. In exchange, the Amerasian claims them as legitimate family on his or her documents, enabling them to accompany the Amerasian to the United

States under the auspices of the Homecoming Act. Amerasians often lack the resources to make the requisite payoffs themselves and thus accept these bogus families as a means of avoiding years of waiting for departure from Vietnam. Amerasians and their legitimate families also often receive payment in gold for this transaction.

Hoa Hao: An independent Buddhist sect, popular in the Mekong Delta region. It was both anti–French and anti–Communist. In the 1940s and 50s, the Hoa Hao maintained its own military forces.

Hoa Lo Prison: A prison in Hanoi, nicknamed the "Hanoi Hilton" by American prisoners who were held there.

hold, on hold: In the terminology of the Philippine Refugee Processing Center, a refugee whose departure to the United States has been delayed or postponed.

Homecoming Act: Also known as the Amerasian Homecoming Act or the Mrazek Act, it allows for Vietnamese Amerasians and specified members of their families to enter the United States as immigrants, while retaining eligibility for refugee benefits.

hootch: In GI jargon, a basic dwelling.

household register: See "family book."

Immigration and Naturalization Service (INS): Interviews applicants for asylum in the United States and rules on their eligibility.

International Catholic Migration Commission (ICMC): In the Philippine Refugee Processing Center, ICMC offers English as a Second Language (ESL), Cultural Orientation (CO), and Work Orientation (WO) classes to refugees seventeen to fifty-five years old and operates the Preparatory for American Secondary School (PASS) program for refugees eleven and a half to sixteen years old.

International Organization for Migration (IOM): Offers health care to refugees in the Philippine Refugee Processing Center.

IOM Card: Enables refugees in the Philippine Refugee Processing Center to obtain selected health care services, including immunization and treatment for communicable diseases. Also enables refugees to obtain medical screening and documentation, as well as transportation.

Joint Voluntary Agency (JVA): Facilitates the search for, and selection of, sponsors for refugees.

Kampuchea Krom: In the Khmer language, the part of South Vietnam previously belonging to Cambodia, which was taken by the Vietnamese in the eighteenth century.

Khmer Krom: Ethnic Khmer (Cambodian) inhabitant of Kampuchea Krom (see Kampuchea Krom).

labor camp: See reeducation camp.

lai den: Black Amerasian. Often used derogatorily.

Lambretta: A three-wheeled vehicle, popular as public transportation in Vietnam.

Ma roc: Refers to any black North African soldier with the French Colonial Army.

MACV: Military Assistance Command, Vietnam.

Mau Thanh: The year of the monkey. Also frequently used to refer to the Communist offensive of 1968, which took place on Tet, the Vietnamese New Year, in the year of the monkey.

monkey house: Prison, jail, reeducation camp, and especially, the detention center at the Philippine Refugee Processing Center.

My den: Literally "black American," but used to refer to black Amerasians, often derogatory.

My lai: Amerasian. Often used derogatorily.

neighborhood: One of the ten sections of the Philippine Refugee Processing Center, each containing refugee billets, classrooms, and a rudimentary clinic.

New Economic Zones (NEZ): Undeveloped tracts of rural land lacking any amenities, to which many South Vietnamese, especially city dwellers having ties with the previous regime, were sent to live and work by the Communist regime after 1975.

number 10: Vietnamese-English slang for very bad, the worst.

Orderly Departure Program: A program created in 1979 to provide a safe alternative to dangerous flight from Vietnam by boat or overland. ODP officers interview applicants in Ho Chi Minh City for resettlement in sponsor countries. The American ODP program has been the main conduit out of Vietnam for Amerasians and their families.

pesos: Philippine currency, valued in August of 1992 at about twenty-two to the U.S. dollar.

Philippine Refugee Processing Center (PRPC): Refugee camp in Bataan province of the Philippines to which Southeast Asian refugees already accepted for resettlement to the U.S. are sent to complete a five-month educational program including English as a Second Language, Cultural Orientation, and Work Orientation prior to their departure for the United States. Three hundred and seventeen thousand refugees passed through the PRPC as of December 1991. Amerasians started coming to the PRPC in 1985.

piasters: See "dong."

Quan Am: Buddhist goddess of mercy.

reeducation camp: Camp in which "undesirables," mainly those previously connected to the South Vietnamese regime or its army or to the American war effort, are imprisoned and subjected to forced labor and political indoctrination.

resettlement agency: Offers various services to refugees and immigrants arriving in the United States. These services often include assistance in house and job search, welfare registration, entry into ESL classes, and counseling.

Saigon Tea: Watery concoction drunk by Vietnamese bar girls. Women working in bars would coax customers to buy them glasses of Saigon tea, for which they received a commission.

split case: Situation in which refugees arriving in the Philippine Refugee Processing Center under the same case number, indicating that they will be housed and resettled together, effectively sever ties and go their own way.

sponsor: American citizen, resident, or agency that agrees to help a specific refugee or refugee family resettle. Sponsors are frequently, though not invariably, friends or family of the resettling refugees.

taxi girl: Prostitute.

Tet: Vietnamese New Year.

Thong Nhat: The "Unification Train" that links Ho Chi Minh City with Hanoi.

titi: A little, a small amount.

troi oi: My God!

Viet Cong (VC): The Communist-led insurgents operating in South Vietnam during the war. The political wing was known as the National Liberation Front. Many South Vietnamese when speaking English use the term VC to denote any Vietnamese Communist.

Viet Minh: Communist-dominated resistance and political organization established by Ho Chi Minh during World War II.

Work Credit: The two hours community service that refugees must perform daily in the Philippine Refugee Processing Center.

world, the: GI jargon for the United States.

Young Adult Services Unit (YASU): Offers counseling service to minors in the Philippine Refugee Processing Center.

xic lo: A pedicab, a bicycle rickshaw. The xic lo functions as a taxi cab and is a popular means of public transportation in Vietnam.

SELECTED BIBLIOGRAPHY

BOOKS AND MONOGRAPHS

Akhmatova, Anna. *You Will Hear Thunder*. Athens: Ohio University Press, 1985.
Bai Juyi. *Bai Juyi: Two Hundred Selected Poems*. Beijing: New World Press. 1945.
Butterfield, Fox. *The Vietnam War: An Almanac*. New York: World Almanac Publications, 1985.
Des Pres, Terrence. *The Survivor*. New York: Oxford University Press, 1976.
Duiker, William J. *Vietnam Since the Fall of Saigon*. Revised edition. Southeast Asia Series Number 56A. Athens: Ohio University Center for International Studies, 1989.
Freeman, James M. *Hearts of Sorrow*. Stanford, Calif.: Stanford University Press, 1989.
Hoang Dao Thuy, Huynh Lua, and Nguyen Phuoc Hoang. *Dat Nhuoc Ta [Our Country]*. Nha Xuat Ban Khoa Hoc Xa Hoi [*Social Science Publishing House*], 1989.
Karnow, Stanley. *Vietnam: A History*. New York: Viking, 1983.
Kuntz, Laurie. *Somewhere in the Telling*. Master's diss., Vermont College 1992.
Lacey, Marilyn. *In Our Father's Land: Vietnamese Amerasians in the United States*. Washington, D.C.: United States Catholic Conference, Migration and Refugee Services, 1985.
Leong, Frederick T. L., and Mark C. Johnson. *Vietnamese Amerasian Mothers: Psychological Distress and High-Risk Factors*. Washington, D.C.: Office of Refugee Resettlement, 1992.
Olson, James S. *Dictionary of the Vietnam War*. Westport, Conn.: Greenwood, 1988.
Santoli, Albert. *Everything We Had*. New York: Ballantine Books, 1981.
_____. *To Bear Any Burden*. New York: Dutton, 1985.
To Welcome the Amerasians. Washington, D.C.: United States Catholic Conference, Migration and Refugee Services, 1988.
Tollefson, James W. *Alien Winds*. New York: Praeger, 1989.
Vickery, Michael. *Cambodia: 1975–1982*. Boston: South End Press, 1984.
Willenson, Kim. *The Bad War*. New York: New American Library, 1987.

ARTICLES, PERIODICALS, JOURNALS, AND BULLETINS

"Amerasians: The Second Attempt to Welcome Them 'Home'." *Information Update* 12 July 1988. Center for Applied Linguistics under agreement with the Bureau for Refugee Programs, Dept. of State.

Fenton, James. "The Fall of Saigon." *Granta* 15 (1985): 27–117.

"Home to America, If Not to Daddy," *The Economist,* 19 May 1990, 40.

Menghetti, Anita, ed. *Amerasian Update,* vols. 42–46, January to May 1993. InterAction and the Lutheran Immigration and Refugee Service under agreement with the Office of Refugee Resettlement.

Ranard, Donald A. "Between Two Worlds: Refugee Youth." *In America* 2 January 1989. Center for Applied Linguistics under agreement with the Bureau for Refugee Programs, Dept. of State.

————. "A Look at Vietnamese 'Gangs'." *In America* 10 February 1991. Center for Applied Linguistics under agreement with the Bureau for Refugee Programs, Dept. of State.

Ranard, Donald A., and Douglas F. Gilzow. "The Amerasians." *In America* 4 June 1989. Center for Applied Linguistics under agreement with the Bureau for Refugee Programs, Dept. of State.

————. "The Amerasians: A 1990 Update." *In America* 9 October 1990. Center for Applied Linguistics under agreement with the Bureau for Refugee Programs, Dept. of State.

"Tracing Services for Vietnamese Amerasians and American Fathers." Washington, D.C., American Red Cross, January 1992.

"The United States Orderly Departure Program." Bangkok, Thailand, ODP/International Catholic Migration Commission.

"The United States Orderly Departure Program." Embassy of the United States of America, January 1992.

"The United States Orderly Departure Program Statistical Summary." December 1991.

Untitled Fact sheet on the Philippine Refugee Processing Center. PRPC Information and Materials Production/ODA, 1991.

CONFERENCE PROCEEDINGS

Amerasian Resettlement. Arlington, Va. June 25–27, 1992. Washington, D.C., InterAction Amerasian Resettlement Program under agreement with the Office of Refugee Resettlement, 1992.

Amerasian Resettlement: Building a Network of Welcoming Services. Los Angeles, Calif. March 15–17, 1991. Washington, D.C., InterAction Amerasian Resettlement Program under agreement with the Office of Refugee Resettlement, 1991.

Amerasian Resettlement: Enhancing the Homecoming. Washington, D.C. March 9–11, 1990. Washington, D.C., InterAction Amerasian Resettlement Program under agreement with the Office of Refugee Resettlement, 1990.

Amerasian Resettlement: Strategies for Success. Richmond, Va. March 7–10, 1989. Washington D.C., Dept. of Health and Human Services, 1989.

DIRECTORY

Amerasian Resettlement Cluster Site Directory, 1993. Washington, D.C., InterAction Amerasian Resettlement Program under agreement with the Office of Refugee Resettlement.

INDEX

293